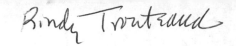

The New Te
Introducing the Way of Discipleship

Wes Howard-Brook

and

Sharon H. Ringe

Editors

ORBIS BOOKS

Maryknoll, New York 10545

Founded in 1970, Orbis Books endeavors to publish works that enlighten the mind, nourish the spirit, and challenge the conscience. The publishing arm of the Maryknoll Fathers & Brothers, Orbis seeks to explore the global dimensions of the Christian faith and mission, to invite dialogue with diverse cultures and religious traditions, and to serve the cause of reconciliation and peace. The books published reflect the views of their authors and do not represent the official position of the Maryknoll Society.

To learn more about Maryknoll and Orbis Books, please visit our website at www.maryknoll.org.

Library of Congress Cataloging-in-Publication Data

The New Testament : introducing the way of discipleship / Wes
    Howard-Brook and Sharon H. Ringe, editors.
        p.   cm.
    Includes index.
    ISBN 1-57075-418-7 (pbk.)
    1. Christian life—Biblical teaching. 2. Christianity and
justice--Biblical teaching. 3. Bible. N.T.—Criticism, interpretation,
etc. I. Howard-Brook, Wes. II. Ringe, Sharon H.
    BS2545.C48 N48 2002
    225.6'1—dc21
                                              2002000852

Contents

Introduction

"I'D LIKE TO FIND A BOOK about the New Testament that's not too academic, but not 'fundamentalist' either, that will help me deepen my understanding of how God is calling me to discipleship of Jesus." This wish, in one form or another, has come to most of the authors of this volume on a regular basis. The Bible has always been meant to be the people's book, yet many people of faith or those puzzling over the question of faith have been turned off by the abundance of books on the Bible that distance the ancient stories from the real-life questions of people's lives. Many books either leave people feeling "stupid" because their authors seem to imply that unless one has a doctorate one cannot possibly engage the biblical narratives. On the other end of the spectrum are the literal-minded volumes that suggest that to bring an inquiring intelligence to the Bible is some sort of blasphemy.

In recent years, a variety of introductory books on the Bible have appeared that attempt to bridge this gap by offering an entry into the worlds of the biblical writers and our audiences. While a number of these volumes are helpful, we have felt that there was still something missing. That "something" was the link between the struggles of our ancestors and our own struggles; between the challenge of discipleship in Jesus' time and in our own.

This book has come out of a movement in biblical studies in recent years that has attempted to tap into the insights of those whose primary place is the academy for the enrichment of those whose primary place is the church and the world. While the effort to wrestle God's Word from the control of the privileged scribal classes goes back to Israel's prophets and to the practice of Jesus, it has been revitalized in recent decades by the vitality of magazines such as *Sojourners* and *The Other Side* and publishers such as Orbis. For us, the publication of Ched Myers's *Binding the Strong Man: A Political Reading of Mark's Story of Jesus* (Orbis, 1988) was seminal. It led to the development of the Bible and Liberation series, in which Wes Howard-Brook and Neil Elliott, contributors to the present volume, have published books on specific parts of the New Testament and of which contributor Richard Horsley is co-editor. Other members of the present collaboration have similarly written books that offer insights into the biblical texts grounded in both scholarship and discipleship.

As powerful as some of these books have been, we know that many people will not jump into the pool of biblical studies by taking on a five-hundred-page work on a single Gospel! Even the shorter, more popularly oriented books written by some of our group on specific pieces of the New Testament are more than many readers will take up as their first step into biblical studies. This volume is intended to serve as that first step.

As co-editors, we have disciplined ourselves and our team to keep each chapter of this book within a tight word limit. We have also made sure that each writer, while speaking in her or his own voice, has connected their New Testament texts to the challenges faced by would-be disciples of Jesus today. Our diversity of starting points has, within this framework, resulted in a diversity of styles and emphases. Some of us begin as scholars who are also people of faith concerned with issues of justice in the world. Others start as faith-based activists and popular educators trying to engage biblical scholarship on behalf of the people with whom we are in community. We are Catholic and Protestant, ordained and lay, female and male, from a variety of cultural traditions. Binding us together is our trust in the One revealed by Jesus and the Way of discipleship which is both our heritage and our invitation.

Our hope is that wherever you may be on the discipleship journey—from experienced traveler to one considering the first step—this book may fan the flame of faith in the Holy One in you and encourage and nourish you on the Way. In that Spirit, all royalties from this book are being offered in equal part to Habitat for Humanity and Witness for Peace in recognition and honor of their work of discipleship.

1

The New World Order

The Historical Context of New Testament History and Literature

RICHARD A. HORSLEY

THE EXPANSION AND CONSOLIDATION of worldwide empire constitute the historical context for the ministry of Jesus, the movement he founded, the mission of Paul, and the literature that communities of Jesus-believers produced. The expansion and consolidation of worldwide empire also constitute the context in which we understand and respond to New Testament history and literature.

IMPERIAL DOMINATION, CLIENT RULERS, AND POPULAR RENEWAL MOVEMENTS IN PALESTINE

The Roman warlords expanded their empire into the eastern Mediterranean in the two generations before Jesus and then consolidated their "ecumenical" domination during the lifetime of Jesus and Paul. Having already taken effective control in North Africa and the Greek city-states, the Romans then relentlessly conquered peoples of the eastern Mediterranean as the power of Hellenistic empires, exhausted from warfare, could no longer maintain their hold.

In contrast to most peoples subjected by the Romans, who soon acquiesced in imperial rule, the Judeans and Galileans (residents of the southern and northern provinces of Palestine, respectively) resisted the initial conquest and periodically revolted against Roman domination, evoking brutal reconquests by the Roman legions. In conquest and reconquest, the Roman armies systematically pursued "scorched earth" and "search and destroy" practices in order to terrorize the population and ferret out all pockets of resistance. The legions destroyed villages, slaughtered the inhabitants, or at least the elderly, and took tens of thousands of the younger and able-bodied to sell as slaves back in Rome and the rest of Italy. A standard feature of the Roman terrorization was the crucifixion of hundreds or thousands on stakes or crosses along the roads, a grim reminder of what would happen to those who rebelled against Roman domination. Right around the time Jesus was born, in the area around Nazareth where he presumably grew up, the Romans had burned the houses and enslaved thousands of people in response to a widespread popular revolt in 4 B.C.E.

In recently conquered territories in the east, the Romans established "indirect rule." Instead of maintaining standing armies there, the Romans installed client kings to control these areas. Although the pretense, and perhaps even the point, was to set up "native" rulers who supposedly had some legitimacy among the people they were to rule, the Romans generally backed figures whom they could rely upon to rule ruthlessly if necessary with military force. In the imperial "grand strategy" of the Romans, it was particularly important to have dependable military strongmen in place in Judea and neighboring areas along the frontier with the "Eastern" empire of the Parthians. Thus, after the high priestly dynasty ruling Palestine from the temple-state in Jerusalem became embroiled in a civil war parallel to the "civil war" between rival Roman warlords, the latter appointed the Idumean strongman with a reputation for ruthless pursuit of Rome's interest in the area as "King of the Judeans." The Judeans and Galileans, however, put up such a fierce and prolonged resistance to Herod's rule that it took him three years to conquer his own people with the help of Roman legions, along with his own mercenary troops. Herod ("the Great") then established sharply repressive rule, with prominent military fortresses throughout his territory manned by well-trained "security forces" and a "secret service" to keep tabs on people who might be disruptive. He then proceeded to milk the productive peasantry with heavy taxation to support his own lavish lifestyle and his massive development projects of public buildings, monuments, and even temples and whole cities constructed and named in honor of the emperor, Augustus.

Prior to the Roman conquest and imposition of Herod, Palestine had been ruled by the temple-state in Jerusalem headed by the Hasmonean dynasty of high priests. Like his Roman warlord sponsors, Herod left the temple and high priesthood in place, quickly getting rid of the Hasmoneans and installing one after another of his own appointees, thus expanding the Jerusalem high priesthood with families beholden to himself. The Pharisees and other scribes and teachers provided the "retainers" who represented the now dependent high priestly aristocracy in helping "govern" the subject territories such as Galilee and Judea itself. The Pharisees, "caught in the middle" as mediators of Roman and Herodian rule to the Judean and Galilean people, but knowledgeable in and committed to "the laws of the Judeans," apparently attempted to lead the people in maintaining the traditional way of life, under the less than optimal conditions of foreign and tyrannical Herodian rule.

Herod shrewdly used the Temple to great advantage in his own sophisticated political maneuvering within the new Roman imperial order. He launched a massive reconstruction of the temple complex in a grand Roman-Hellenistic style, a huge "development" project that took many decades to complete. One of the most grandiose temples of antiquity, the Jerusalem temple thus became one of the ancient "wonders of the world." It also became a center for worldwide Jewry (with Herod as its patron). Jews from Diaspora communities (and others) who could afford to travel or wanted to go on a sort of pilgrimage visited the newly famous city and its temple. Some of these "Hellenist" Jews were attracted to the nascent Jesus movement in Jerusalem, the best known being the martyr Stephen and Saul of Tarsus, soon to become the great apostle to non-Israelite peoples.

The Jerusalem temple-state had originally ruled only the small territory/people of Judea, as a subordinate unit of the Persian and then the Hellenistic empires. The Hasmonean high priesthood, established by the leaders of the Maccabean Revolt against Hellenistic imperial repression of the traditional Judean way of life, had step by step extended the temple-state's rule over Idumea to the south and Samaria and Galilee to the north. The Samaritans and Galileans, presumably descendants of the northern Israelites who had rebelled against the Davidic monarchy and its temple eight hundred years previously, again came under Jerusalem rule only about one hundred years before the birth of Jesus. Although not often recognized by New Testament scholars, the difference in historical experience between the Galileans and the Jerusalemites must have been a very important factor in the emergence and program of Jesus and his movement. On the one hand, Galileans would likely have resented the tithes, offerings, and taxes they had to render up to the temple and the priesthood. On the other, as a result of the renewed imposition of Jerusalem rule, they would have become more aware of being part of the whole people of Israel, with its rich heritage of resistance to and freedom from oppressive rulers, as embodied most significantly in the Passover festival, which celebrated Israel's liberation from bondage under the Egyptian pharaoh. It is only on the basis of this renewal of Galilean awareness of belonging to Israel and its liberationist heritage that we can explain why Jesus focused his prophetic indictment of rulers on the Jerusalem high priesthood and temple rather than on the Herodian ruler of Galilee.

After the death of Herod in 4 B.C.E. and the brutal Roman suppression of the revolts that ensued in every major area of his realm, Caesar Augustus installed his son Antipas as ruler over Galilee and Perea (the Transjordan), while establishing the direct Roman rule of a governor over Jerusalem and Judea, leaving the temple-state and high priestly aristocracy in power. For the first time in their history, Galileans now had their ruler located directly in the area. (Herod) Antipas proceeded to rebuild the fortress city of Sepphoris on a lavish scale as the "ornament" of his realm, then within twenty years also built the completely new city of Tiberias as a second capital overlooking the "Sea" of Galilee—across the lake from the village of Capernaum, where Jesus and his disciples later apparently established the headquarters from which they operated in building their movement in the villages of Galilee and nearby areas. For Galileans in particular, then, the severe economic pressures entailed in Antipas's massive building projects compounded their already desperate situation resulting from the previous multiple demands for tithes to the temple, tribute to the Romans, and taxes to Herod. Judging from the social banditry—Robin Hood-like thefts from the wealthy to be given to the poor—that escalated in scale during the first century, as peasants could no longer make a living on their parcels of land, families and village communities, the fundamental forms of Israelite society, were beginning to disintegrate from hunger and heavy indebtedness. It cannot be coincidental that these are precisely the problems Jesus addresses in his preaching and attempts to renew family and village communities (see especially Luke 6:20-49; 12:22-31; Mark 10:2-31).

Not just in Galilee, but throughout Roman-dominated Palestine, the popular distress, disintegration of family and village life, and discontent deepened during Jesus' lifetime and the first decades of the Jesus movements. Although no Herodian king continued over Judea itself, the Romans kept the temple and the high priesthood intact, which meant that the peasants were required to render tribute to Caesar as well as tithes and offerings and other taxes to the temple and the priests. Because of the surplus wealth piling up in the temple, which also served as a bank under the control of the high priestly families, enterprising aristocratic priests and descendants of the Herodian family actively manipulated peasants into debts so that they could live off of the exorbitant interest payments—forbidden by certain Mosaic covenantal laws, which conveniently went unenforced. Archaeological explorations have unearthed evidence of extensive agricultural estates and of the mansions built in the "New/Upper City" of Jerusalem at this time, apparently by the high priestly and Herodian families. The Jewish historian Josephus reports that these powerful wealthy families became more and more predatory on their own people during the first century C.E. The four principal high priestly families, among whom the actual office of high priest was rotated in frequent new appointments by the frequently changing Roman governors, were of course maintained in power by their Roman sponsors.

The discontent and social disintegration that resulted from the oppressive structures imposed by the Romans and the exploitative political-economic practices of the multiple layers of rulers—Roman, Herodian, and high priestly—provided the conditions for periodic protests, renewal movements, and even massive popular revolts. Judea and Galilee produced the most frequent and extensive resistance for well over a century, from the imposition of Roman rule and Herod the Great to the great revolt of 66-70 C.E.

The frequent protest movements and the extensive revolts were clearly rooted in the distinctive Israelite tradition of liberation from oppressive rulers and Mosaic covenantal principles of justice in the people's common social-economic life. The standard old Christian historical picture of Jesus protesting the legalism of the Pharisees in favor of a direct spiritual relationship with God and of Paul breaking with the parochial particularism of "Judaism" in favor of the new, universal spiritual religion of "Christianity" is a gross oversimplification unrecognizable in ancient sources, including New Testament literature. It is even historically false to imagine that there was a standard Jewish "Law" shared by both the Jerusalem rulers and the Judean and Galilean villagers. As in traditional agrarian societies in general, the Galilean and Judean peasants had their own "little" or popular Israelite traditions, cultivated orally in village communities over the generations, as distinct from the "great" or elite tradition, partly written on sacred scrolls, cultivated and interpreted by professional intellectuals such as "scribes" and "Pharisees." The "great" and "little" traditions, of course, while parallel and sharing much in common, emphasized what was in the interest of the ruling elite and ordinary people, respectively. Emphasis in the "great" tradition thus lay on the support of the temple and the priesthood, with heavy focus on the Jerusalem monarchic and temple traditions. The popular tradition focused heavily on the exodus and the Mosaic covenant, which had formed the foundation of early Israel, along with the prophets who had led popular revolt against or resistance to oppressive rule, such as Elijah.

Occasionally a radical minority of dissident scribal retainers engaged in protest against or resistance to Roman or Herodian oppression. The Pharisees refused to take the required oath of loyalty to Herod and the emperor. Later, as Herod lay dying, two respected Jerusalem teachers inspired their students to cut down the Roman eagle that the king had erected above a gate of the temple—and were torturously executed for their act of defiance. When direct Roman rule was imposed in 6 C.E., a group led by a "teacher" named Judas of Gaulanitis and a Pharisee named Sadok led a movement to refuse to pay the tribute, called the "Fourth Philosophy" (the first three were the Pharisees, the Sadducees, and the Essenes—the latter probably the same as the Qumran community that left the Dead Sea Scrolls). Josephus says that they shared the beliefs of the Pharisees, except that they were more dedicated to acting on them. In good Mosaic covenantal theology, they insisted that since God was their exclusive Lord and Master, they could not possibly pay the tribute to Caesar, which was tantamount to serving another Lord (the political-economic being utterly inseparable from the religious). Several decades later, at mid-first century, a related group of "teachers" called the "Dagger Men" (*Sicarioi*), in their frustration at the high priestly collaboration with the Romans, began surreptitiously assassinating particular high priestly figures under cover of the press of festival crowds in the temple courtyard.

Most of the agitation, protests, and movements, however, emerged among the common people. As in most preindustrial capital cities, where the population is economically dependent on the rulers who reside there, ordinary Jerusalemites had little leeway to protest the politics and practices of their high priestly patrons. Nevertheless, the protests periodically pressed by the "mob" in Jerusalem were not the actions only of peasants on pilgrimage during festival time. The prime time for anti-Roman protest was at the Passover festival, which celebrated the liberation of the Israelite ancestors from Egyptian bondage. In a repressive practice that must have only exacerbated the tensions at Passover time, the Roman governors brought a cohort of troops into

Jerusalem and stationed them atop the porticoes of the temple courtyard where the pilgrims gathered. Not surprisingly, the symbolic as well
as physical face-off occasionally did erupt into vigorous protest and
brutal repression. Surely the most remarkable popular protest came in
response to the emperor Caligula's order to install his bust in the temple, a blatant act of symbolic aggression that exacerbated resentment at
Roman domination. In protest the Galilean peasants refused to plant
the crops on which the Romans depended for their precious tribute.
The Roman Legate of Syria recognized exactly what was about to happen: instead of an orderly harvest from which Rome would take its
share in tribute, the peasant resistance and resultant hunger from lack
of a harvest would produce "a harvest of banditry," which was already
common because peasants could not both meet demands for tribute and
taxes and feed their families.

Most important in relation to Jesus and his movement surely were
two distinctively Israelite types of popular movements that arose in
reaction to Roman, Herodian, and high priestly rule. In both cases these
popular movements are clearly informed by deeply rooted Israelite traditions. After the death of Herod the Great, the revolts in every major
district of the realm, movements that attacked royal fortresses and
established effective popular control of their areas for months or even
a few years, took the form of "messianic" movements, with the people
acclaiming their leader as "king." These movements were clearly patterned after the stories of how the Israelites had collectively "anointed"
("messiah-ed") Saul and then David as king to lead them against Philis-
tine domination. The popular messianic movement in Galilee was
located around Sepphoris in villages such as Nazareth just about the
time Jesus was born. The brutal Roman devastation of the area and the
enslavement of the people would have left the surviving inhabitants of
the area in deep social-spiritual trauma for generations. Again seventy
years later, the largest movement active in the great revolt of 66-70 took
the same form of a messianic movement patterned after the young
David, the prototypical popular messiah. In a significant symbolic as
well as geopolitical act in the aftermath of the Roman destruction of
Jerusalem, the Roman imperial lords ceremonially executed the "messiah" (Simon bar Giora) in their triumphal procession in Rome as "king
of the Jews." Thus, Jesus was not the first popular "messiah" of this
period, nor was he the only one executed as "king of the Jews."

The other distinctively Israelite type of movement contemporary
with Jesus was the popular prophetic movement. In the cases known
through Josephus's histories, a prophet named Theudas led his follow-

ers out to the wilderness of the Jordan to experience the waters divided and the way opened for what appears to have been understood as a new exodus or new entry into the land. Theudas clearly envisioned a new divine act of deliverance patterned after the exodus or entry into the land led by Moses and Joshua, respectively. An Egyptian Jewish prophet led his followers from villages up to the Mount of Olives opposite the temple, from which they would see the walls of the city fall, giving them access apparently to a liberated city—clearly a new Joshua leading a new divinely engineered battle of Jericho. The occurrence of several movements of both types right around the time of Jesus indicates that two distinctively Israelite scripts were alive in the popular tradition cultivated in village communities in accordance with which the people could mount movements of resistance to oppressive rulers and renewal of Israelite society. We have hardly begun to explore, by careful reading of the Gospels as whole stories, how these traditional Israelite "scripts" were adapted by Jesus and his followers in the movement they inaugurated in Galilee.

The movements of Jesus-followers that emerged in Galilee, Jerusalem, and elsewhere in Palestine developed and expanded in precisely this period of deepening conflict between rulers and ruled and social disintegration that led to the great revolt in 66-70. These "Jesus-movements" must thus be understood in the context of several other popular movements that sought a divinely inspired renewal of Israel led by a prophet like Moses, Joshua, or Elijah over against the temple, the high priesthood, the Herodian rulers, and their Roman imperial patrons. Speeches and sayings of Jesus and stories about Jesus that eventually found their way into the Synoptic Gospels, Mark, Matthew, and Luke were developed and performed during these first decades of the movements. The series of speeches of Jesus that are not in Mark but can be discerned in parallel form in Matthew and Luke, called "Q" (short for *Quelle,* the German term for "source") is commonly believed to have been cultivated in a Jesus movement probably in Galilee around mid-first century. Mark is the only canonical Gospel that may have originated, perhaps in Galilee or a nearby Greek-speaking region, prior to the Roman destruction of Jerusalem in 70.

RELIGION AND POWER IN THE ROMAN IMPERIAL ORDER
IN THE GREEK CITIES

While Jesus movements were expanding in Palestine, the community of Jesus-followers based in Jerusalem and other "free-lance" apostles such as Saul of Tarsus were taking the "good news"—that in Jesus' death and resurrection God was fulfilling the promises to Abraham— well beyond Palestine into Jewish communities in eastern Mediterranean towns and cities. Damascus, whose Syrian culture was still very much alive underneath its veneer of western culture, was an important early center from which the movement was spread by Saul/Paul and others. More important in the wider spread of the movement was the great city of Antioch, one of the three most important metropolitan centers of the Roman empire. Rome had made Antioch, which lay close to the frontier with the Parthian empire to the east, the center of its political-military power in the East. Antioch thus provided the basis from which the Romans invaded Palestine in repeated reconquests to put down popular rebellions. The city—paved in marble as a gift from Herod the Great—had a very large Greek-speaking Jewish community, a portion of which joined the splinter movement of Jewish Jesus-believers. Antioch quickly became the major base from which Peter, Paul, Barnabas, and others spread the movement in the wider eastern Mediterranean (see Acts 13:1 and the conflict Paul describes in Gal. 2:11-13). According to Acts 11:26 the term *Christianoi* was first applied to Jesus-believers in Antioch.

In somewhat the same way as they have tended to stereotype ancient Jews and Judaism, Christian interpreters have also tended to stereotype the Hellenistic world into which Paul and other apostles carried their mission. Although all areas had been affected by earlier Hellenization in the spread of the Greek language even into villages and the establishment of cities as the "civilized" urban centers from which the surrounding countrysides were dominated, significant differences remained between Galatia and Thessalonica or between Philippi and Corinth. Galatia in central Asia Minor, like Judea and Galilee, had only recently come under Roman rule and begun to experience the impact of Hellenistic "civilization" in language and urbanization. Philippi and Thessalonica, small cities in Macedonia, north of Greece proper, had been overlaid with colonies of Roman soldiers, who became the new urban elite—with the attendant resentments of the previous elite and further demotion in status of the indigenous common people. Ephesus is perhaps the principal site of Paul's mission that one could characterize as a typical large Hellenistic city, with its mix of general Greek culture and more recent Roman political-cultural influences overlaying the city's indigenous urban culture.

The Roman imperial order was very different in major Greek cities such as Corinth and Ephesus from the situations in Palestine and Galatia, where Roman military power had only recently pressed "civiliza-tion" upon the people and the landscape. With regard to literature, phi-losophy, and religion, the Romans held the more sophisticated culture of the Greek cities in high regard. That did not stop the Roman war-lords from simply devastating a given city in retaliation for resisting the empire's inevitable advance. In the case of Corinth—the site of Paul's mission about which we are perhaps best informed from ancient sources—in one massive exercise of military violence, the Romans anni-hilated one of the most illustrious classical Greek cities and carried off its great cultural treasures to Rome (just as modern Western imperial elites looted the cultural treasures of Greece, Egypt, and the Middle East). After maneuvering Corinth and the Achaean league into war, in 146 B.C.E. Roman armies destroyed the city, slaughtered the men, and enslaved the women and children—thereby serving notice to other Greek cities that Rome would tolerate no resistance to its advancing domination of the Aegean world and the eastern Mediterranean. A cen-tury later, in 44 B.C.E., Rome founded a colony at the site of ancient Corinth as a base for the control of commerce and the perpetuation of imperial rule in Greece. Whereas most Roman colonies, such as those in Philippi and Thessalonica, comprised mainly army veterans, the colonists sent to Corinth were recruited from the urban poor in Rome, half of them being freed slaves (Strabo, *Geogr.* 8.6.23). This gave the city a very mixed population, those from the Roman mob probably having been peasants displaced from the Italian countryside and the freedpersons having been (descendants of) slaves taken in Roman con-quests of eastern Mediterranean peoples. Given this mixture of rootless and displaced people of "inauspicious" origins, there must have been an acute lack of social coherence and common cultural heritage and an acute awareness of the lack of "social status" in this burgeoning metropolis that became the center of commerce and Roman control of Greece.

Any Greek city, but particularly one of such highly composite popu-lation as Corinth, would have been vulnerable to two closely interre-lated major developments in the early empire. After Octavian had defeated Mark Antony at the battle of Actium (near Corinth) in 31 B.C.E. and had effectively become the emperor "Augustus," the wealthy and powerful elite of the Greek cities quickly moved to ingratiate them-selves with the emperor and imperial family. Pyramids of patronage, which had already come to structure political-economic relations in Rome itself, quickly spread into the Greek cities. Under the emperor at the apex of all such pyramids, the magnates of each city or province who controlled vast amounts of land and commercial ventures established pyramids of patron–client relations that extended relentlessly downward into the population. A high percentage of the population of a city was thus personally as well as economically dependent on a more wealthy patron. On the cultural level, wealthy and powerful patrons developed a taste for having a "house philosopher" or other intellectual or spiritual guru as well as other services provided by clients in various lines of work.

These very magnates, who became the most powerful heads of patronage networks, also took the lead in the Greek cities' development of the honors to the emperor. The "emperor cult" has been dismissed by many scholars of early Christianity as empty forms and mere personal flattery of the emperor. But this is because they work with a concept of religion that has not only been reduced to individual faith or belief, but has also been separated from politics and the exercise of power. That is a peculiarly modern Western understanding, however. In most historical societies religion and political-economic life were inseparable. The emperor cult developed by the Greek cities in response to the imperial impact on their lives in fact provides a vivid illustration of how power relations can be constituted by religion.

The elite of the Greek cities built the emperor cult directly into and upon the established "civil religion" of the city. They installed statues of the emperor into the temples of their gods, such as Asclepius, Aphrodite, Apollo, Athena, or Demeter, which lined the *agora,* or city center. They constructed new temples to the emperor, often in the center of the city, and added shrines to the emperor at various points around the perimeter. Thus the presence of the emperor (absent in Rome!) came to pervade public space; it was physically and visually all around the city-dweller. The urban elites also renamed major festivals such as the Olympic Games for the emperor—the Caesarean Games—and, where no such festival already existed, they created one in the emperor's honor. In proclamations, public performances, and inscriptions prominent in public places the emperor was acclaimed as the "Lord" of the world, as the "Savior" who had brought "peace and security" to the world (e.g., 1 Thess. 5:13). The appropriate response of the people, of course, was to declare their loyalty (*pistis* in Greek, *fides* in Latin, usually translated "faith" in English-language Bibles). Indeed, even the very calendar of urban life was rearranged as the emperor's birthday was proclaimed not only the beginning of the new year but the beginning of a new era. And all of the building projects, shrines, and festival games, which involved the entire population of the city (probably the only occasions all year when the poor were able to eat meat), were sponsored by the urban elites. Their names were inscribed in prominent places; they were "elected" (by the elite city council) to the most prestigious city offices; and they were themselves honored at the very festivals they sponsored. The Roman imperial order thus pervaded the economic and religious fabric of life in the Greek cities through the closely linked networks of patronage relations and imperial cult that restructured urban life both spatially and temporally. Little wonder that the Romans did not need to keep occupying troops in or near these cities and that maintaining the empire required the development of minimal bureaucracy in Rome, where the *familia Caesaris,* "emperor's household" of managerial slaves, could handle things adequately.

Modern interpreters living in a society that thinks in terms of a large "middle class" tend to project a broad continuum of statuses onto the political-economic structure of ancient Greek and Roman urban life. In antiquity, however, there were simply no "middle" classes or statuses. It is potentially misleading to think that communities of Jesus-believers included members from "across the social spectrum," because there was no such spectrum similar to what we imagine. Nor should we imagine that the early "assemblies" of Jesus-believers were, in effect, a proletarian movement. We must be much more precise about the differences between ancient and modern Western social structures. Modern Western societies have nothing comparable to the extremes of wealth and poverty in the Roman empire. The only wealthy people were the extremely wealthy elite, who comprised a tiny percentage of the overall population. Virtually all others were poor by our standards. Among the vast majority who were poor, there were some with adequate food and shelter, more whom we would classify as marginal, and many who were more destitute. Perhaps most difficult for us to understand is the chattel slavery that simply went unquestioned and unchallenged by most people in the Roman empire. The huge households—and extensive farms—of the wealthy and powerful were run by slaves. But even families of modest means had a slave or two in their households.

Because literature and written records such as inscriptions are almost always left only by the literate elite, we have little sense of what ordinary people were thinking and doing—unless of course they made trouble for the elite, who then complained about them in literature. Thus, we do not know much about the very people that Paul and other Jesus movement organizers reached in their work. We can only survey a few of the ways that elite Greeks and Romans made sense of and sought transcendence of their lives in the Roman imperial order.

The intellectual elite attempted to make sense of the new imperial world order in terms of various philosophies. Most influential in the general worldview of literate antiquity was Stoicism. Since Alexander the Great had established a "worldwide" empire that first brought the Greek city-states under an overarching political order, thus relativizing the old Athenian and other civil-religious traditions and identities, Stoics and others thought of the universe as one cosmic "city-state" (*kosmopolis*), of which the "constitution" (*politeia*) was reason (*logos*) and in which those creatures who shared reason (*logos*) were citizens (*politeis*). That is, with one's sense of belonging now to the universal order, and no longer to a local civic order, went a liberating sense of individualism, being a citizen of the universal rational order insofar as one cultivated one's individual reason—through philosophy.

Not all members of the elite were so sanguine about the new world order, however. Some experienced it as dehumanizing. Under the Roman imperial order that operated through the pyramids of patronage headed by the emperor and whose local power relations were constituted by the imperial cult in the various cities, Greek "democracy" (which was far more restrictive than modern democracy) had long since been replaced by a tiny oligarchy that ran affairs in each imperial city. Even many Greek and Roman elites, therefore, felt their lives to be determined by the fickle finger of the goddess Fate (*Tychē, Fortuna*), whose statues were ubiquitous in the ancient Roman world, so that people could appease her in hopes of avoiding her whims. Those who could afford the cost sought initiation into the mystery religions devoted to such goddesses as Isis, the Queen of Heaven. Spiritual seekers could enter cloisterlike compounds walled off from the streets and, in the inner sanctuary of the goddess all decorated with exotic Egyptian figures and hieroglyphics, could adore the statue of the blessed Queen of Heaven from the opening ritual at daybreak until 2:00 P.M. Individuals specially chosen by this Egyptian-derived goddess, who in her love as the divine mother had saved them from the evil designs of Fate, underwent an elaborate all-night ritual initiation in which they conversed face to face with all the gods of the upper and lower worlds and at dawn were elevated on a dais and displayed to previous initiates in the guise of the sun as consort to Isis, the moon. That is, she had become not only their divine mother but their divine lover and very personal savior. At least the elites could avail themselves of mystery religions, a "New Age"-like means of individual transcendence of the weight and stress of life under the imperial order.

Not all "Eastern" religions were so tailor-made to the Greco-Roman elite. For centuries Diaspora Jews had established communities in many Greek, Egyptian, and Mesopotamian cities. Although we are not certain of their presence in all of the cities of Paul's mission, these Jewish communities must have provided the basis from which cells of Jesus-believers split off to form separate communities. Moreover, these Greek-speaking Jewish "assemblies" (synagōgai) provided the model for the foundation of "assemblies"(ekklēsiai) of Jesus-believers. They provide the best-known, and perhaps the only, case of groups that were not simply religious associations but semi-separate self-governing communities that had their own religious-political identity and agenda different from those of the dominant imperial or local civil order. In some cases, at least the intellectual elite of such communities had become acculturated into the dominant Hellenistic culture and philosophy. The Wisdom of Solomon and the scriptural interpretation of the Alexandrian Jewish philosopher Philo, for example, articulate a mystical theology that owes much to Hellenistic philosophy. Many of the members of these Hellenistic Jewish Diaspora communities must have been (former) slaves taken by Roman armies in the various conquests of Palestine.

The vast majority of people in Greece, Asia Minor, or anywhere else in the Roman empire, of course, were peasants living in villages and towns subordinate to and exploited by the urban elites. It has been fashionable in New Testament studies to treat "early Christianity" as if it were exclusively an urban phenomenon. This is surely because our sources, such as New Testament literature itself, are from urban situations. There is increasing awareness, however, that the Jesus movements spread also in villages and towns. Besides (the possibility of) "Q," the Didache (Teaching of the Twelve Apostles), and even the Gospel of Mark having originally been developed in and addressed to village communities in Syria, there is evidence in the letters of the younger Pliny to the emperor Trajan in the second decade of the second century for thriving communities of Jesus-believers in the villages of northwestern Asia Minor (Pontus-Bithynia).

These letters also indicate that Roman officials, even governors such as Pliny, did not know quite what to make of or what to do with such communities. And is it any wonder, since the "assemblies" of Christ-followers which organized in both cities and villages did not fit any form that the Roman officials recognized? In the second century, opponents of the movement known by then as "Christians" noted the intense solidarity and mutual assistance among the members of such communities. Ignatius of Antioch, one of the first bishops of the assemblies, in a pattern borrowed from hierarchical imperial society, ironically enough on the way to his martyrdom in Rome, denounced some assemblies for using common community funds to buy their fellow members out of slavery, indicating that the members' solidarity extended even to the most fundamental economic basis of their common life. From the outset the movement appears to have taken a clear anti-imperial stance, operating through organizing "assemblies," rather than direct agitation against the imperial order or its official representatives.

It is uncanny how the most basic terms Paul used to preach the gospel and to compose his letters were borrowed from Roman discourse in order to present an alternative to the Roman imperial order: Christ, who had been crucified by the Romans, not Caesar, was the true "Lord" and "Savior" (Phil. 3:18-21) and the subject of the gospel, and those who joined the assemblies were to maintain exclusive "loyalty" to Christ. If we stated the agenda of Paul's mission in modern terms, it seems clear that he was building an international anti-imperial alternative society embodied in local communities. However megalomaniac and paternalistic he may have been personally, his principal concern was to see the assemblies maintain their solidarity until their Lord should return and finally establish the new age, of which they were the anticipatory communities.

RESOURCES FOR FURTHER STUDY

Garnsey, Peter, and Richard B. Saller. *The Roman Empire: Economy, Society, and Culture.* Berkeley: University of California Press, 1987.

Hanson, K. C., and Douglas E. Oakman. *Palestine in the Time of Jesus: Social Structures and Social Conflicts.* Philadelphia: Fortress Press, 1998.

Horsley, Richard A., with John S. Hanson. *Bandits, Prophets and Messiahs: Popular Movements at the Time of Jesus.* Harrisburg, Pa.: Trinity Press International, 1999.

Horsley, Richard A., ed. *Paul and Empire: Religion and Power in Roman Imperial Society.* Harrisburg, Pa.: Trinity Press International, 1997.

Saldarini, Anthony J. *Pharisees, Scribes, and Sadducees in Palestinian Society: A Sociological Approach.* Grand Rapids: Eerdmans, 2001.

2

Matthew's Gospel

The Disciples' Call to Justice

MICHAEL H. CROSBY, O.F.M.CAP.

WHO IS THE "MATTHEW" OF MATTHEW'S GOSPEL?

TRADITION HAS ATTRIBUTED the "First Gospel" to the disciple named Matthew: the one who sat "at the tax booth" and followed Jesus (9:9). Today, however, that "Matthew-the-tax-collector" view of authorship is held by few. While such a disciple may have been the original inspiration for the Gospel, the final form as we have it today seems to have been the work of a Gentile Christian well-versed in the Hebrew Scriptures but whose mistakes about the Hebrew world (i.e., 21:2 vs. 21:7) indicate an outsider's knowledge.

An analysis of the text and its language suggests that Matthew's audience of house churches was a socially marginalized community of Greek-speaking people living in the late first century. They were already separated from main elements of the Jewish religion; hence Matthew speaks of "their" scribes (7:29) and especially "their" synagogues (4:23; 9:35; 10:17; 12:9; 13:54; 23:34). According to John P. Meier, there was conflict in Matthew's church between conservative Jewish members and Gentile members. Matthew's task was to offer a resolution through an "inclusive synthesis."[1]

Given this historical context—especially for us readers today, who are called to put into practice "everything" Jesus has taught (28:20)— the Matthew (*Matthaios*) of the First Gospel appears likely to have been a representative appellation for any disciple (*mathētēs*) who has been taught (*mathēteutheis*) and who understands (*synienai*) the implications of what has been taught. This involves putting the teachings of Jesus into practice.[2] In this sense the question immediately before the core passage of the Gospel stands out: "Have you understood (*synienai*) all this?" Jesus asks upon completing the third discourse on the parables (13:1-53), which sets the disciples apart from those who see but do not perceive and hear but do not listen since they do not understand (13:13). When they answer "Yes," he says to them: "Therefore every scribe who has been trained (*mathēteutheis*) for the kingdom of heaven is like the master of a household (*oikodespotēs*) who brings out of his treasure what is new and what is old" (13:52).

Of all the Gospels, only Matthew uses the word *mathēteutheis*. It can mean to be "one learned" in the teacher's ways, "one discipled" to a teacher, or one who puts into practice the master's teachings. Here it is used of any "householder." Later it will identify Joseph of Arimathea (27:57). The final time can be found in the Great Commission, or final words of Jesus on the day of resurrection. Having earlier said that he had been "sent only to the lost sheep of the house of Israel" (15:24) and having himself sent his own apostles only "to the lost sheep of the house of Israel" (10:6), the resurrected Jesus now breaks all boundaries. This demands that those now united to him do the same by going into the *whole world*: "Go therefore and make disciples (*mathēteutheis*) of all nations, baptizing them in the name of the Father and of the Son and of the Holy Spirit, and teaching them to obey everything I have commanded you. And remember, I am with you always, to the end of the age" (28:19-20). Ultimately, then, all persons who make the words and works of the Gospel of *Matthaios* are to be its *mathēteutheis*. As such they are to be its final redaction in the world entrusted to them.

THE SETTING OF MATTHEW'S GOSPEL

The first appearance of the adult Jesus in Matthew's Gospel establishes its basic theme: that he has come to inaugurate God's reign of justice, in fulfillment of the Law and the Prophets. Before he begins his public life, Jesus "came from Galilee" (3:13). At the opening of his ministry Matthew sees Jesus' mission not only to Israel but to "Galilee of the Gentiles" (4:15); Jesus goes "throughout Galilee." He concludes his ministry by extending his power to the disciples at Galilee (28:16).

More than any other evangelist, Matthew highlights the Galilean connection of Jesus. This seems to be Matthew's way of universalizing Jesus' message beyond the geographical and ideological boundaries circumscribed by the image and reality of Judea and/or "Israel" as well as that of the empire.

During his ministry, Jesus was identified as one who healed, preached, and taught (4:23-24; 9:35) in a way that attracted public attention (i.e., "crowds"). He also seems to have been the leader of a rural and village-based sectarian faction of wandering charismatics that originally attracted alienated Jews. He is portrayed as calling his own disciples from a patriarchal household (4:18-22) into a free association that reflected an alternative, more collegial grouping that would challenge empire and its way of thinking. While some of these disciples would remain house-based, others would imitate Jesus in the way he went from town to town, always drawing on the hospitality of households along the way (10:1-15).

Within a few decades of Jesus' death and resurrection, however, a gradual change took place among his disciples. Those followers of Jesus who before had been mobile were becoming sedentary or house-based. A message that originally appealed to the poor and marginalized now attracted the middle and upper strata of society. A transition was being made from the rural and village culture of Palestine to Greco-Roman urban culture, from the Aramaic to the Greek language, from an ethnically homogenous constituency that was largely unlearned, relatively poor, and of lower social status to an ethnically heterogeneous one that included people more educated and more financially secure and successful. The latter, while attracted to the person of Jesus, struggled with the received message concerning the poor. It was the task of Matthew to make clear to them that true discipleship did not demand being poor. Rather it involved being "discipled" to Jesus in a way modeled by Joseph of Arimathea. He could be rich and still be a disciple—provided that, in the face of poverty, he would be just in the way he shared his resources in light of Jesus' need for his tomb (27:57-60).

Because Matthew's Gospel assumes readers of greater prosperity and urbanization than the audience of Mark's Gospel, his original audience could have been based in Antioch (Why else would Jesus' fame or honor be extended as far as Syria? [4:24]), a place of some prosperity, but there, nevertheless, the poor were always with them (26:11). The readers' discipleship demanded they be just and do good in imitation of how God's reign or way was revealed in Jesus' attitude toward the poor.

Because Matthew's Gospel laid such stress on conversion of life as the fundamental requirement for entering God's reign, it has often been called the "Gospel of the Kingdom." At the same time, because it is unique among the four in using the word *ekklēsia*, it has often been called the "Gospel of the Church." However, since both the "church" and the political kingdom of empire were structured around the household, I find the notion of house (*oikia* and/or *oikos*) to be at the core of a contemporary understanding of Matthew's world. In fact, I have written elsewhere that, because the household represented the basic unit of life in the empire, be it "economic and social as well as the life of the local church," the notion of "house" must be viewed "as a self-evident, 'primary assumed metaphor'" in understanding Matthew's Gospel.[3]

The *oikia/oikos* involved persons and resources. The ordering (*nomos*) of each household was determined by the kind of relationships that took place among these persons (male/female, parent/child, master/slave) and the resources that were available (house, net, boat, land, monies). In the first-century Mediterranean world, households tended to be based on the prevailing system of the empire; thus the majority were patriarchal. Jesus, however, envisioned a new kind of household under the paternity (not the patriarchy) or reign of God that would serve as an alternative to the prevailing model. This notion of *ekklēsia* refers, Douglas R. A. Hare, notes, "not simply to the local Christian assembly but to the whole movement." At the same time, Matthew's threefold use of the word for "church" suggests that the Matthean groups were associated in some way with Gentile Christianity.[4]

As someone formed from birth in Roman Catholicism, I had only one of the three Matthean passages about "church" drilled into my head: "You are Peter, and on this rock I will build my church" (16:18). This was done in a way that would reinforce the patriarchal pattern of the papacy built on Jesus' empowering Peter with the keys to bind and loose (16:19). This was the only Scripture passage we were taught to remember. Our entire "faith" was anchored in this text, much as John 3:16 is used in some fundamentalistic and therefore ideologically oriented approaches to the Scriptures. Never was I taught that the same power to bind and loose in the church is given collegially as well—to the community itself (18:18). This makes one aware of how easily a Gospel such as Matthew's can be used ideologically (and idolatrously) for the sake of a tradition that can often "void the word of God" (15:6).

The "tradition" that is reinforced by such a selective use of the Scriptures limits power and authority in the church to that approach to morality exercised by those defined by Matthew 16 (the church defined by Peter), not Matthew 18 (the church of the people). As a priest in the Roman Catholic Church, I find such a selective use of the Scriptures— used to limit authority in the church to one group over another—as an abuse of the Scriptures and the intent of Jesus Christ as articulated by Matthew.

Despite the overemphasis of one of the binding and loosing passages over the other to buttress the Petrine dimension of the "church," it is evident that baptism serves as a core requirement for entrance into this church (28:16-20) and that the eucharistic memorial serves as a sign of the disciples' fidelity in recalling and embracing Jesus' self-donation of his life (26:26-29).

THE STRUCTURE OF MATTHEW'S GOSPEL

That Matthew sees Jesus as the founder of an alternative group, a kind of egalitarian community within a patriarchal system, seems quite clear when one considers how the Gospel is structured. Building on this notion of a new kind of household of disciples, we can discern in Matthew's Gospel a chiastic structure. (A chiasm is a text in which various elements or phrases are arranged to form a concentric pattern, thus drawing special attention to a central point.) At the center of the chiasm and, therefore, of the entire Gospel, is the passage wherein Jesus articulated the difference between his own disciples (inside "the house") who do God's will and those in the crowd "outside." In a critical nuance of Mark, Matthew first presents Jesus speaking in parables to the "crowds" outside the house, but as the parable chapter (13) develops, he left "the crowds and went into the house" (13:36), where Matthean disciples would hear the Gospel read in assembly. As a prelude to this chapter on the parables, Matthew narrates:

> While he was still speaking to the crowds, his mother and his brothers were standing outside, wanting to speak to him. Someone told him, "Look, your mother and your brothers are standing outside, wanting to speak to you." But to the one who had told him this, Jesus replied, "Who is my mother, and who are my brothers?" And pointing to his disciples, he said: "Here are my mother and my brothers! For whoever does the will of my Father in heaven is my brother and sister and mother." (12:46-50)

In this passage Matthew distinguishes between the blood family "outside" the house and those "inside." However, changing his Markan source (which speaks about those "who sat about him" [Mark 3:34]), he points specifically to those "disciples" (*mathētai*) *in* the house as those who do God's will. He refers to them as a new kind of family: his "brother and sister and mother." What Jesus earlier asked of his disciples—the breaking of patriarchal familial bonds (4:22; 8:21-22)—the Gospel now makes even clearer. In the new family of disciples blood counts for nothing. What counts is being a disciple who does the will of the heavenly Father and embraces the pattern of God's reign within the empire. The structure of Matthew's Gospel revolves around being disciples of Jesus in the household of the heavenly Father rather than servants in a world defined by empire. The implications for Jesus' disciples living in the world involve for them what it did for him: the cross—the sign of being publicly rejected by society not only for noncompliance with its norms but for subversion of the system itself (16:24-26; see 16:21; 17:22-23; 20:17-19).

The structure of Matthew's Gospel can be presented in the following scheme, which shows an alternating pattern of narrative and discourse, all bracketed by a prologue and a concluding climax.

PROLOGUE:	Genealogy, Birth and Infancy (1:1-2:23)
NARRATIVE:	Baptism, Temptations, Capernaum (2:24-4:25)
DISCOURSE:	Beatitudes and Justice in the House (5:1-7:29)
NARRATIVE:	Authority and Healing (8:1-9:38)
DISCOURSE:	Mission to and from the House (10:1-11:1)
NARRATIVE:	Rejection by this Generation (11:2-12:50)
DISCOURSE:	Parables of God's Reign for Householders (13:1-13:53)
NARRATIVE:	Acknowledgment by Disciples (13:54-17:23)
DISCOURSE:	House Order and Church Discipline (17:24-19:1)
NARRATIVE:	Authority and Invitation (19:2-22:46)
DISCOURSE:	Woes to the House of Israel and a Blessing for Just Deeds (23:1-26:1)
CLIMAX:	Passion, Death, and Resurrection (26:2-28:20)

In Matthew's sculpting of the Gospel, the Prologue serves as a summary and preview of core themes in the Climax. Both make it clear that Jesus' reign is that of God "with" us (1:23; 28:20). Matthew presents the announcement of Jesus as "king of the Jews" (2:2; 27:37) as a threat to the religious representatives of the empire. This threat results in their efforts to destroy him. As Matthew sees both the infancy narrative and the passion, death, and resurrection events, both evidence that "this man was God's Son" (27:54). Indeed, as John P. Meier notes:

"The passion narrative at the end of the gospel is mirrored in miniature [in the infancy narrative] especially in chap. 2." Such themes include Jesus' rejection by the Jews, acceptance by the Gentiles, persecution unto death and restoration to life through God's intervention on behalf of Jesus, the Christ.[5]

WHAT IS THE PURPOSE OF MATTHEW'S GOSPEL?

The people's allegiance to Rome and its imperium was strictly governed through the religious leaders. The means for maintaining their control revolved around their interpretation of the Law—the religious code of belonging (and not belonging). Specifically this involved adherence to the holiness code or the "righteousness" or justice code as it was defined by them. The basis for this was the Holiness Code itself as expressed in Leviticus: "The Lord spoke to Moses, saying: 'Speak to all the congregation of the people of Israel and say to them: "You shall be holy, for I the Lord your God am holy"'" (Lev. 19:1-2).

Through the centuries a very detailed codification of the Law defining how this holiness would be ensured became the warp and woof of the entire life of Israel. With the fall of Jerusalem and the temple in 70, Pharisaic notions of holiness became even more dominant. At the same time, this approach took on even greater political (belonging to a group) and religious (blessed by God) overtones and implications.

In the language (and, therefore, the culture) of the day, holiness meant to be "set apart." Apartness involved a kind of political apartheid embedded in religious codes of belonging. Being set apart or being holy became defined as being pure. Purity was equated with being clean. Being clean meant being free of those defined as "unclean," impure, and therefore not holy. These were sinners and outsiders. As Marcus Borg notes: "Purity was political because it structured society into a purity system. . . . The ethos of purity produced a politics of purity—that is, a society structured around a purity system."[6] In the face of this prevailing "politics of purity" based on a restrictive notion of justice, Matthew presents Jesus as the just one who does good by a life of mercy and compassion grounded in a more general notion of justice. In the process, Matthew shows that baptism is the way "all justice" will be fulfilled (3:15).

Baptism was to become the sign of one's decision to live within the empire under another kind of reign. Unlike today's overly individualistic interpretation of the Scriptures, first-century baptisms had little to do with personal salvation. They represented a public commitment to live in society as a disciple of the one doing the baptism. On the one hand, it involved a repudiation of the society's underlying patterns; on the other, it witnessed to an alternative way of living that would affect one's world. Since religion was embedded in the political economy, embracing John's baptism was a religious act with political and economic implications; it was meant both to turn around one's life and to subvert one's world (3:2).

Matthew presents Jesus' submission to John's baptism as a repudiation of society's underlying patterns, including the ways of the religious leaders (3:1-10). He also understood baptism to involve a commitment to usher in the reign of God with its demand of personal conversion and social transformation (3:11-12). Specifically this would be expressed via the God-sanctioned commitment "to fulfill" all justice (3:15) as the *sine qua non* for entering the reign or the way of God. In a world alienated from God's vision of right order, Matthew's vision of John and Jesus involved a radical way of reordering life on behalf of justice as core to the Gospel.

In Matthew the "reign" of God that set Jesus apart from John, from his contemporaries, and especially from the religious leaders involved *exousia,* or authority. At the end of the Sermon on the Mount Matthew recalls: "Now when Jesus had finished saying these things, the crowds were astounded at his teaching, for he taught them as one having *exousia,* and not as their scribes" (7:28-29). From the beginning the contrast between Jesus' exercise of authority or his "reign" and that of those in the religiously reinforced imperial system is made clear. It's not just a "them" versus "us" situation; it's his authority versus that of "their scribes." Until the last words of the Gospel, when *exousia* is given the disciples to "make disciples of all nations" (28:18-19), Matthew's portrayal of Jesus contrasts his authority with that of the representatives of the empire (8:9) and the religious leaders (21:23-27 [4x], see 9:6). What he had been given by God (28:18) and gave to "his twelve disciples" (10:1), he now gives to empower the whole community (9:8)—including us who try to live by Jesus' pattern of life.

As in the other Synoptics, the life and ministry of Matthew's Jesus revolve around proclaiming "the reign of God" in contrast to all other forms of power and authority. In that culture of empire where only one reigned—namely, Caesar—the very notion of another "reign" had political overtones. At the same time, since religion was used in the empire to serve as the divine cement that buttressed imperial control over peoples' lives, to call for entrance into the reign of God demanded a commitment to alter existing power relationships which stood opposed to God's way of justice or right ordering. Thus, upon learning "that John had been arrested" for his preaching another reign, and having struggled with the temptation to make the empire's ways his own (4:1-11), Jesus took up the mantle of John's baptismal cry. "From that time" he too began to proclaim the need to change one's ways and one's world: "Repent, for the kingdom of heaven has come near" (4:17).

The parables make it clear that entering God's reign involves a conversion dynamic that invites us to subvert the underlying pattern of life in the world. As John Dominic Crossan has shown, all the parables can be described by images that invite the reader to seek, find, sell, or buy.[7] The parabolic process of entering this reign, or submitting to its authority, finds its finest expression in the seeking and finding, selling and buying defined in Matthew 13:45-46: ". . . the kingdom of heaven is like a merchant in search of fine pearls; on finding one pearl of great value, he went and sold all that he had and bought it." This dynamic not only defines the process of coming under the reign of God; it represents a subversion of the same process of seeking and finding, selling and buying that lies at the heart of today's contemporary empire: the market economy. The central projection of global capitalism, like the central preaching of Jesus, involves coming under one or the other authority: God's reign or the reign of the market; both involve the same process of seeking, finding, selling, and buying.[8]

Like his embrace of John's baptism, at the core of Jesus understanding of God's reign lay one task: the fulfillment of all justice. Like baptism, Jesus' fulfillment of "all justice" or "right order" involved a repudiation of the existing social patterns of the empire as religiously sanctioned by the prevailing arbiters of the Law, the religious leaders. Thus, in the first of the core teachings of Jesus in Matthew (the Sermon on the Mount [5:1-7:29]), Jesus tells his disciples that unless their justice "exceeds that of the scribes and Pharisees, you will never enter the kingdom of heaven" (5:20).

The reason for this new interpretation of the Law and the Prophets brings us to the second dimension of justice or doing good as perceived by Matthew, which also links to baptism: the creation of an alternative way of living based on the example of Jesus himself. For Matthew, following Jesus requires that the disciples create a new kind of household under the authority of God rather than the existing authorities—be they of Caesar or the religious leaders. As members of this new household of faith they would usher in the reign or way of God on earth as it was in heaven by imitation of God's holiness or justice: "Be perfect (*teleios*), therefore, as your heavenly Father is perfect (*teleios*). Such perfection would have to be expressed in a way that surpassed simple observance of the commandments; it would be defined by a community whose members had left the traditional households (19:29) to create a new household of faith based on the fulfillment of a justice established by a reordering of life on behalf of the poor (19:16-22) and those alienated from society because of their disabilities.

For those scandalized by this understanding of discipleship, Matthew returns in chapter 11 to show, that, even John the Baptist needed to rethink what it meant to be identified with Jesus. After the second key discourse (10:1-11:1), the author writes:

> When John heard in prison what the Messiah was doing, he sent word by his disciples and said to him, "Are you the one who is to come, or are we to wait for another?" Jesus answered them, "Go and tell John what you hear and see: the blind receive their sight, the lame walk, the lepers are cleansed, the deaf hear, the dead are raised, and the poor have good news brought to them. And blessed is anyone who takes no offense at me." (11:2-6)

Matthew's understanding of God's messianic presence is inseparably identified with solidarity with the very ones rejected by the prevailing religiously sanctioned social order.

We have already noted how Jesus came to John's baptism to "fulfill" the Law and the Prophets in order to live out their intent, not merely their interpretation by John or the other religious leaders. This involved the implementation of justice or the establishment of right relations among people and their resources in a way that would reveal the reign or perfection of God. As Matthew sculpts the person and message of Jesus in his words and deeds, we find him reconstructing the traditional code of exclusion defined by purity and cleanliness in favor of one defined by inclusion grounded in justice, mercy, and compassion. More specifically, Matthew shows Jesus accomplishing this new way of imitating God's holiness or perfection in the way he presents Jesus' approach to key pillars of the Jewish religion: the Territory, the Temple, the Torah, the Table, and the Touch.

Beyond the Territory of Israel
to the Boundaries of Another Reign

In the agrarian culture of Matthew, territory defined boundaries, beginning with the constitution of the house. Beyond the household "belonging" was extended in ever-diminishing circles. Those furthest from one's household represented territory beyond one's own. This was alien, even "enemy," environment.

From the first words of the Gospel, Matthew makes clear the royal nature of Jesus' background. The genealogy reflects the traditional patriarchal group boundaries Jesus inherited (1:1-17). But, as Jesus remains faithful to the tradition, he does so with a twist. While Matthew makes it clear that Jesus is of the royal Davidic household, at the same time he expands the patriarchal definition of belonging to show that the lineage of "the Christ" is meant to include those normally outside the boundaries: four women (Rahab, Ruth, the wife of Uriah, and Mary).

Next, by having those beyond King Herod "and all Jerusalem with him" (2:3) be the "wise men from the East [who] came to Jerusalem" (2:1), Matthew again expands the boundaries. In the process he also shows that experiencing the reign of God found in the one "born king of the Jews" demands a new kind of worship. This worship involves a reordering of one's resources: "On entering the house, they saw the child with Mary his mother; and they knelt down and paid him homage. Then opening their treasure chests, they offered him gifts of gold, frankincense, and myrrh" (2:11). Authentic religion in the midst of empire not only has political implications; it must have economic significance as well.

The reordering of one's life, relationships, and resources will later become part of the core teaching of Jesus (see 4:18-22; 8:18-22; 19:16-30). It demands a break with the pattern of the empire: "Do not store up for yourselves treasures on earth, where moth and rust consume and where thieves break in and steal; but store up for yourselves treasures in heaven, where neither moth nor rust consumes and where thieves do not break in and steal. For where your treasure is, there your heart will be also" (6:19-21). Recognizing the enslavement of the mind that comes from "what you will eat or what you will drink" or "what you will wear," Matthew's Jesus invites his followers to be given over in their hearts to another reign based on God's way of justice: "Strive first for the kingdom of God and his righteousness, and all these things will be given to you as well" (6:33).

Next, while Matthew does have Jesus circumscribe his ministry and that of his disciples to the "house" of Israel alone, almost from the beginning, intimations of a wider circle of believers connected to him is made clear: "And great crowds followed him from Galilee, the Decapolis, Jerusalem, Judea, and from beyond the Jordan" (4:25).

God's people, Israel, were to be shepherded by this one "born king" not "of the Jews" (since "the Jews" was not a term used at that time) or the Judeans, but the Galileans and the Pereans as well (4:25). All were to come under the authority of this one called "'Emmanuel,' which means 'God is with us'" (1:23). After Jesus is labeled "King" of the Judeans by "the soldiers of the governor" (27:27-29), it is the outsiders—"the centurion and those with him"—who proclaim his authority beyond any human kind to that of divinity itself: "Truly this man was God's Son" (27:54).

Finally, with the resurrection inviting the disciples of Jesus to go beyond Judea and Jerusalem "to Galilee, to the mountain to which Jesus had directed them" (28:16), all geographic boundaries are broken when Jesus opens up the world as his territory for evangelization. Now he commands that disciples be made (*mathēteutheis*) of all nations (28:19). Now, going beyond Judea and empowered at Galilee, Matthew makes clear what he intimated earlier: Jesus is fulfilling what had been spoken through the prophet Isaiah:

> Here is my servant, whom I have chosen,
> my beloved, with whom my soul is well pleased.
> I will put my Spirit upon him,
> and he will bring justice to the Gentiles.
> He will not wrangle or cry aloud,
> nor will anyone hear his voice in the streets.
> He will not break a bruised reed or quench a smoldering
>   wick
> until he brings justice to victory.
> And in his name the Gentiles will hope. (Matt. 12:18-21)

While Matthew describes Jesus as breaking boundaries of geography and ideology, especially once he is risen, he also shows how Jesus could be overly circumscribed by them. At the same time, however, even here he shows that human need and the cry for mercy elicited from Jesus his *exousia* in the form of healing in a way that manifested his alternative model of observing the holiness code. The classic example of Jesus being defined by his cultural patterns of restriction, yet being able to transcend them, revolves around the time Jesus left the "land of Gennesaret" (14:34) "and went away to the district of Tyre and Sidon" (15:21). There he was confronted by "a Canaanite woman from that region [who] came out and started shouting, 'Have mercy on me, Lord, son of David: my daughter is tormented by a demon'" (15:22).

Elaine M. Wainwright has written that the traditions around this story of Jesus and the Canaanite woman show us "two very different readings of Jesus and of the reign of God movement within Matthean households."[9] Faithful to the cultural codes that demanded a Jewish male shun someone "different" (a woman and a Gentile), "he did not answer her at all" (15:23). Matthew recalls Jesus' self-imposed limitation of his evangelizing. He attributes to Jesus the exclusivistic statement "I was sent only to the lost sheep of the house of Israel" (15:24) and an ethnic slur used by Judeans against "enemies" such as Canaanites. He calls her a member of "the dogs" (15:26). However, given her persistent cry for "mercy" (15:22-23), Matthew shows Jesus extending the mercy he had limited to the other children of David to her because of her "great" faith (15:28). Mercy, in Matthew, finds Jesus redefining the holiness codes characterized by separation and removing the boundaries that demanded that exclusive control of God's reign be in the hands of the chosen few.

Beyond the Temple's Boundaries to Include
Those Previously Rejected from It—Even on the Sabbath

At the time of Jesus, people's participation and placement in the temple depended on their classification. Such circumscription defined one's belonging to "the House of Israel." By the time the final version of Matthew was written, the temple had been destroyed and the synagogue had taken its place. Hence a new kind of classification system to determine communal belonging was demanded.

In showing how Jesus identified with the very ones the system had rejected from the temple, Matthew's Jesus declares to the religious leaders that "something greater than the temple is here" (12:6). In this one, mercy will define belonging rather than the temple's sabbaths, rules, and rituals. Moving on toward Jerusalem, with the temple as its center, Matthew describes Jesus' entrance into Jerusalem and the temple itself (21:1ff.) as an act of subversion of the system. In contrast to the way the "king" or other leaders of the empire would make a formal entrance into the capital city with horse and chariot to parade their authority and reign, "Jesus sent two disciples, saying to them, 'Go into the village ahead of you, and immediately you will find a donkey tied, and a colt with her; untie them and bring them to me. If anyone says anything to you, just say this, "The Lord needs them"'" (21:2-3).

As Jesus entered Jerusalem, "a very large crowd spread their cloaks on the road, and others cut branches from the trees and spread them on the road. The crowds that went ahead of him and that followed were shouting, 'Hosanna to the Son of David'" (21:9). As King Herod "and all Jerusalem with him" were frightened at the first announcement to the world of "the child who has been born king of the Jews" (2:2-3), so now "the whole" of Jerusalem "was in turmoil, asking: 'Who is this?'" (21:10).

Making his formal entrance into this religiously sanctioned seat of Rome's power, Jesus "drove out" and "overturned" those practices and forces that undermined the temple's integrity in order to re-dedicate it to authentic holiness. It was to return to being a house of prayer in contrast to "a den of robbers" (21:13). In this setting "robbers" were not just those greedy ones who extorted and exploited the poor and kept people marginalized; at a deeper level, robbers were those who had stolen the people's identity as belonging to God alone. Thus "the blind and the lame came to him in the temple, and he cured them" (21:14).

It seems interesting that here in the temple of Jerusalem Matthew uniquely presents Jesus not as teaching but as one healing, making whole—which was a deeper threat to the authority of the leaders. That the "chief priests and the scribes" saw what he did and realized the reaction of the people to his display of power and authority and even "the children crying out *in the temple*, 'Hosanna to the Son of David,'" they became angry" (21:15). This anger of theirs first would lead them to challenge his authority *in the temple* (21:23-27). Then, when they realized that his exercise of authority threatened to take away their kingdom in favor of "a people that produces the fruits of the kingdom" (21:43)—such as those tax collectors and prostitutes who followed "the way of justice" (21:31-32)—they "realized that he was speaking about them." Consequently they "wanted to arrest him" (21:45-46).

Of all four accounts of the "cleansing" of the temple, Matthew's version makes it clear that a restored temple finds Jesus at its heart, with those once excluded coming into his presence (21:14). The implications of Jesus' activity were clear to those exercising authority that might exclude the outsiders. According to Letty Russell: "Like Jesus in the temple, those who are 'house revolutionaries' do not wish to destroy the house of authority. Quite the contrary, they wish to build it up again as a new house in which the authority of God's love and care for the outsiders is clearly seen."[10] Indeed, when the reign of God's mercy-filled justice is the order of the household, those "outside" are received "inside."

This necessitated more than ever that "belonging" to Israel be strictly restricted to smaller groups who had proved their fidelity; these would revolve around boundaries called "synagogues." With the temple destroyed, "their" synagogue became the predominant locale for word and worship rituals. However, even here the notion of mercy in response to human needs must dominate all other approaches to religion. After allowing his hungry disciples to begin "to pluck heads of grain and to eat" on the Sabbath (12:1) and then riposting the Pharisees with his own challenge: "If you had known what this means, 'I desire mercy and not sacrifice,' you would not have condemned the guiltless. For the Son of Man is lord of the Sabbath" (12:7-8).

Immediately after this "he left that place and entered their synagogue" (12:9), only to be confronted by a man "there with a withered hand" (12:10). Trying to undermine Jesus and find him guilty of violating the Law, the synagogue leaders "asked him, 'Is it lawful to cure on the Sabbath?' so that they might accuse him" (12:10). Declaring "it is lawful to do good on the Sabbath" Jesus "restored" the man's withered hand (12:12-13). This was enough for the Pharisees to go out and conspire as to how Jesus might be destroyed (12:14).

Reinterpreting the Torah to Ensure the Law's True Purpose: Right Relations among All

The Law had always been part of the glue that would hold the people of Israel together. However, when the temple was destroyed and Jerusalem fell in 70, the highest political body of Judaism—the Sanhedrin—vanished. Fearing the loss of identity for themselves and the people, some Pharisaic scribes were able to reestablish the main authority of the high council at the imperial city of Jamnia through a renewed stress on the Law. They—and their interpretation of the Law—would now constitute the power that would hold the people together. Through a stringent obedience to the purity codes contained in the Law, the Pharisees believed, Israel would be able to maintain its identity by isolating itself from those it defined as "impure" who lived in the empire.

In many ways, then, the Law took on an even greater force in the people's lives at the time the First Gospel was written than it had at the time of Jesus. Indeed, while Territory and Temple helped define the people, now only Torah and Table would be sources of meaning for the people. As a result it might be likely that Matthew retro-read into the text the situation experienced by his community as it stood outside the synagogues of Israel. Law is the glue of structures; by going beyond the Law (at least the scribal or Pharisaic interpretation of it) to reorder relationships to include the excluded, Matthew's Jesus showed that mercy must be at the heart of the household ethos he came to proclaim (9:13).

In this context of a justice grounded in mercy, Matthew reinterprets Jesus' approach to the Law, or Torah. On the one hand, he accepts the need for the most scrupulous observance (5:18-19), but, on the other hand, he shows how he has come "to fulfill" the Law and the Prophets (5:17): via a justice that embraces mercy in a way that reveals the reign of God's holiness or perfection. This he explicates in six examples (5:21-48) of how the Law and the Prophets are to be observed in a way that would truly fulfill their intent (5:17). Grounding himself in the existing societal understanding of the Law as defined by the leaders (at Jamnia?) he invited his disciples to embrace a deeper way of reordering relationships in their world. Now he declared to his followers that unless their justice (the basis of the Law and the Prophets) "exceeds that of the scribes and Pharisees, you will never enter the kingdom of heaven" (5:20).

Building on the received tradition, Matthew shows Jesus going beyond the interpretation defined by the scribal Pharisees to a new way of living in merciful justice in Jesus' house of disciples. Now his followers could not just refrain from murder, they must refrain from its source: that kind of anger that severs familial ties. Instead they must seek to be reconciled with their opponents (5:21-26). As his followers, they must not only refrain from adultery; they must commit their entire selves to a new kind of fidelity (5:27-30) that would be expressed in ways that could not even lead to adultery (5:31-32). As his followers, they would stand on their own word, instead of echoing society's codes about the taking of oaths (5:33-37). In a culture of oppression determined by honor challenges and ripostes meant to shame, he invited his followers to embrace a nonviolent way to deal with one's enemies and those in need (5:38-42). And, finally, and probably most importantly, in a world defined by reciprocal relationships circumscribed by those of one's own household and kin in opposition to "your enemy," Matthew's Jesus demanded of his disciples that they love their enemies and pray for their persecutors "so that you may be children of your Father in heaven," whose sun rises on the evil and the good and whose rain is sent on the just and unjust (5:43-47).

Welcoming Those Systemically Excluded to Become Part of Table Fellowship

As noted above, with the loss of territorial definition and the Temple, Torah and Table became the two poles around which Israel's life would revolve. Sharing in this life was defined clearly by notions of table fellowship. For the Jamnian Jews, table fellowship served as a microcosm of the ideal community. It mirrored the social order or structure of justice envisioned for the nation. Israel's unique union with God was thus perceived in terms of table fellowship (Ps. 23:5; 78:19; Isa. 25:6; Ezek. 39:20). Jacob Neusner has shown that, especially after 70, the Pharisees became a kind of "table-fellowship sect,"[11] establishing themselves as ultimate authorities among the people in a way that demanded exclusion of non-Jews as a sign of covenantal fidelity. But, for Matthew's Jesus, this was not enough.

As Matthew portrays Jesus (and therefore, what is essential for discipleship), Jesus' form of table fellowship set him apart from the scribes and other reformers such as the Pharisees. Jesus' actions show his acceptance of the basic Pharisaic insights. Yet he went further and mirrored the need for a more humane and merciful reordering of the basic patterns of table fellowship. We have already seen how Jesus' original rejection of the Canaanite woman involving images of table fellowship ("It is not fair to take the children's food and throw it to the dogs" [15:26]) was reordered in response to her faithful cry for mercy. Such mercy must prevail at every table; it must constitute the core of every community of disciples.

Perhaps the most significant entry showing the reordering around table fellowship that was to characterize the Matthean Jesus can be found when he is "in the house" after his call of Matthew. By sitting at the same table in his own house with the excluded and outcasts, called "sinners and tax collectors" (9:10), Jesus challenged the existing social order. He invited it to turn from a model that excluded to one more open to all. Sharing a meal with others in that ranked society symbolized equality with them; inviting the marginalized to table made them equals. Jesus' approach to table fellowship not only was expressed in his equal treatment of people—especially those outside the system. It also led to him being perceived as their "friend" (11:19). The Pharisees viewed such an approach as subverting their conviction of what Israel needed for true social ordering.

The story of the king's wedding feast for his son (22:1-14), which Matthew recalled from one of his sources shared with Luke ("Q"), makes it clear that, when table fellowship reflects "the reign of God," the inevitable invitation will go beyond those "who had been invited" originally "to the wedding banquet" but who would not come (22:3-8), to include "everyone" who can be found on "the main streets" (22:9).

If "insiders"—be they the scribes and Pharisees of Jesus' day, the judaizers of Matthew's day (or those who exclude in any day [28:20])—insist on limiting table fellowship, they face exclusion themselves: "I tell you, many will come from east and west and sit at table with Abraham, Isaac, and Jacob in the kingdom of heaven, while the sons of the kingdom will be thrown into the outer darkness" (8:11-12).

With this passage we turn to its context: the healing touch of Jesus that revealed the in-breaking of God's messianic reign of mercy and justice which makes people whole (11:1ff).

Touching the Untouchables with Healing to Announce God's Reign

In the first-century world, human pathology was seen more as a familial dilemma or a social problem than as an individual's plight. People did not look so much at the symptoms as at the relational dynamics. Depending on people's sickness, they could be defined as "unclean" and, therefore, unable to participate in wider social interaction. Furthermore, a significant function of the priests in this culture involved the power to declare people clean or unclean, touchable or untouchable, or ostracized from the community. For someone to be declared clean, independent of the defining power of the religious leaders, served notice to them—and the wider culture—that another power was now at hand.

The first of Jesus' miracles in the Gospel according to Matthew involved a triptych of healings: the leper (8:1-4), the servant of "a centurion" (8:5-13), and Peter's mother-in-law (8:14-15). Matthew presents each of these as a manifestation of the in-breaking of God's reign of restorative healing of the people who, at the worst, represented those alienated from society and who, at the best, were merely tolerated in that social system.

In the first of the healings, Jesus is approached by the person most feared in the first-century Mediterranean world: the leper. According to the Law, a person's leprosy (which covered many skin diseases, including what we know as psoriasis today) demanded that that individual be excluded from the community until declared healed and ritually purified. Once declared "clean," the person had to make a sin offering (Leviticus 13-14). While all the Synoptic Gospels narrate the story of the leper's situation and Jesus' healing, only Matthew places the story first (8:1-4). By beginning with the event, the reader realizes that Matthew's intent is to portray Jesus as the one whose caring touch can break all boundaries and make those most alienated whole and restored.

In the second miracle story we find another outsider—a centurion—pleading for the life of his servant. We also find the second use of the word *exousia* in Matthew. After hearing about the plight of the servant, "Jesus said: 'I will come and cure him.' The centurion answered, 'Lord, I am not worthy to have you come under my roof; but only speak the word, and my servant will be healed. For I also am a man under authority (*exousia*) . . .'" (8:7-9).

A leader representing the empire itself can acknowledge openly a higher authority; in Matthew, it will be clear, the religious leaders cannot (21:23-27). In this passage we also find contrasted the faith of an outsider and that of "the heirs." The first elicited Jesus' merciful healing; the latter elicited his sharp retort: "Truly I tell you, in no one in Israel have I found such faith. I tell you, many will come from east and west and will eat with Abraham and Isaac and Jacob in the kingdom of heaven, while the heirs of the kingdom will be thrown into the outer darkness, where there will be weeping and gnashing of teeth" (8:10-12).

The third of the triad of healings involves Jesus touching the hand of Peter's fevered mother-in-law in a way that restored her so that "she got up and began to serve him" (8:14-15). Matthew shows Jesus breaking many boundaries, but not the one that exists in the majority of households to this day: the women serve the men!

That Matthew sees these first three of Jesus' healings as fulfilling the messianic hopes of the people is clear from his next words: "That evening they brought to him many who were possessed with demons; and he cast out the spirits with a word, and cured all who were sick. This was to fulfill what had been spoken through the prophet Isaiah, 'He took our infirmities and bore our diseases'" (8:16-17).

As he presents Jesus and what it means to be part of the reign of

God, Matthew makes it clear that healing and restoration constitute God's holiness or reign and are, at their core, the way of messianic mercy. Even more than mercy, the notion of compassion (*splagchnizomai*) goes even beyond selective mercy (to this person or that group) to be extended in *every* case in ever-widening circles of people who are marginalized and in need—even to "the crowds." We find this in the five times the verb *splagchnizomai* is used.

Whenever Matthew uses *splagchnizomai* (translated as "having a heart moved with compassion") we find it in the middle of a structural triad. The triad begins with the description of some kind of need (being harassed and helpless like sheep without a shepherd [9:36], being sick [14:14] or hungry [15:32], being caught in a huge debt [18:24-25], or simply being blind [20:30]). Second, these situations of need elicit *splagchnizomai*, a movement coming from deep within one's bowels. Finally, the need is not only acknowledged and the heart is not only moved with compassion; something must be done to address the need the heart has felt.

Thus, this pattern of seeing a need, being moved with compassion, and doing something about the problem demands imitation. The final story involving *splagchnizomai* narrates how, upon Jesus' heart being "moved with compassion," he touched their eyes in a way that enabled them to regain their sight. However, now they could not only see; they could walk in his footsteps. They too could put into practice his words and deeds: "Immediately . . . they followed him" (20:34). Following Jesus demands that we embrace the new way of holiness: the life of compassion.

WHO IS THE MODEL DISCIPLE IN MATTHEW?

In considering authentic following of Jesus, we understand the nature of true discipleship. And when we examine Matthew's Gospel to discover who an authentic disciple might be, we do not locate such a person in any of the apostles—even Peter (who receives the most prominent place of anyone in Matthew's version). Rather we find Jesus pointing to an outsider, one who "did not count" in that society (see 14:21; 15:39). He proclaims that the deeds of a woman—at a table—are the model of discipleship; they should be embraced everywhere until the end of the ages: "Truly I tell you, wherever this good news is proclaimed in the whole world, what she has done will be told in remembrance of her" (26:13). In Matthew's version we read:

> Now while Jesus was at Bethany in the house of Simon the leper, a woman came to him with an alabaster jar of very costly ointment, and she poured it on his head as he sat at the table. But when the disciples saw it, they were angry and said, "Why this waste? For this ointment could have been sold for a large sum, and the money given to the poor." But Jesus, aware of this, said to them, "Why do you trouble the woman? She has performed a good service for me. For you always have the poor with you, but you will not always have me. By pouring this ointment on my body she has prepared me for burial. Truly I tell you, wherever this good news is proclaimed in the whole world, what she has done will be told in remembrance of her." (26:6-13)

We have already seen that the true disciple is the one "like the master of a household who brings out of his treasure what is new and what is old" (13:52). What is there about this woman, in this household, at this table, with her alabaster jar of very costly ointment, that makes Matthew's Jesus describe her as the model disciple? How, in her anonymity, is she being elevated to be the archetype of authentic discipleship for all time? How might a reader in today's consumer culture find in her a way of life that can be imitated?

First of all, we must set the context: it is a house (*oikia*). In the first century, a household involved *persons* (husbands and wives, parents and children, masters and slaves, and sometimes others of the kin). A household also included various *resources* (land, buildings, boats, nets, money). How persons related to each other and their resources defined whether the household would be patriarchal or more egalitarian. How the house would be ordered or regulated (*nomos*) defined the economic (*oikonomia*) as well as religious (for us, *ekklēsia*) relationships. These cultural "givens" must be understood if we are properly to grasp the power of this final story before Jesus' betrayal by Judas Iscariot (26:14).

The scene takes place in the house of "Simon the leper." Herein a person culturally prohibited from initiating communication with a man—"a woman"—"came to" Jesus. The text highlights the dynamics that took place "in the house" between two persons "at table." The woman came to Jesus with a resource representing wealth (signifying the economic situation of the "house churches" to whom Matthew addressed the Gospel?): an "alabaster jar of very costly ointment." In a gesture recalling an earlier story of a generosity-beyond-what-is-just with one's resources (20:13-15), the woman pours the ointment "on his head as he sat at the table" (26:6-7). In this opening sentence (26:6-7) are structured all the dynamics for what Matthew considers proper household interactions: people in mutual relationships with resources that are shared generously. All occur "at the table." This represents the new kind of household relationships that are to be structured in every community of disciples that remains faithful to Jesus' teachings.

When "the disciples" protest that the "ointment could have been sold for a large sum, and the money given to the poor" (26:8-9), Matthew reveals how Jesus rejects the notion and, in the process, outlines what it means to be an authentic disciple. His vision of discipleship does not canonize the poor, as does Luke (Luke 6:20-21). It goes deeper—to the need for a reordering of one's resources on behalf of the poor in a way that will make things right in terms of both of economics and religion (26:12).

The unique word Matthew's Jesus uses to describe the woman's action—"a good service for me"—is *kalon ērgasato eis eme*. The work that God began in the beginning (see Genesis 1), which Jesus came to do and which now is continued by this disciple, is envisioned as "good." Her "good work" was not to be poor but to respond to Jesus' projected poverty: to "prepare me for burial" (26:12). In Jesus' eyes, according to Matthew, good works are those which meet the needs of others (11:2, 5). People are blessed (11:6; see 5:3-13) when their work imitates Jesus' works (11:2), when they direct their resource to meet the needs of other persons (25:31-46) in a way that will enable the world to see the "good" that they do (5:14-16).

The concept of "doing"—in contrast to "saying"—and "doing good" in contrast to "doing evil" or nothing at all in the face of injustice and evil is central to Matthew. Doing God's will is linked with putting morality and spirituality into practice (6:1; 23:3), bearing fruit (3:8, 10; 7:16, 17 [2x], 18 [2x], 19, 20; 12:33 [3x]; 21:19, 34, 41, 43), as well as being and doing good (5:45; 7:11 [2x]; 12:34; 12:53 [3x]; 19:16, 17 [2x]; 20:15; 22:10; 25:21, 23). These notions of doing good and bearing fruit are also connected in Matthew with being just (*dikaios* [1:19; 5:45; 9:13; 10:41; 13:17, 43, 49; 20:4; 23:28, 29, 35; 25:37, 46; 27:19, 24]) and the practice of justice itself (*dikaiosynē* [3:15; 5:6, 10, 20; 6:1, 33; 21:32]). Those in the household who do justice are those who will enter the reign of God. Those doing the will of God in justice determine who in the households or who gathered with Jesus in the house will enter God's reign.

In Matthew, unlike what some in today's world would have us

believe, Jesus does not condone poverty by saying "you will always have the poor with you." Rather he honors all those who, following the model of this woman, use their resources to do good in a way that brings about God's reign of justice and proclaims the holiness of God's name on earth as in heaven (6:9-13). Such teaching is what must be proclaimed to "all nations." Those discipled to Jesus can be assured that, if they remain faithful to their baptism in an alien empire and "obey everything" he has commanded, his words will serve as comfort in their lives even if they are flogged in "their synagogues" or "dragged before governors and kings" (10:17-18): "Remember, I am with you always, to the end of the age" (28:20). Until the end of the age, "what she did" must be what we must do as well.

NOTES

1. John P. Meier in Raymond E. Brown and John P. Meier, *Antioch and Rome: New Testament Cradles of Catholic Christianity* (New York: Paulist, 1983), 51.

2. For a thorough approach to Matthean discipleship, see Michael J. Wilkins, *The Concept of Disciple in Matthew's Gospel as Reflected in the Use of the Term* Mathētēs, Novum Testamentum Supplement 59 (Leiden/New York/Copenhagen: Brill, 1998).

3. Michael H. Crosby, *House of Disciples: Christ, Economics, and Justice in Matthew* (Maryknoll, N.Y.: Orbis, 1988), 11.

4. Douglas R. A. Hare, "How Jewish Is the Gospel of Matthew?" *Catholic Biblical Quarterly* 62 (2000): 269.

5. John P. Meier, *Matthew* (Wilmington, Del.: Michael Glazier, 1980), 2.

6. Marcus J. Borg, *Meeting Jesus Again for the First Time: The Historical Jesus and the Heart of Contemporary Faith* (San Francisco: HarperSanFrancisco, 1994), 50.

7. John Dominic Crossan, *In Parables: The Challenge of the Historical Jesus* (New York: Harper & Row, 1973).

8. Michael H. Crosby, O.F.M.Cap., *Spirituality of the Beatitudes: Matthew's Challenge for First World Christians* (Maryknoll, N.Y.: Orbis, 1981), 39-40.

9. Elaine M. Wainwright, *Shall We Look for Another? A Feminist Rereading of the Matthean Jesus,* Bible and Liberation Series (Maryknoll, N.Y.: Orbis, 1998), 92.

10. Letty M. Russell, *Household of Freedom: Authority in Feminist Theology* (Philadelphia: Westminster, 1987), 63.

11. Jacob Neusner, *From Politics to Piety: The Emergence of Pharisaic Judaism* (Englewood Cliffs, N.J.: Prentice-Hall, 1973), 80.

RESOURCES FOR FURTHER STUDY

Balch, David L., ed. *Social History of the Matthean Community: Cross-Disciplinary Approaches.* Minneapolis: Fortress, 1991.

Borg, Marcus J. *Meeting Jesus Again for the First Time: The Historical Jesus and the Heart of Contemporary Faith.* San Francisco: HarperSan Francisco, 1994.

Crosby, Michael H. *House of Disciples: Church, Economics and Justice in Matthew.* Maryknoll, N.Y.: Orbis, 1988.

———. *Spirituality of the Beatitudes: Matthew's Challenge for First World Christians.* Maryknoll, N.Y.: Orbis, 1981.

Love, Stuart. "The Household: A Major Social Component for Gender Analysis in the Gospel of Matthew." *Biblical Theology Bulletin* 23 (1993): 21-31.

Luz, Ulrich. *Matthew in History: Interpretation, Influence and Effects.* Minneapolis: Fortress, 1994.

———. *The Theology of the Gospel of Matthew.* Cambridge: Cambridge University Press, 1995.

Malina, Bruce J., and Richard L. Rohrbaugh. *Social-Science Commentary on the Synoptic Gospels.* Minneapolis: Fortress, 1992.

Stanton, Graham N. *A Gospel for a New People: Studies in Matthew.* Louisville: Westminster/John Knox, 1993.

Wainwright, Elaine M. *Shall We Look for Another? A Feminist Rereading of the Matthean Jesus.* Maryknoll, N.Y.: Orbis, 1998.

3

Mark's Gospel

Invitation to Discipleship

CHED MYERS

In our time we have not finished doing away with *idols* and we
have barely begun to listen to *symbols*.
—*Paul Ricoeur*

THE GREAT HEBREW PROPHET ISAIAH envisioned a day in which Israel's
God would "destroy on this mountain the net that is cast over all peoples, the veil that is spread over all nations" (Isa. 25:7). According to
the evangelist Mark, that day dawned in the life, death, and resurrection of Jesus of Nazareth. Mark believed that the story of Jesus was so
extraordinary that he needed to invent a new literary genre. He called
this "gospel" (Mark 1:1, 15), a term he wrested from Roman imperial
propaganda (news of a Roman military victory in the provinces or of
the ascent of a new Caesar was carried abroad as "*euangelion*"). But
Mark is a decidedly anti-imperial story of liberation.

This Gospel was written almost two millennia ago to help imperial
subjects learn the hard truth about their world and themselves. Mark
does not pretend to represent the word of God dispassionately or
impartially, as if it were universally innocuous in its appeal to rich and
poor alike. This story is by, about, and for those committed to God's
work of justice, compassion, and liberation in the world. To the religious, Mark offers no "signs from heaven" (8:11f.). To scholars or
politicians who refuse to commit themselves, he offers no answer

(11:30-33). But to those willing to risk the wrath of empire, Mark offers the way of discipleship (8:34ff.).

An action-based hero narrative, Mark is unlike Roman biographies in that its main characters are drawn not from the elite classes but from plain folk. Jesus is portrayed as a healer and an exorcist, but in contrast to popular tales of magicians common to that period, Mark downplays the miraculous, emphasizing instead the empowerment of Jesus' subjects ("Your faith has healed you" [5:34; 10:52]). Repudiating the authority of both the Judean ruling class and the Roman imperium, Mark's Jesus envisions social reconstruction from the bottom up. His practice of radical inclusiveness among women, outcasts, the poor, and the unclean questions all forms of political and personal domination. This Jesus calls for a revolution of means as well as ends, enjoining his followers to embrace nonviolence and to risk its consequences. At the center of the story stands the contradiction of the cross—life given, not taken—representing the only power that can remove the "veil" over the nations.

CONTEXT AND INTERPRETATION OF THE GOSPEL

There is probably no part of the Bible that has been more the subject of both popular commentary and scholarly investigation than the Gospel of Mark. It has a long and fascinating history of interpretation (see Kealy 1982). As the earliest story of Jesus, it has preoccupied critical scholarly efforts to reconstruct the life of the historical Jesus (or, more modestly, the history of the earliest Christian communities). Each new epoch of modern biblical criticism has used Mark as a crucible in which new reading strategies are tested, established, and overthrown. The historical-critical methods of form and redaction analysis that prevailed throughout most of the twentieth century cut their teeth on Mark (Perrin 1976). In turn, on the basis of work in Mark, these methods were dethroned in favor of literary and other, postmodern approaches (Anderson and Moore 1992). Mark "remains tantalizingly at the center of critical pursuits" (Bilezikian 1977, 11).

Meanwhile, outside the academy, Mark has, as the shortest and "plainest" of our four Gospels, traditionally been used in the church for evangelism and Christian formation. It has also animated many alternative Christian communities in the Anglo-American world over the last thirty years. This "radical discipleship" movement arose among those in First World churches (Catholic and Protestant) who were thirsting for the "whole gospel for the whole person for the whole world." Exposure to the uncompromising call to commitment in Mark was for many, including myself, the invitation to a "second conversion" and fired our battle against acculturated Christianity.

As the great Markan scholar Eduard Schweizer (1960, 21) put it, for Mark "one cannot know who Jesus is until one shares his way with him." This compelled our movement to look also to the various subversive discipleship traditions that have persisted throughout church history, from the fifth-century monastic communities to the twentieth-century Confessing Church. But we have always returned to Mark, under the tutelage of activist sages such as John Vincent in England, Athol Gill in Australia, and William Stringfellow in the United States (see Gill 1989). It is the contention of this movement (and of this chapter) that Mark remains a manifesto for Christians today who would be *radical.* That is, Mark helps us to return to the *roots* of our faith tradition as well as to probe the *roots* of the dysfunction, violence, and injustice that haunt our world (see Myers 1994).

The reading strategy I use and recommend draws upon three major new approaches that have emerged in Gospel scholarship since the 1970s: the sociological, the literary, and the "ideological" (see Myers 1988, 3ff.). It treats the text as a narrative, analyzing form and content. It also assumes that the narrative reflects an ideological point of view, which in turn is a response to real social, economic, and political circumstances. Thus, the *narrative* strategy found in the text reflects, directly or indirectly, a *sociopolitical* positioning and practice within a given historical context. It is also incumbent upon interpreters to state their own preconceptions and concerns openly. As readers, we must clarify our own social circumstances and perspectives, in order to see how Mark's strategies might correlate with or illuminate our context (e.g., the African American reading of Mark by Brian Blount [1998] or the Japanese feminist approach of Hisako Kinukawa [1994]). If we read Mark *as scripture,* we must also allow Mark to "read" us.

There are various opinions about when, where, and why Mark was written, and, as is the case with all books of the Bible, we can never be sure. Church tradition, and up until recently most scholars as well, holds that the Gospel was written in Rome by a Jewish-Christian author for a predominantly Gentile audience. I agree, however, with the growing number of scholars who place the production of Mark in or near northern Palestine (see Kee 1977, 176ff.).

Whether or not one dates the text before or after 70 C.E.—the year the Romans destroyed the Jerusalem temple, thus ending a four-year popular Judean revolt—influences how one interprets Mark's polemic against that temple system. Some assert that Mark wrote after the war, trying to justify theologically the Christian community's rift with Judaism, and perhaps even the Roman victory (see, e.g., Brandon 1968). I disagree. Mark's vigorous criticism of the temple state is primarily *political and economic*, not theological, and would have been superfluous once the temple no longer stood. I therefore propose a date sometime during the Judean revolt (66-70 C.E.). The urgency reflected particularly in the "apocalyptic" sermon of Mark 13 is more understandable if the Gospel was produced during the conflicted and dangerous days of the military struggle between the Judean nationalists and the Roman counter-insurgency campaign (see Myers 1988, 413ff.).

Mark's Greek is relatively poor, suggesting that it may have been his second language (as it was for most literate Palestinians). The text is peppered with Latin and Semitic idioms. The Latinisms (e.g., in 5:9; 12:16; or 15:15) have been interpreted as evidence of the text's Roman origins. But in every case they are socioeconomic and administrative terms and thus could simply reflect Roman linguistic penetration in the colonized culture of Palestine. Mark occasionally explains a Jewish practice (e.g., 7:3, 11), indicating that this text was also for Gentile Christians. But there is far more about Judean culture that he simply assumes, for example the revering of the "mountain" of the temple (11:23); the abhorrence of pigs (5:11f.) and antipathy toward foreigners (7:24-30); and the privileges of the scribal elite (12:38ff.). Mark's narrative may also reflect a rural bias, since cities are always places of conflict for Jesus (see 1:45), whereas the sea (3:6; 4:1), the wilderness (1:35; 6:31), and the field (4:26-32) are places of reflection and renewal.

Mark was the first to shape a *textual* narrative from the various oral traditions about Jesus that circulated among the early Christians. This had a double significance. First, unlike other early collections of sayings, such as the *Gospel of Thomas,* Mark composed an action story that wove together varied episodes into a sustained plot with developed characters. Indeed, Jesus' sayings play a smaller role in Mark than in any of the subsequent Gospels; action is primary. This reflects Mark's view of discipleship as costly social *practice* (in contrast to, e.g., the bias toward detached religious contemplation that is found in some early Gnostic writings).

Mark also employs symbolic motifs from the contemporary tradition of popular Jewish resistance literature known as apocalyptic (other biblical examples would be Daniel and Revelation). Yet the Gospel is neither a heavenly vision nor a fantastic hero tale, but a decisively *realistic* narrative of struggle anchored in the concrete terrain of Roman Palestine. His portrait of everyday people and recognizable places, of the unequal distribution of social power and privilege, and of political conflicts and their consequences would have been all too familiar to his first audiences.

In writing about Jesus, Mark was, in a sense, constraining the oral tradition. Perhaps he was concerned with the way in which the sayings could be manipulated to legitimate practices that were contrary to those of Jesus. This may be reflected, for example, in Jesus' debate with the Pharisees in 7:1-13, in which he pits the authority of the written Torah against their oral tradition. Indeed, throughout the story Mark's Jesus repeatedly appeals to the Hebrew Scriptures to justify his practices or to attack those of his opponents. He employs Scripture offensively (11:17) and defensively (2:24ff.) and argues interpretation with scribes (12:24ff.), Pharisees (10:2ff.), and Sadducees alike (12:10). This suggests that Mark was passionately engaged in the struggle over how and by whom the sacred tradition was best read.

Mark's strategy also employed Scripture for his own narrative purposes. His direct citations (which come from a Greek version known as the Septuagint) are sometimes conflated (as in 1:2-3 and 10:19), other times reimagined (2:25; 11:1ff.). His allusions are often brief but unmistakable: to the exodus escape from Pharaoh's army in an exorcism (5:13); to Moses at Sinai in the Transfiguration (9:2ff.); or to the Deuteronomic Jubilee in the notoriously misused phrase "the poor will always be among you" (14:7 = Deut. 15:4, 11). More often he simply adapts older stories to new circumstances:

- portraying John the Baptist as an Elijah figure (1:6 = 2 Kgs. 1:8)

- invoking Sabbath mandates to justify Jesus' direct action in a grainfield (2:24ff. = Exod. 23:10f.)

- recontextualizing prophetic seed/tree parables (Ezek. 31; Dan. 4) in Jesus' agrarian metaphors (4:30-32)

- recounting the disciples' crossing of the sea in terms of the Jonah story (4:38 = Jonah 1:5f.)

- renarrating Elisha's bread "miracle" in Jesus' wilderness feedings (6:35-44 = 2 Kgs. 4:42-44)

- invoking Daniel's heavenly courtroom scene to ground Jesus' vocation as the "Human One" (8:38f. = Dan. 7:9-14)

- reiterating Isaiah's parable of the vineyard in order to criticize absentee landlords (12:1-10 = Isa. 5:1-10)

Thus the Markan text reshaped tradition while at the same time endeavoring to "normalize" it. This strategy simultaneously brought the historical Jesus of Nazareth alive in the present *and* distanced him. On one hand, Jesus was not to be embalmed for the sake of reverence, but followed, which means continually recontextualizing his teachings and practices. On the other hand, this Jesus is not under the control of the way one might experience him: he is the Jesus of *this* story and *these* demands. The Gospel is both "open" and "closed," affirming the dialectic between canon and context that characterizes every community committed to a living tradition.

Mark drew upon many of the rhetorical traditions of his time, including various parts of the Hebrew Bible, apocalyptic literature, rabbinic stories, wisdom sayings, and even Greco-Roman tragedy (see further Roth 1988; Tolbert 1989). But his "Gospel" represented a new genre in the literature of antiquity.

To what extent is Mark a *reliable* source for the "historical Jesus"? This is a very modern question, and while it has preoccupied several generations of scholars, it would not have interested a first-century audience. They, like all traditional peoples, did not make an absolute distinction between "facts," "myths," and symbols. I do not think Mark's Gospel is fiction, as does the more skeptical tradition of modern historical scholarship (e.g., Mack 1991). Neither, however, do I think it is best handled merely as a window to "what actually happened" (as does, for example, the Jesus Seminar; see Funk 1998). I do not believe there is history without interpretation. I do believe Mark was a faithful interpreter (and certainly more reliable than any contemporary theologian!) of the earliest traditions, who "shows" and "tells" us about the life and meaning of Jesus of Nazareth.

STRUCTURE OF THE GOSPEL

We can and should approach the Gospel with the native skills we routinely use to interpret stories: looking for plots, characters, and settings. The relationship between narrative *form* (composition and structure) and *content* is also crucial to interpretation. The components of literary structure are the following:

- *sentences* (the basic building blocks of discourse)
- *episodes* (a series of related sentences around a common event or theme)
- *minor sequences* (episodes that are linked around a theme or plot development)
- *major sequences* (a "sequence of sequences" articulating a continuing plot line of the story)
- *overall architectural pattern* (this can sometimes define a *genre*)

Each component has its own (or sometimes more than one) internal structure, and these can be analyzed for clues to Mark's purpose in writing.

There have been numerous proposals for how one might outline the composition of Mark (summarized in Kee 1977, 60ff.). No one of these is conclusive, because ancient storytelling, like a complex tapestry, has multiple dimensions. Mark, though at first glance a deceptively simple, quickly moving story, is no exception. Its texture is rich and layered. For example, a single Markan *episode* (the healing of the blind man at Bethsaida [8:22-26]) can be viewed as having at least three different compositional functions: (1) It can be seen as part of a *minor sequence* of healing episodes that articulate the theme of spiritual "deafness" (7:31-37 and 9:14-29) and "blindness"(8:22-26 and 10:46-52). (2) It can also be seen as the front end of a doublet (along with Mark 10:46-52) that "frames" a *major sequence* of Mark, namely, the teaching cycle from 8:27 through 10:45, which I call the "discipleship catechism." (3) This episode (along with the one that follows it, 8:27-30) is a narrative bridge between the two halves of the story (*overall architecture*). These three compositional "designs" cut across each other, but they are not mutually exclusive.

Having affirmed that there are a variety of ways to "read" the composition of Mark, let me offer one model. The first half of the Gospel (1:1-8:21) takes place largely in and around Galilee, with Capernaum and the Sea of Galilee representing the gravitational center of the narrative world. It introduces the characters and plots and focuses on the healing work of Jesus and the call to discipleship. Its *minor* and *major sequences* may be outlined as follows:

1:1-20	Prologue/call to discipleship
1:21-3:35	First campaign of challenge: around Capernaum
4:1-34	First sermon: parables
4:35-8:10	First campaign of affirmation: around the Sea of Galilee
8:11-21	Symbolic epilogue to first half

The second half of the story (8:22-16:8) deals with Jesus' journey to Jerusalem and its consequences, and focuses on Jesus' teaching and the cost of discipleship:

8:22-9:13	Second prologue/call to discipleship (the "confessional crisis")
9:14-10:52	Second campaign of affirmation: from Bethany to Jerusalem
11:1-12:44	Second campaign of challenge: around the Jerusalem temple
13:1-37	Second sermon: apocalypse and parables
14:1-15:39	Arrest and execution of Jesus (passion narrative)
15:40-16:8	Symbolic epilogue to second half

At the end of Mark's story, our attention is directed suddenly *back* to Galilee and the prospect of following Jesus anew (16:7). This gives the narrative as a whole a sort of circular character, reopening the discipleship adventure that had tragically closed with the scattering of the community (14:50f.) and Jesus' execution by the authorities (15:16-47). This architecture compels the reader to keep rereading the story so as to "understand" ever more deeply its meaning (Mark 8:21).

There is a rough symmetry between the constituent sequences in each of these halves, or "books," of Mark.

Narrative Sequence	*Book I*	*Book II*
(A) Prologue/call to discipleship	1:1-20	8:22-9:13
(B) Campaign of challenge	1:21-3:35	11:1-12:44
(C) Extended sermon	4:1-34	13:1-37
(D) Campaign of affirmation	4:35-8:10	9:14-10:52
(E) "Passion" tradition	6:14-29	14:1-15:39
(F) Symbolic epilogue	8:11-21	15:40-16:8

While these elements do not necessarily appear in corresponding order in each half, the parallels are unmistakable. We will get a feel for the narrative strategy of Mark by looking at them more closely.

(A) Each *prologue* introduces the essential symbols, characters, and plot complications of the respective "books." Each takes place in the context of "the Way" (1:2f.; 8:27) and discusses the relationship between Jesus and John-as-Elijah (1:6; 8:28). In both prologues, Jesus is confirmed as the anointed one by the divine voice (1:11; 9:7) in conjunction with symbolism drawn from the exodus tradition (wilderness [1:2, 13]; mountain [9:2]). Each articulates a call to discipleship (1:16-20; 8:34-36) specifically in regard to Peter, James, and John (1:16, 19; 9:2). In Book I Jesus calls disciples to follow him in overturning the structures of the present social order, but because these disciples' understanding is suspect, Jesus must, in the prologue of Book II, extend a "second" call to follow, in which he introduces the central symbol for the rest of the narrative: the cross.

(B) What I call the *"campaigns of challenge"* consists of a series of conflict stories. The first sequence dramatizes Jesus' criticisms of the authorities in the provinces of Galilee (1:21ff.). The second, set in Judea and Jerusalem, narrates Jesus' confrontation with the political stewards of the public order at the seat of its power: the temple (11:1ff.). Both campaigns involve actions aimed at delegitimizing the current social arrangement. In the first half of Mark these are predominantly healings and exorcisms, while in the second half they are mostly verbal jousting and symbolic direct action. Each campaign centers on dramatic acts of "civil disobedience" (2:23-27; 11:12-25) that provoke the authorities to conspire to arrest Jesus (3:6; 12:12). Each culminates with an object lesson concerning the system's exploitation of the poor (3:1-5; 12:38-44) and closes with Jesus' ideological polarization from the scribal establishment (3:22ff.; 12:35-44).

(C) Each of the above campaigns is followed by a narrative moment of reflection, in which Jesus offers an extended *sermon*. The first begins as an address to the crowd (4:1), but ends in a private explanation to the disciples (4:10-34). Conversely, the second sermon begins as a strictly private revelation (13:3-5) but concludes with a warning addressed to "all" (13:37). Both sermons rely heavily on apocalyptic symbols and include parables about seasons and trees (4:26ff.; 13:28ff.) and the command to "Watch!" (4:12, 24; 13:5, 9, 23, 33). The aim of both teachings is to exhort patience and discernment concerning the coming of God's kingdom in history.

(D) Complementing the two campaign sequences of challenge are major sequences that function primarily to legitimate the alternative

social practice of the discipleship community. I refer to these sections as *campaigns of affirmation.* In both cases Mark relies heavily on the narrative device of repetition and the plot of a journey. The first sequence features a broad double cycle of socially significant actions:

- Two sets of double healings (5:21-43; 7:24-37) represent a practice of overcoming class and ethnic exclusion.
- Two wilderness feedings (6:33-44; 8:1-10) represent a practice of economic sharing with the poor.
- Two boat journeys across the Sea of Galilee (4:35-41; 6:45-52) represent a practice of overcoming social segregation between Jew and Gentile.

The second affirmative sequence, which I prefer to call the *discipleship catechism,* employs a triple cycle of teaching. It is framed by two healing stories of blind men as noted above, and unfolds along a journey south to Jerusalem. Each cycle consists of a "portent" in which Jesus anticipates his death at the hands of the Jerusalem authorities, which is followed by the disciples' "blindness" and ensuing instructions that center on a paradox:

Site Portents	*"Blindness"*	*Teaching*	*Paradox*
Caesarea to 8:31 Philippi	8:32f.	8:34-37	save life/ lose life
Galilee to 9:3	19:33f.	9:35-10:31	first/last
Judea on way to 10:32-34	10:35-39	10:40-45	greatest/ Jerusalem least

This teaching cycle addresses issues of status and power that are social (9:38-10:16), economic (10:17-31), and political in nature (10:35-45).

(E) There is nothing in the first half of Mark comparable to the extended *passion narrative* of Jesus' last days as a fugitive—his arrest, political trial, and execution (14:1ff.). However, a semblance of symmetry is maintained by the account in Book I of the last days of John the Baptist (6:14-29). Both prophets are arrested for their political criticisms of the ruling elite (John of Herod, Jesus of the priestly aristocracy). Both are railroaded as victims of court intrigues in accounts that smack of parody (6:21-28; 14:53-15:15). Both narratives conclude with the prophet's execution and burial in a tomb (6:29; 15:46).

(F) The Gospel's general structural symmetry is completed in the respective *"symbolic epilogues."* Here Mark attempts to interpret the

meaning of the events he has recounted. In the third and final boat journey, which closes Book I, Jesus poses questions to his disciples that
force them to review his previous symbolic actions. Mark is implicitly
challenging the reader to review the story in order to see what we have
missed: "Do you not yet understand?" (8:21). Similarly, the empty
tomb scene at the end of the story directs the disciples (and the readers)
to return to Galilee (16:7), where the adventure began. As in 8:21, this
ambiguous ending undermines our attempts to draw triumphal conclusions, inviting us instead to resolve the narrative crisis through only our
own discipleship. That is, whether the risen Jesus who continues the
journey is actually "seen" or not depends on whether or not *we ourselves* follow him.

The symmetrical structure of Mark, using the rhetorical strategy of
repetition, functions to emphasize several "theses," including the following:

- Divine intervention occurs at the margins of society, not at its center.

- The Way of Jesus is in conflict with the ordering of power in
  Roman Palestine.

- As a healer/exorcist, Jesus always attends both to the pain of individual bodies *and* to the roots of repression/ oppression in the
  body politic.

- The kingdom of God demands radical change, radical commitment, and yet also radical patience.

- Human beings (including disciples) are profoundly "blinded" to
  the kingdom because of our patterns of denial.

At the structural center of this bipartite model, functioning somewhat like a fulcrum, is the "confessional crisis" (8:27-9:1). Thus, at the
heart of Mark's Gospel is the assertion that the messianic vocation—
and our discipleship as well—is defined by redemptive suffering, not triumph.

This or any other structural model of Mark can only offer a sort of
"roadmap" to aid the reader in navigating the fascinating terrain of the
Gospel. But the map is not the territory. Nothing can substitute for
careful reading of the story itself.

STORY LINES OF MARK

Rhoads and Michie's *Mark as Story* (1982) is a useful introduction to analyzing a Gospel narrative. They summarize the general tenor of Mark's storytelling style as follows:

> The narrative moves along quickly, and is a lively representation of action, with little summary. The narrator "shows" the action directly, seldom talking about it indirectly. Episodes are usually brief, the scene changes often, and minor characters appear and then quickly disappear. The reader is drawn quickly into the story by means of this fast-paced, dramatic movement. The brevity of style and rapidity of motion give the narrative a tone of urgency. Whereas early in the narrative the action shifts rapidly from one location to another, the end of the journey slows to a day-by-day description of what happens in a single location, Jerusalem, and then an hour-by-hour depiction of the crucifixion. (1982, 45)

The first person on stage is John the Baptist (1:2-6), an Elijah figure who portends divine judgment (Mal. 4:5) yet who also embodies Isaiah's promise that the exodus "Way" will be reopened (Exod. 23:20; Isa. 40:3). After introducing Jesus, John disappears, resurfacing only in the flashback of 6:14-29 and in subsequent allusions (8:28; 9:11-13; 11:27-33). Jesus' baptism is the first of three "apocalyptic moments," in which a heavenly voice intervenes in the narrative (1:11; see 9:7; 15:34). After a brief wilderness sojourn that might be likened to a sort of "vision quest" (Myers et al. 1996, 7), Jesus announces his mission in Galilee. His simple message summarily dismisses the two classic excuses religious people use to avoid change or responsibility, namely, that the domain of divine justice is beyond this world and in the hereafter. "The time is *now*," proclaims Jesus, "and the place is *here*" (1:15).

Jesus' first initiative is to begin creating a community around him. Three key disciple characters (who will represent the inner circle of the community) are briefly introduced in the first call to discipleship (1:16ff.). Mark next shifts to the first public scene in a Capernaum synagogue (1:21ff.), where the scribes, who will emerge as Jesus' arch-opponents, surface indirectly. A confrontation with a demon begins Jesus' inaugural ministry cycle around the Sea of Galilee, a campaign of exorcism and healing (1:32f.; 2:1ff.).

Jesus establishes a social practice of inclusivity which defies established group boundaries (eating with sinners [2:15f.]), purity restrictions (contact with lepers [1:41ff.]), and economic norms (expropriating food for the hungry [2:23ff.]). This in turn provokes conflict with the local civic leadership: first the scribal (1:22; 2:6) and priestly (1:43) sectors, then the Pharisees (a series of three episodes beginning in 2:15ff.). In the course of the story virtually every identifiable ruling faction in Judean society will oppose Jesus. The first campaign has a double culmination. A public challenge in a synagogue ends with the formation of a political coalition (the Pharisees and Herodians represent the Galilean political elite) that begins plotting Jesus' murder (3:1-6). Soon after, a shouting match with government investigators ends in ideological polarization (3:22ff.). Between these episodes Jesus consolidates his new community (3:13ff.) even as he breaks with his own kin (3:31ff.).

After each confrontation with the authorities, Jesus withdraws (1:35; 3:7; 4:1). In a kind of narrative pause (4:2ff.), Jesus offers an extended reflection concerning the paradoxes of the kingdom's infiltration into history. He next embarks on the first of several stormy boat crossings of the Sea of Galilee (4:35ff.), which will traverse between "Jewish" and "Gentile" territory (see Kelber 1979, 30ff.). Upon his arrival on the "other side" of the sea, Jesus initiates his ministry among Gentiles with another dramatic exorcism (5:1ff.).

Jesus next returns to Jewish territory for two interrelated healing episodes (5:21ff.; we will look closely at this episode in the final section below). Traveling to his hometown he experiences more rejection (6:1ff.), and then dispatches his disciples on their first solo mission (6:7ff.). Inserted between their departure and return (6:30f.) is the flashback account of John's arrest and execution by Herod (6:14ff.). The remainder of the first half is a continuation of symbolic actions, including more boat journeys (6:46ff.; 8:14ff.) and healings (7:24ff.), two wilderness feedings (6:34ff.; 8:1ff.), and a dispute with the Pharisees over social boundaries and table fellowship (7:1ff.).

Throughout this middle section, the crisscrossing of the sea and the recurring debate concerning "the loaves" (6:51f.; 8:14-21) aim to dramatize the struggle to overcome the enmity between Jew and Gentile—an ancient rift in the Mediterranean world. The healings and brief teaching section (7:14ff.) signify Jesus' repudiation of caste and class barriers. Book I closes with Jesus' attempt to tutor the disciples (and the readers) concerning the real meaning of his symbolic action (8:14-21).

In the second half of Mark, the narrative sites of boat and sea are abruptly abandoned, and a new journey is begun. After the transitional

Bethsaida healing (8:22-26), the first scene opens in Caesarea Philippi. This is the northernmost reach of the narrative, which then turns south with Jesus' slow march to Judea. From here on the story is dominated by the anticipatory force of the showdown in Jerusalem, articulated in the first of three "portents" (8:31f.; see 9:31f.; 10:32-34). In the second prologue, three major plot developments are suddenly brought into focus. First, the growing conflict between Jesus and his own followers erupts into full-scale confrontation (8:29ff.). This tension will continue to escalate until its tragic conclusion in 14:50. Second, the mystery surrounding the identity of Jesus deepens when he rejects Peter's "orthodox" confession of the Christ (8:29). As readers, we are now off balance, for we had been led from the beginning of the story to believe that Jesus was in fact the Messiah (1:1). Finally, the real consequences of Jesus' conflict with the authorities is revealed. He exhorts that his followers be prepared to reckon with execution by the Romans for insurrectionary activity (8:34ff.). This second call to discipleship is confirmed by the divine voice in the second apocalyptic moment, the Transfiguration (9:2-8).

The next section consists of a triple cycle I call the "discipleship catechism on nonviolence" (see Beck 1996). Each time Jesus anticipates his execution at the hands of the Jerusalem powers, the disciples are unable (unwilling?) to grasp or embrace this destiny (see 10:32). Each time Jesus responds by teaching them about power and service. This section addresses the internal organization of the community, including marriage and family (10:1-16), group boundaries (9:38-50), leadership (10:35-45), and possessions (10:17-31). By the time it draws to a close with a second blind man story (10:46-52), the traveling band has arrived at the outskirts of Jerusalem.

The second "campaign of challenge" is a series of running debates as Jesus moves in and out of Jerusalem. It commences with a theatrical procession (11:1ff.), a symbolic gesture (11:12-14, 20-25), and a dramatic direct action in the temple (11:15-20). With this nonviolent assault Jesus declares his opposition to the temple-state and the way it was legitimated through appeals to the old Davidic monarchy (12:35-37). One by one he engages in rhetorical battle with the various ruling factions, whose every objection is met by Jesus' counterarguments. First the representatives of the temple power structure (chief priests, scribes, and elders) try to intimidate Jesus (11:27ff.). Next come the Pharisees and Herodians (12:13ff.). After locking horns with the archconservative Sadducees (12:18ff.), Jesus turns for a final offensive upon the ideology of the scribal class (12:28-40).

In each of these debates Jesus appears to prevail, finally silencing his antagonists (12:34). Throughout most of this section the disciples are waiting offstage, reappearing only at the bitter culmination of the section (12:43). In the story of the "widow's mite" Jesus sharply repudiates the temple economy's exploitation of the poor. He then dramatically exits the temple for the final time and, alluding to his very first parable (3:25), predicts that it is a "house that cannot stand" (13:1-2). Taking a seat on the Mount of Olives, a traditional site for judgment (see Zech. 14:4), he offers his second extended discourse on apocalyptic patience (13:3ff.). Jesus exhorts his followers to reject the claims of nationalist patriots in their commitment to a restored temple-state (13:5-23). Instead, they should hold out for a more genuinely revolutionary transformation of the world, in which the domination system itself unravels (13:24-37).

As Jesus withdraws to suburban Bethany, the plot to arrest him is in full swing (14:3). At this point, the narrative takes on the sinister hues of covert machinations. The authorities infiltrate Jesus' community, one of the disciples collaborating with the undercover operation (14:10f.). Meanwhile, the hard-pressed community has gone underground (14:12-16). Mark offers a tragic/pathetic portrait of the community celebrating the Passover feast in hiding, riddled by doubt and suspicion (14:17-21). In stark counterpoint, Jesus emphasizes his solidarity with them (14:22-25), insisting that although their defection may be inevitable, the discipleship story will not end (14:28). True to his prediction, the disciples buckle under pressure and flee when Jesus is seized by state security forces (14:32-52). At this point the discipleship story collapses and the trial narrative begins.

The double trial and torture of Jesus is narrated in parallel fashion (14:53-15:15). This functions to equate the Judean ruling class and the Roman imperialists in their common rejection of Jesus, who submits to the railroading in defiant silence. While the disciples hover in the shadows (14:66-72; 15:40f.) new characters come onto the stage: the high priest, the Roman procurator Pilate, a fellow prisoner Barabbas. The narrative builds to a crescendo of irony, culminating in the crowd's insistence that the dissident terrorist Barabbas be spared and the nonviolent dissident Jesus be executed (15:6-15). Amid the derision of his triumphant opponents, Jesus is summarily crucified, and the story appears to reach its tragic end (15:21-32).

Jesus' death, the story's third apocalyptic moment, brings to a climax Mark's symbolic representation of the "Human One" (15:33-38). Not only did Jesus three times anticipate the execution of this messianic persona (8:31; 9:31; 10:33f.); he also thrice portended the "appearance" of the Human One as a sign of the "end of the world" (8:38f.; 13:26f.; 14:62). Here at the cross, as his opponents look on, Jesus expires and the sun goes dark. This is Mark's apocalyptic finale, but only for those with "eyes to see," for the dishonoring of Jesus continues in the post-mortem responses of both a Judean and a Roman representative (15:39-46).

In the second epilogue it is three female followers, who have endured the ordeal of Jesus' crucifixion without abandoning him, who are revealed as true disciples (15:40f., 47ff.). Attempting to give Jesus the dignity of proper burial, they encounter a mysterious "young man" presiding over an empty tomb (16:5ff.). In Mark's third call to discipleship these women are invited to follow Jesus to Galilee, with the promise that the gospel narrative will resume there. The story ends with their (and our) understandable reaction of both "trauma and ecstasy" (16:8) at the realization that the discipleship adventure, like the tomb itself (16:4), has been unexpectedly reopened.

It has been argued that the basic "syntax" of a plot consists of five essential elements: (1) mandating; (2) acceptance or rejection of mandate; (3) confrontation; (4) success or failure; (5) consequence (Via 1985, 40ff.). It is not hard to see each of these elements in the story line as I have outlined it. Jesus is mandated at baptism, accepts the mandate to proclaim and embody the kingdom, and continually skirmishes with opponents of this mission. Whether the cross represents success or failure depends of course on one's point of view. From Mark's point of view it demonstrates that his portrait of Jesus as Messiah is indeed reliable—but only in terms of how Mark has redefined messianic characteristics!

In addition to this main plot, we can abstract three distinct subplots, each with a different subject. The first subplot involves Jesus' attempts to create and consolidate a discipleship community. Here the subjects are regular working folk he summons to follow. Though mandated to carry on Jesus' work (1:17; 3:14; 6:7), the Way is first unintelligible to these disciples (6:53; 8:17ff.) and is eventually resisted once its consequences are made clear (8:32; 9:38; 10:35-39; 14:27-42). This tragedy is, however, reversed by the persistence of a few women and the promise that because Jesus lives, the story *and its mandates* will go on (14:27f.; 16:6f.).

The second subplot is Jesus' liberative ministry of healing, exorcism, and proclamation. The subjects are the poor and oppressed, who typically in Mark are part of the "crowd." The mandate arises in the opening synagogue exorcism, in which the crowd first recognizes that Jesus' authority exceeds that of their scribal overlords (1:22). Jesus' clear priority for the poor is demonstrated in the healing of two females, as we shall see below (5:21-43). His social location is characterized by intimate communion with the outcast (1:40-45; 14:3), the disabled (2:1-12), the despised (2:13-17), and the marginalized (6:33-44; 8:1-10). By the time Jesus arrives in Jerusalem, it seems that the crowd has accepted his mandate for a new social order, hailing him as popular king (11:1-10). In the end, however, the crowd (like the disciples) abandons Jesus. Manipulated by the authorities into supporting his execution, the poor thus tragically remain under their control (15:11-15).

Mark's third subplot is Jesus' confrontation with the dominant social order. The subjects are the various groups of the political elite: scribes, Pharisees, Herodians, and ruling Jerusalem clergy. Jesus delivers his mandate to them several times in the first campaign of direct action. He critiques the public purity and debt system (2:10, 28) and issues a Deuteronomic challenge to choose an ethos of justice and compassion over one of domination (3:4; see Deut. 30:15-20). This mandate is rejected by the authorities then (3:6) and throughout the story (6:26; 7:1f.; 8:11; 11:27-33; 12:13; 14:1f.). Jesus again confronts each of the elite groups during the second campaign narrative, disrupting temple commerce and appearing successfully to silence his opponents (12:34). But eventually the forces of Judean and Roman state power join to vanquish him. The surprising consequence is that they behold the advent of the Human One on the cross, to their shame (15:29-32; see 14:62). Their ultimate demise is symbolized by the cosmic darkness and rending of the temple curtain (15:38; see 13:24-27).

These three narrative strands function to articulate the key aspects in Jesus' messianic mission: confronting the dominant public order, nurturing an alternative social order, and embodying solidarity with the poor. All three subplots contribute to and converge in the climactic passion narrative. In the next-to-last scene of the story we see the defecting disciples, the disillusioned crowd, and the hostile authorities, all juxtaposed to Jesus, who alone goes the way of the cross.

THE GOSPEL IN AN EPISODE: A READING OF MARK 5:21-43

As a popular educator I frequently use the Gospel of Mark for Bible study and social analysis with denominational leadership, churches, and faith-based activist groups. Sometimes I have only a brief time with a group—even as short as one sermon or an hour workshop—to communicate the essential themes of Mark's story of Jesus. On such occasions I have found the best "summary" episode in Mark to be the healing of two females in 5:21-43. I therefore conclude this brief introduction to Mark with a closer look at that tale, which represents a kind of "microcosm" of the Gospel as a whole.

This episode is a classic example of a "Markan sandwich," in which he wraps one story around another in order to compel the reader to interrelate the two. We pick up the narrative on the heels of Jesus' dramatic exorcism of the Gerasene demoniac on the "other side" of the sea (5:1-20), after which Jesus returns to "Jewish" territory (5:21).

The setting of the first half of this story is the "crowd" (5:21, 24, 27, 31). Jesus is approached by a synagogue ruler who appeals for a healing intervention on behalf of his daughter, whom he believes to be "at the point of death" (5:23). Jesus departs with him (5:24), and since Jesus has already healed many different people to this point in the story (1:30-34, 40-42; 2:10-12; 3:5, 10), we fully expect this mission will be accomplished. On the way, however, Jesus is hemmed in by the crowds (5:24). The narrative focus zooms in upon a woman whose condition Mark describes in detail with a series of descriptive clauses:

- she had been with a flow of blood for twelve years;

- she had suffered much under the care of many doctors;

- she had spent all her resources yet

- she had not benefited, but grown worse instead. (5:25f.)

The purity code stipulated that menstruating women should be quarantined (see Lev. 15:19ff.), though in this period these strictures probably were not applied to the poor. Still, it would have been highly inappropriate for a hemorrhaging woman to publicly grab a "holy man"! But Mark focuses instead on the way she had been bankrupted by profiteering physicians who had exploited her without addressing her condition.

The woman's approach to Jesus is in stark contrast to that of Jairus. The latter was frontal and assertive: he acknowledges Jesus' honor (lowering himself before him) in order to request a favor. She, on the other hand, reaches out anonymously from behind in the crowd, seeking to touch Jesus covertly and somehow effect a magical cure. Jairus addresses Jesus directly, as would befit male equals (5:23), while the woman talks only to herself (5:28). Jairus is the "head" of both his household (speaking on behalf of his daughter) and his social group (the synagogue). The woman is nameless, homeless, and alone: poor, sick, and ritually impure. In other words, Mark is portraying two characters that represent the opposite ends of the social spectrum.

At the moment of contact between Jesus and the woman (5:29), however, the power dynamics of the story begin to be reversed. Her body is healed—whereas from the perspective of the purity code *Jesus* should have been contaminated. Indeed, Mark tells us that power had been transferred (5:30). Does this comment signal a magical transaction, or is it a symbol of "empowerment" and a clue to the social reversals to come?

When Jesus stops to inquire what has happened, the whole narrative, which was in motion toward Jairus' house, grinds to a halt. A struggle now ensues:

Jesus: "Who touched my clothes?"

Disciples: "You see the crowd yet ask, 'Who touched me?'"

Jesus looked around to see who had done it. (5:30-32)

To the disciples this interruption is an inconvenience attributable to the anonymous crowd, with whom they are unconcerned. Jesus, however, insists on encountering the human face of the poor.

The woman emerges from the margins of the story to center stage, and it is her turn to fall in front of Jesus, suggesting that she is now an equal to Jairus. Finding her voice, "she told him the *whole* truth"— including, no doubt, her opinion of the purity system and the medical establishment (5:33)! One might legitimately wonder how long her story took, further delaying Jesus from his original mission. After listening patiently, Jesus acknowledges her rightful status as "daughter" in the family of Israel and acclaims the faith evidenced by her initiative (5:34). His commendation grants her a status *exceeding* that of Jesus' own disciples, who have been shown to be "without faith" (4:40)!

But what of the original "daughter"? Jairus is informed by some servants that she has died (5:35). The phrase "while Jesus was still speaking" functions to overlap the utterances, as if gain and loss are voiced simultaneously:

Daughter, your faith has made you well. Go in peace.

Your *daughter* is dead. Why trouble the Teacher further?

By attending to this importunate woman Jesus appears to have defaulted on his original task. Will the story end in tragedy? Undeterred, Jesus ignores this "interpretation" of events and exhorts Jairus to believe. The shock cannot be missed: he is instructing a leader of the synagogue to learn about faith from this outcast woman (5:36)!

The scene now shifts to Jairus's household. There, mourning turns to derision at Jesus' insistence that the girl only "sleeps" (5:39). Jesus is not being coy; "being asleep" will emerge later in the story as a symbol of lack of faith (13:36; 14:32ff.). He throws the onlookers out and takes the girl's hand (5:41), thus for a second time in this episode defiling himself by touching a body that is ritually unclean in the extreme (a bleeding woman, a corpse). After he raises the girl back to life the witnesses are "beside themselves with great astonishment" (5:43), a reaction that will occur only one other time in Mark: at *Jesus'* resurrection (16:6).

This episode portrays Jesus in the tradition of the prophet Elisha, who raised the dead son of a woman of Shunem (2 Kgs. 4:8-37). This may help explain why Mark's story ends with Jesus' instruction to give the girl "something to eat" (5:43). For just as the story of Elisha's restoration of the young boy is followed by one in which he presides over a "feeding miracle" during a famine (2 Kgs. 4:38-44), Jesus will shortly do the same with a hungry crowd in the wilderness (Mark 6:35ff.).

In the art of narrative, every detail is there for a reason, and Mark's "aside" that the girl was twelve years old is a good case in point (5:42). She has lived a life of privilege for twelve years and is just on the edge of puberty (i.e., ready to start menstruating). In contrast, the bleeding woman had suffered deprivation for twelve years and is permanently infertile. In the same way in which fifty stars and thirteen stripes on the U.S. flag symbolize the number of states and original English colonies, the number twelve here symbolizes the tribes of Israel (see 3:13). This "coincidence" represents the key to the social meaning of this doublet. Within the "family" of Israel, these "daughters" represent the privileged and the impoverished, respectively. Because of this inequity between these two "socialized bodies," the body politic as a whole (represented by Jairus as head of household/synagogue) is "on the verge of death."

As Jairus learns, the healing journey with Jesus must take a necessary detour that stops to listen to the pain of the crowd. Only when the outcast woman is restored to true "daughterhood" can the daughter of the synagogue be restored to true life. *That* is the faith the privileged must learn from the poor. This story thus *shows* a characteristic of the sovereignty of God that Jesus will later also *tell*: The "last will be first" and the "least will be greatest" (10:31, 43).

This story of "good news to the poor" embodies in a nutshell Mark's manifesto of radical discipleship. Writing in the midst of the pressure and suffering generated by the Roman–Judean war of 66-70 C.E., Mark beckoned readers to "have ears to hear" (4:9) and "eyes to see" (10:51f.). This Gospel still invites its audience to "wake up" (13:37) and "turn around" (1:15); to speak truth to mountains of domination (11:23) and cast out demons (3:14f.); to row against the storms of ethnic division (6:48) and give the hungry something to eat (6:37); and to take up our cross and follow Jesus (8:34). It is a story whose symbols, if heeded, can yet animate us to do away with the dehumanizing idols of today.

RESOURCES FOR FURTHER STUDY

Anderson, Janice Capel, and Stephen Moore
    1992   *Mark and Method: New Approaches in Biblical Studies.*
              Minneapolis: Fortress.

Beck, Robert
    1996   *Nonviolent Story: Narrative Conflict Resolution in the Gospel of Mark.* Maryknoll, N.Y.: Orbis.

Bilezikian, Gilbert
    1977   *The Liberated Gospel: A Comparison of the Gospel of Mark and Greek Tragedy.* Grand Rapids: Baker.

Blount, Brian
    1998   *Go Preach! Mark's Kingdom Message and the Black Church Today.* Maryknoll, N.Y.: Orbis.

Brandon, S. G. F.
    1968   *Jesus and the Zealots.* New York: Scribner.

Funk, Robert, and the Jesus Seminar
    1998   *The Acts of Jesus: What Did Jesus Really Do?* San Francisco: Harper & Row.

Gill, Athol
    1989   *Life on the Road: The Gospel Basis for a Messianic Lifestyle.* Homebush West, Australia: Lancer.

Kealy, Sean
    1982   *Mark's Gospel: A History of Its Interpretation.* New York: Paulist.

Kee, Howard C.
    1977   *Community of the New Age: Studies in Mark's Gospel.* Philadelphia: Fortress.

Kelber, Werner
    1979   *Mark's Story of Jesus.* Philadelphia: Fortress.

Kinukawa, Hisako
1994   *Women and Jesus in Mark: A Japanese Feminist Perspective.*
            Maryknoll, N.Y.: Orbis.
Mack, Burton
1991   *A Myth of Innocence: Mark and Christian Origins.* Philadel-
            phia: Fortress.
Myers, Ched
1988   *Binding the Strong Man: A Political Reading of Mark's Story
            of Jesus.* Maryknoll, N.Y.: Orbis.
1994   *Who Will Roll Away the Stone? Queries for First World
            Christians.* Maryknoll, N.Y.: Orbis.
Myers, Ched, Marie Dennis, Joseph Nangle, Cynthia Moe-Lobeda, and Stuart
    Taylor
1996   *"Say to This Mountain": Mark's Story of Discipleship.* Mary-
            knoll, N.Y.: Orbis.
Perrin, Norman
1976   "The Interpretation of the Gospel of Mark." *Interpretation*
            30:115ff.
Rhoads, David, and Donald Michie
1982   *Mark as Story: An Introduction to the Narrative of a Gospel.*
            Philadelphia: Fortress.
Roth, Wolfgang
1988   *Hebrew Gospel: Cracking the Code of Mark.* Oak Park:
            Meyer-Stone.
Schweizer, Eduard
1960   *Lordship and Discipleship,* Studies in Biblical Theology 28.
            London: SCM.
Tolbert, Mary Ann
1989   *Sowing the Gospel: Mark's World in Literary-Historical Per-
            spective.* Minneapolis: Fortress.
Via, Dan
1985   *The Ethics of Mark's Gospel—In the Middle of Time.*
            Philadelphia: Fortress.

4

Luke's Gospel

"Good News to the Poor" for the Non-Poor

SHARON H. RINGE

INTRODUCTION

IF YOU HAVE BEEN READING your way through the New Testament, you may be tempted to skip over most of Luke. After all, you have already read essentially the same story twice, in the Gospels of Matthew and Mark. Sure, there are some stories in Luke that the others do not have—the parables we know as the Prodigal Son and the Good Samaritan, for example, and the stories about the shepherds who herald Jesus' birth. Those and other passages unique to Luke would offer a rich feast all by themselves. To limit oneself to such supplementary reading, though, would miss the real importance of this Gospel, which is carried in the big picture of Jesus that the author paints.

This author, whom tradition has named Luke but who really is anonymous (like the authors of the other three Gospels), admits that this project is not the first of its kind. The preface sets out the purpose behind the writing and tells us a lot about what to expect from this account of "the events that have been fulfilled among us" (1:1-4). The author, whom for convenience we also will call Luke, proposes to offer "an orderly account" of these events. The resources on which the author is drawing have been shaped to accomplish a specific purpose, namely, that readers "may know the truth concerning the things about which you have been instructed."

Several points in this preface are worth our attention. First, Luke is writing something that he understands not primarily as a missionary document designed to draw people to this story for the first time, nor even as an introduction to instruct newcomers to the faith. He is writing to clear up some things for people already part of the community gathered around the memories and proclamation about Jesus. That leads to the second important point in the preface, namely, the meaning of "truth." We modern readers might assume that his purpose is to get the facts right. We might imagine him doing careful research and sorting through the evidence in order to tell us exactly what Jesus said and did. A few more of the clues in this same preface, however, might help us to reassess that assumption.

The style of the introductory verses (a modern equivalent might be something like the notation on a thesis or term paper, "submitted in partial fulfillment of the requirements of" a course or degree), as well as the polished and elegant language in which this document is written, establishes the author as a learned person. Tradition has called him a physician and identified him with the companion of Paul reflected in the first person plural ("we") accounts of the travels reported in the book of Acts. Actually there is nothing to suggest that he was a physician in the specialized sense we think of today, but rather that he was a scholar with knowledge about many matters—"life sciences" included. His project, which includes both the account of Jesus' life that we call the Gospel of Luke and his second volume, which we know as the Acts of the Apostles (which begins with a similar preface and retells several of the events that follow Jesus' resurrection), marks him as a historian. In the ancient world being a historian meant not someone interested principally in factual accuracy, but rather someone committed to moral instruction through a recounting of events and deeds from the past. We should recognize the "order" that shapes the Gospel, then, as the shape of the story that the author deems most effective in helping the audience understand the stories of its founder and of the early years of the community in a way that informs their understanding of who they are and how they should live. In other words, the purpose is to shape and ground the community's discipleship.

The fact that our author appears to be well educated places him among the elite of his society, since education was not popularly available in the ancient world. He also identifies his audience as part of the elite. The address to "most excellent Theophilus" makes use of a title of honor and respect. The name itself may refer to a specific person, but it may also be a symbolic name that encompasses a group of people. It means "Friend of God," and it may suggest that a fair number of the people in the community to which Luke is writing belong to a group of Gentiles known as "God-fearers" who clustered around the edges of the synagogues without fully converting to Judaism. They were drawn to the moral principles and the accounts of God's acts on behalf of the people that are conveyed by the Torah and by the prophets (24:27), but they did not take on observance of all of the Law. People from this group tended to be of a fairly high economic and social class. They may have held back from converting to Judaism in order not to jeopardize their social and business relations by too close an affiliation with a group that kept itself separate from many of the practices of the commercial, social, and political elites of Roman imperial society. The early church attracted many from this community as a way to express their belief in the God of Israel, but at a bit more distance. The Greek name Theophilus also suggests that this audience is far removed from Palestine, where Jesus' own ministry took place. Most likely it was a community in a Hellenistic city, perhaps even as far away as Greece, but in any event part of the "Diaspora" (the "Dispersion" of the Jews to territories outside of Palestine) that accelerated after the Roman–Jewish war of 66-70 C.E. The fact that the second volume looks back on events of the early decades of the church's life suggests that Luke wrote in the final decades of the first century, perhaps 85-95 C.E.

Data such as these that we can identify in the opening verses and overall design of Luke's work suggest why his project is especially important and especially challenging for us who want to live lives of justice-seeking discipleship in privileged parts of the world of the early third millennium. The challenge comes from two directions. First, the Gospel seems directed to a community that includes some people who are poor as well as the elites we have identified. Note, for example, the radical language of direct address in the blessings and woes in Luke 6:20-26: "Blessed are you who are poor . . ."; "But woe to you who are rich." The picture of such an economically mixed community fits with the fact that religious affiliation in the Roman world was usually determined by the allegiance of the well-to-do householders, who would bring with them all members of their households—slave, freeborn, and freedpersons alike—some of whom would have no resources of their own. From this and other passages, it is clear that the heart of the Gospel, which is carried strongly in the traditions stemming from Jesus' own ministry, is a word of "good news" directed especially to those suffering from poverty and other consequences of imperial structures and policies. The "non-poor" receive in this Gospel a message that challenges their place of privilege and exhorts them to change their lives accordingly. That is the first challenge to us "non-poor" as well, who have a stake in the very systems and institutions that create the suffering we deplore in our own day. To hear the Gospel as "good news" calls us to a life contrary to business as usual, and contrary to what our culture identifies as our best interests.

The second challenge comes as we look closely at the ways Luke has negotiated the first challenge. On at least two key points, he has pulled his punches. Luke's Gospel is often called the "Gospel of the poor" because he writes about the poor and other marginalized groups more directly and more often than do the other Gospel writers. If we read carefully, though, we note that he talks *about* the poor, but most often *to* the well-to-do concerning their responsibilities for the poor within the structures that still maintain some in poverty. "Charity" or "almsgiving" becomes the immediate practical response he urges, in order to move toward the vision carried by such agenda-setting texts as the Magnificat (1:46-55) and the reflections presented as Luke's programmatic sermon in Nazareth (4:16-30). As we work our way through this Gospel, we need to pay careful attention to such compromises, to see whether, in engaging in the art of the possible, the author has risked betraying the message with which he began—a risk always at hand for us too, as we try to be faithful disciples in a context of privilege.

Related to Luke's treatment of the economic agenda is his treatment of the issue of gender. This Gospel is also often considered a Gospel that favors women. Indeed there are more stories that feature female characters in this Gospel than in any of the others. Quantity, however, may belie quality. When we look at the roles these characters play in the story of Jesus, we find that they are the very traditional roles played by women in the Hellenistic world of the Roman empire. They bear children (chaps. 1 and 2). They are passive like Mary of Bethany, learning meekly at Jesus' feet (10:38-42), with no challenge to use what she has heard in preaching, teaching, healing, or casting out demons, as the male disciples are instructed to do. Mary's sister Martha—clearly a female-head-of-household in the modern jargon—is scolded for her efforts to carry out the cultural and religious mandates of hospitality to guests in her household. Women are the beneficiaries of Jesus' ministry of healing and forgiveness as well, without ever joining the men in carrying out the same tasks (e.g., 7:36-50; 13:10-17). They support Jesus' movement with their money (8:1-3), though Luke does not explain how they happen to have disposable wealth in a context where resources usually came under the control of a male (husband, father, or even son). In short, women are portrayed as part of the movement of Jesus' followers, but in traditional roles. The book of Acts shows a similar trend, as the lists of prominent women missionaries whom Paul greets at the end of his letters are reduced to just a few who get a brief mention. To me, as a woman concerned with the dignity and equal rights of all women in my own context, Luke's compromises on this matter provide little cause for confidence. In fact, my assessment of this evidence explains why I am perfectly content to use masculine pronouns to refer to the author, without challenging the traditional assumption that Luke is a male. As in the case of economic issues, so also in the matter of gender, his stake in the dominant culture and society of his own day seems to have set limits on the scope he can imagine for the new world under divine sovereignty that is the focus of Jesus' ministry—the reign, dominion, kingdom, project, or "kin-dom" of God.

STRUCTURE OF LUKE'S GOSPEL

Luke's "orderly account" of Jesus' life and ministry can be viewed from several angles. First, it is generally "biographical," in that it begins with accounts of Jesus' conception and birth, pauses to highlight the circumstances of his call into public ministry, and then proceeds through an account of that ministry to its conclusion in arrest, administrative hearings, sentencing, and execution. In a bridge from the story of Jesus to the story of the early church, there are accounts of appearances of the risen Christ and commissions of the followers to continue the story. I put "biographical" in quotation marks, however, because this is not a factual report of specific events or teachings of Jesus in the order of their occurrence, such as we might expect from a modern biography.

Within that basic temporal framework, then, we need to look for other patterns. The geography is also interesting. The story starts in Nazareth, with the annunciation to Mary (1:26-38). Stories of Jesus' birth and childhood (chap. 2) center in Jerusalem and especially in the temple. His encounter with John the Baptist is set in "the region around the Jordan" (3:3), and he is said[1] to remain in that wilderness area dur-

---

[1] To speak accurately, I would need to qualify every reference to an action or teaching of Jesus by words such as "Luke said that Jesus said [or did]" or "as Luke portrays Jesus." I have not done so, but I will trust that you recognize that in each case we are talking about the Gospel text and not claiming "historical" facts about Jesus of Nazareth.

ing his time wrestling with Satan (4:1-13). The start of his ministry takes him home to Nazareth, from which he is driven out after the first description of a public act of ministry (4:16-30)—not an auspicious beginning! He never returns there, but rather the first part of his ministry is set elsewhere in the region of Galilee. There he teaches, calls followers, engages in a ministry of healing, and has several hostile encounters with representatives of the religious elites. In 9:51 he "sets his face to go to Jerusalem," and he begins a long journey that ends only when he finally arrives there in 19:28. The actual route is not the point of the journey. Rather, it resembles the journey of the Israelites told in the book of Deuteronomy. That account, which is presented as the "last will and testament" of Moses, contains all that he considered essential for them to know before his death at the edge of the promised land. Similarly, Luke's journey narrative is replete with teachings (and a few stories about Jesus) designed to prepare the followers for their life without Jesus. The story inches forward during the time in Jerusalem, taking four chapters to follow Jesus through those dramatic and traumatic days in the city that is at once holy and the home of the Roman occupiers and their supporters among the local elites. Unlike Matthew (whose resurrection accounts are all said to take place in Galilee), Mark (who tells of no appearances but only sends the followers to Galilee where Jesus will meet them; see Mark 16:7), and John (whose appearance stories are divided between Galilee and Jerusalem), Luke's Easter accounts all take place in Jerusalem and its suburbs. The community remains there until they "have been clothed with power from on high" (Luke 24:49) and sent out to proclaim "repentance and forgiveness of sins . . . in his name to all nations" (24:47). Luke's second volume appropriately begins there also, with the assignment that they will be sent out from there by the risen Christ to "be my witnesses in Jerusalem, in all Judea and Samaria, and to the ends of the earth" (Acts 1:8). The trajectory that began with Jesus' expulsion from Nazareth, we are told, will not end until the testimony concerning him encompasses the whole world!

This grand promise reaches our day, however, through centuries of the abuse of power by churches that came to be identified with various imperial powers. The "testimony" or witness of those churches carried the threat of death at the hands of the public authorities if one did not accept it, and the culture and self-interested political, military, social, and economic projects of the imperial powers themselves were the gift wrappings of the Gospel. From our vantage point we have to acknowledge that a dangerous Roman imperial rhetoric seems to have shaped

Luke's vision. That recognition, coming in the context of this volume, whose writers live in the middle of a country that humbly calls itself "the last great superpower," lends a note of caution to what might be considered yet another structural rubric of Luke's work. He seems to present it as the saga of the Holy Spirit—a power present at Jesus' conception, enfolding him at his baptism, accompanying him in the wilderness, "anointing" him for his ministry of "good news to the poor," and embodied in him until he surrenders it at his death. That same Spirit then gives birth to the church at Pentecost, and, as Justo González says, Luke's entire second volume could well be called the "Book of the Acts of the Holy Spirit."

Luke's challenge and ours come clearly into focus. How does he speak or write about an experience so thoroughly powerful and life-giving that he attributes it to the Holy Spirit itself, without having his voice and words fall captive to the very rhetoric of power and domination that the Gospel confronts and—by God's grace—overcomes (as the freedom song says) in God's own "some day"? How do we read his words as calls to the costly and joyful discipleship that holds open a space for that Spirit to continue its work in the imperial systems and ideologies that claim to structure our world, and from which we benefit in many aspects of our lives?

Getting Down to Specifics

A strategy that might help our task of reading Luke through the lenses of justice-seeking discipleship is to move from looking at the grand design of Luke's project to examine some of the specific stories and teachings that make it up. That closer look might help us recover the critical voice of the Gospel and enable us to identify points where Luke's own biases and interests risk subverting it. Any number of texts could serve us well in this study. I have chosen most of those I will examine from the ones unique to Luke's Gospel. I have also chosen texts that contribute to the three angles of vision from which Luke approaches the issue of discipleship in his Gospel: the identity of the one we are to follow, specific teachings about discipleship, and the modeling or teaching-by-apprenticeship through which the followers of Jesus are led.

Not surprisingly, the early sections of the Gospel develop a picture of Jesus' identity. The birth narratives (chaps. 1 and 2) develop that picture by the intertwining narratives of the annunciations, births, liturgical recognitions, and childhoods of Jesus and John the Baptist. The dynamics of the parents' lives and the rhythms and timing of conception, gestation, and birth set the pace of the story. By the accompanying drama and the sheer number of verses devoted to the telling, it is clear that Jesus' story will be Luke's focus. The town of Bethlehem, adoring shepherds, and angels' songs all add their familiar accents to our introduction to Jesus. Interspersed among the parts of the narratives, though, is another significant device by which Luke lets us know what we are facing. The hymns or canticles—Mary's song in 1:46-56; Zechariah's in 1:68-79; the angels' in 2:10-14; and Simeon's in 2:29-32—sing the meaning of Jesus.

The vocabulary and style as well as the content of these hymns echo psalms and prophetic oracles of the Hebrew Bible, but we search in vain for Luke's sources. He seems to have married form and content to compel his readers to connect God's story being made known in Jesus to those biblical traditions by which they already know God's will and presence. Each hymn is focused on or directed to God—"the Lord," "Savior," "Lord God of Israel," "Master." God's gracious acts on behalf of God's people are connected to the awaited one (1:68-79) and to the newborn child (2:29-32). Visions from such oracles as Isaiah 52:7-11 and 60:1-22 reaffirm that the redemption God has in mind for God's people Israel, in fact encompasses Israel and "the nations" alike (1:55, 68-73, 78-79; 2:10, 32). God is both faithful to God's promises and free to mediate blessings in unexpected ways, and at the heart of the faithfulness and the freedom of God is Jesus.

The best known of these songs is the Magnificat (1:46-56). Its content echoes Hannah's song or prayer found in 1 Samuel 2:1-10. Hannah's story is of an older woman who finds herself expecting a child late in life, to her great surprise, which is really more like Elizabeth's story here than Mary's. The song is set where the two expectant mothers come together, and it is said to have been evoked in response to Elizabeth's words recognizing the child that Mary will bear (1:42-45). Perhaps early in the tradition it began as Elizabeth's song, but so true did it ring to the picture of Jesus that Luke's Gospel attributes it to Mary, the bearer of this child of God. Just as she gives birth to the child, so she also articulates his calling in a hymn of praise to the God who is present in the child and, through the child, in the world at large.

The God who is portrayed in this hymn countermands the imperial ethos of Roman-occupied Palestine and of our own day as well. In the song, the mighty and the powerful lose their places of privilege, and the wealthy cease to accumulate even more ("are sent empty away"). The

lowly, in turn, are lifted up and the hungry fed. But losing one's privilege and being "sent empty away" does not mean destruction. It means
that the gap between rich and poor does not continue to grow. The revolutionary longing for a reversal of position—when the lowly replace
the mighty and lord it over them, and the poor now have a chance to
exploit the rich—thus looks in vain for support here. All of this level-
ing of privilege and confrontation of longing came to focus in Jesus. Little wonder that the one whom the angels' song greeted as "good news
of great joy for all the people" (2:10) came to represent such bad news
that only his execution promised to get rid of the threat—a conclusion
in which people from across the social spectrum are said to collude
(23:13-25).

Luke's Gospel proceeds by the "deductive" method. Instead of the
gradual "inductive" unfolding of dimensions of Jesus' ministry and
mission that we find in Mark, Luke not only has the agenda-setting
birth narrative, but his Gospel begins the story of Jesus' public ministry
with a clearly programmatic public introduction (4:16-30). Right on
the heels of the accounts of Jesus' baptism and testing in the wilderness
(3:21-22; 4:1-14), we meet him in his hometown of Nazareth, in the
synagogue, on a sabbath. The picture is of a simple gathering of the
congregation, with at least one reading from the Scriptures and an
interpretation of it.

Both the Scripture reading and the surrounding narrative tell us a lot
about how Luke views Jesus. The text is one of several that call for the
practice of the "Jubilee." The most famous and explicit of these texts,
all of which stem from the time after the leaders of Israel returned from
exile, is in Leviticus 25. There the fiftieth year—a "sabbath of sabbath
years" or super-sabbath—interrupts business as usual with a call for
debts to be canceled, those imprisoned due to unpayable debts to be set
free, the land to be given a "rest" or a fallow year, and land that had
been sold to obtain cash needed for survival to be returned to its original family or clan owners. The oracle in Isaiah 61:1 does not refer to a
cyclical repetition like the laws of Leviticus, but the Hebrew word
translated "release" is an unusual word found only in conjunction with
Jubilee texts. There is a link of content as well as vocabulary. Leviticus
25 calls for a once-in-a-lifetime arrest to the progressive accumulation
of land and other wealth in a few hands and gives all members of society a chance for a fresh start. Two theological reasons are given for
these laws: God's liberation of Israel from slavery in Egypt, as a model
for our human response in covenant loyalty to God (Lev. 25:38); and
God's sovereign ownership of the land, which prevents humankind

from any permanent sale of it (Lev. 25:23). These laws obviously sounded like wonderful news to the debtors and poor people of the land and bad news to the creditors and wealthy people. The principles of the Jubilee—release and liberation for the oppressed and good news to the poor *in the name of a sovereign God*—came to be linked to the longing for God's reign or "kingdom" in such texts as Isaiah 61. That reign too would require a disruption of business as usual, in the form of a cancellation of the demands of all the other authorities and institutions that claim sovereignty over human life, in the name of the divine sovereignty about to be established.

In Jesus' day, the link of this Jubilee text to the inaugural celebration of God's reign would have been precious to his hearers, who longed for freedom from Roman occupation, release from the suffering caused by the indebtedness that resulted from the burdensome tax structure imposed by Rome and its allies, and relief from the burdens of the patronage system (see pp. 10-11), which limited options throughout their daily lives. In Luke's surrounding narrative of the events at Nazareth, the initial amazement and positive reaction of the townspeople (4:22) reflect that view of the text as expressing God's alternative to the system that was causing their suffering. Suddenly, though, things go sour, so much so that by the end of the account the same townspeople are seeking Jesus' death. What happens to provoke the shift?

First, we must say that it wasn't the result of a poor sermon! In fact, Luke's account gives us no interpretation of the text itself. Rather, what is talked about is how the fulfillment of the text will take place. There again, the Hebrew Bible provides the keys. Jesus links the fulfillment of this text to the way God is said to have acted in the stories of Elijah and the widow of Zarephath (2:25-26; cf. 1 Kgs. 17:8-24) and of Elisha and Naaman the Syrian (4:27; cf. 2 Kgs. 5:1-14). In these stories, God's saving help does come to Israel in times of crisis, but it begins first with these two outsiders. In other words, while the text from Isaiah reminds the hearers of God's promises and God's faithfulness, these other references remind them of God's freedom. Their response expresses the rage of people who find their assumptions of privilege and an inside track to blessing contradicted. Were there some such in Jesus' audience? Probably. But the bite would have been felt acutely in Luke's community, both as they had begun to make assumptions about their own privileged place in God's plan because they were followers of Jesus (see 3:8), and as they recognized the costliness of the disruption in business as usual that this text from Isaiah portrays as our initial encounter with the reality of God's reign.

Jesus survives this mob action and leaves Nazareth for good, to initiate his ministry throughout Galilee and its environs (4:31-9:50). This long section of the Gospel contains some teachings about discipleship, but a more important dynamic is Jesus' demonstration through his own ministry of what is required of his followers as they prepare to assume their role in his agenda. This section develops the Jubilee motifs introduced in 4:16-30 in two key points.

In 6:20-26, the beatitudes and parallel woes that comprise part of what interpreters call the Sermon on the Plain (which is parallel at many points to Matthew's longer and better known Sermon on the Mount) seem to be an actual interpretation of Isaiah 61:1 attributed to Jesus. Here he interprets the content of that oracle, and does so in a pattern of reversal and contrast that echoes the Magnificat. Those whom the world's values pity or scorn are those who will experience blessings in this vision of God's project, and those who are honored according to the values of imperial society will experience the other side of life. Matthew's Gospel elaborates the list of blessings (Matt. 5:3-12), while Luke addresses directly ("you") both the poor, hungry, weeping, and excluded members of his audience and the wealthy, sated, laughing and honored ones: all are present. All are confronted with the dramatic changes ahead for those who take seriously what they are seeing and hearing in Jesus' company.

Chapter 7 recapitulates the steps of 4:16-30, but in reverse order. The stories of Elijah and Elisha are echoed in the stories of the (Gentile) centurion's faith (7:1-10) and the widow's son (7:11-17). The visit to Jesus from disciples of John the Baptist (7:18-23) brings the question about Jesus' identity: "Are you the one who is to come, or should we wait for someone else?" The question is troubling, because according to Luke, John has known Jesus since their childhood, and they have been involved in a common (even perhaps overlapping) mission to proclaim the good news to the people (3:18). It is even a more troubling query, because no direct answer is given. In response to a question about his identity, Jesus answers by pointing to what is taking place around him. That description presents a paraphrase of Isaiah 61 and related texts that draws us back to the reading in the Nazareth synagogue. Presumably we readers should recognize that indeed this is the awaited "Coming One." We are given no confirmation that John has made this connection, however. The question hovers over the stage of the Gospel narrative, while Jesus praises the prophetic presence of John in 7:24-35.

If we look closely at the paraphrase of the Jubilee motifs from the texts of Isaiah found in the response to John, however, we are struck by something missing. There is no mention of "release" or "forgiveness." Luke's story of the anointing of Jesus by the woman at the banquet in Simon's house (7:36-50) fills in that blank. Unlike the anointing stories in Mark 14:3-9; Matthew 26:6-13; and John 12:1-8, the problem identified by the onlookers in this story is not the extravagance of her act, which wastes money that might have gone to the poor. Instead, the issue is her character: she is "a woman of the city, a sinner." What her sin was is not specified, but the host—a Pharisee—apparently knows enough to be horrified that Jesus allows her to touch him. Jesus attempts to clarify his actions by telling a parable. The parable tells of the forgiveness of a debtor who owes much and one who owes little, and then asks which one will love the forgiving creditor more. The answer is self-evident to the host: cancellation of a large debt would evoke greater gratitude, which is equated with love. Jesus then turns to the woman and declares that her sins are forgiven "for she loved much."

Does forgiveness evoke love, or does love earn forgiveness? Which came first (since the grammar does not make that clear)? With that debate, we, like the host in the story, miss the point, since really forgiveness and love are inseparable. Together they express the moment of the woman's fresh start in life, without the burdens of what she and everyone else "know" about her. We also are apt to miss two important details. One is that in the little parable the word for "forgiveness" is a word whose root is common to the word "charity." It is forgiveness with strings attached. When Jesus announces the woman's forgiveness, however, the word is the one found in the Jubilee texts, which could be translated "release" or "letting go"—forgiveness with open hands. The second detail that we risk missing is ignored by the host in the story as well: calculating relative debts is an exercise of the privileged. For the poor and those who live on the margins of society, even a tiny debt is a matter of life and death. The woman in the story has none of the religious capital of Simon the Pharisee. She is a "sinner." Furthermore, since she enters the story as one of the street people who would be brought into such a home to consume the leftovers of a banquet as an additional act of charity on the part of the host, she is apparently not part of his economic circle either. In her story, the Jubilee release that Jesus mediates is the epitome of good news of a new "reign," the likes of which neither she nor Jesus' critics have seen before.

The section that tells of Jesus' time in Galilee ends with another portrait of Jesus' identity (9:7-50). Human followers, heavenly voices, celestial visitors, and the forces of evil all answer the question left dangling in the earlier episode of the visit from John's disciples. This is indeed the Anointed One, child of God, embodiment of God's sovereign authority in the face of every other power that can confront him. Just as the section began with his precipitous departure from Nazareth, so it ends with the dramatic announcement that he has "set his face to go to Jerusalem" (9:51). Galilee is now part of his past, and the Holy City holds his future.

One might suppose that the short distance from Galilee to Jerusalem would be quickly covered, and geographically it would be. Theologically, though, the trek covers a long preparation for Jesus' impending absence from them—one last chance to bring the principal implications of his ministry together to inform their continuing discipleship. The account of the journey with its catalogue of essential teachings extends from 9:51 to 19:28. It includes some of the best-known teachings in Luke, and if they are read one by one, their very familiarity makes them hard to encounter afresh, because we have been told so many times what they are "supposed to" mean. Nevertheless, if we read Luke's "travel narrative" at a single sitting instead of one passage at a time, their cumulative impact is almost impossible to avoid.

The Jubilee motifs continue throughout this section. For example, the groups of people identified as the particular focus of the great joy that is to characterize the Jubilee in Isaiah 61:1—persons who are poor, lame, blind, or maimed—are the guests specifically sought out in the teachings on banquet etiquette in 14:7-14 and in Luke's version of the parable of the banquet (14:15-24; see Matt. 22:1-10).

The affirmation of God's coming reign, the sayings about forgiveness (with the specific word for monetary "debtors" in 11:4), and the petition for bread (a crucial aspect of the commitment to trust God rather than human agricultural production for one's sustenance) in Jesus' prayer in 11:1-4 all reaffirm the importance of the Jubilee in Jesus' ministry. Two principal details distinguish Luke's version of the prayer from the more familiar version in Matthew 6:9-13. First, Luke lacks the parallel constructions and rhythms that give Matthew's prayer the aura of having been polished into a central part of the church's liturgy. Luke's seems to be a simpler and more basic teaching on prayer. Second, the saying on bread in Luke asks for the bread "each day," instead of Matthew's "this day." That change of wording confirms the difference in verb tenses of the petitions, with Matthew's (the aorist tense in Greek) pointing to a one-time request, and Luke's (the present tense in Greek) asking for repeated actions, both in the petition for bread and in the petition for forgiveness. That second difference from the version in Matthew fits with the emphasis of this section of Luke's Gospel on preparation of the followers for long-term accountability to Jesus' teachings, rather than for a dramatic and imminent final divine drama.

The shift to a long-term perspective in Luke's version of the prayer gives coherence to the other teachings in this section of the Gospel as well. There are a few warnings about the impending future (e.g., 11:37-13:9; 17:1-10, 20-37), but by far the bulk of the teachings are reminders about the values that are to shape daily interactions (e.g., 10:25-37; 11:5-13; 13:10-17; 14:1-24; 15:1-32; 16:1-31; 17:11-17; 18:1-14), and specific teachings about discipleship and missionary activity (e.g., 9:57-62; 10:1-32; 13:22-35; 14:25-35; 18:15-19:28). Repeatedly, these teachings confront assumptions about the value and worth of persons and about criteria for wise or prudent behavior that would have been taken for granted by people, like many in Luke's audience, who were succeeding in the terms dictated by their Roman imperial context. For example, in this section of the Gospel we find parables about an ethnic outsider who demonstrates the compassion required by Torah (10:29-37) and an ungrateful and irresponsible son who is restored to the status of heir (15:11-32). With the disciples we hear the commandment to disdain the obligations, privileges, and benefits of family connections (14:25-35).

While Luke is not in the business of designing full-blown alternative economic models, he does present several hints about the need to open up subversive spaces within the imperial economic system. For example, the parable of the rich man and his poor neighbor Lazarus (16:19-31) spins out in graphic detail the sort of reversal of fortunes forecast in the Magnificat. The eternal suffering of the rich man is not attributed to his being a particular scoundrel, but simply to his having settled for business as usual and having not heeded "Moses and the prophets," who have provided plenty of warning about what God requires.

The story of the rich ruler who wants to inherit eternal life (18:18-30) introduces us to a man who tries to avoid the fate of the rich man of the other story. He wants to "inherit eternal life." His economic model is the one where he lives: estates and inheritance are taken for granted, and he wants to be sure his portfolio is in order. We are told that he has led an exemplary life, but that he "lacks" one thing. Paradoxically, what he lacks is a lack of wealth. In order to acquire that lack, he is told to sell all that he owns and distribute the money to the poor: not an option in his life plan! Even Peter's attempt to depict himself and the other followers as having made the grade stops short of the radical challenge to give everything away (18:28). What is even more striking is that Luke (like Matthew in 19:28-29) uses an image from the world of investments to reassure any in the audience who might be put off by the insanity of the claim: they will "get back very much more in this age, and in the age to come eternal life" (18:30). The subversive economic space that is the space of discipleship is still justified in the rhetoric of the dominant order!

Near the end of the journey narrative, Zacchaeus again adjusts the terms of the challenge, but with a successful result (19:1-10). Zacchaeus is introduced as a toll collector—not a positive character for either Jesus' followers or Luke's audience. Pious, observant Jews would look with revulsion at toll collectors, who would have been pawing through the packs and gear of the merchants and other travelers who passed the toll station, in order to assess the appropriate levy. Thus, they would have been ritually unclean. Luke's audience, in the time of increased tension in the Roman empire near the end of the first century, would have been acutely aware that toll collectors were servants of the imperial overlords. Finally, "everyone" knew that toll collectors lined their pockets by overcharging their victims. In fact, they were expected to earn their own salaries by adding a surcharge to what they had to render to Rome, but many practiced what amounted to "fraud." In this story Zacchaeus, the quintessential outsider on religious, political, and ethical grounds, does not even admit to fraud. Nevertheless, he agrees to give half of his wealth to the poor and to more than meet the requirements of Torah to make restitution if he has defrauded anyone (Exod. 22:1-4; Num. 5:7; Lev. 6:5). When he has made this pledge, he is told that "salvation" has come to his house, and he is called a child of Abraham. In this touching story—the last narrative before the journey to Jerusalem is completed—a space is held open in the economic order where God's values (known in Torah as well as in the teachings of Jesus), and not the rules of the empire, prevail. It is a tiny space—a crack, barely, in the complex structures of the dominant economic order—but it sounds a note of hope as the journey ends.

Luke is ever the realist, though. The hope-filled story of Zacchaeus is followed by a parable, "because he was near Jerusalem, and because they assumed that the reign of God was to appear immediately" (19:11-27; see also Matt. 25:14-30). As Luke tells this story, it is not a parable about the reign of God, but a parable reminding them that we are not there yet. It is a parable that takes us into our investment portfolio, with a classical picture of skilled and not-so-skilled investors, where those who earn the big profits are praised and get even more wealth to invest, and the cautious ones lose even what they have. In the hyperbole of the parable, they do not just lose their jobs, but they are executed by the irate king whose wealth they were to manage. But remember that this is not a parable about how things are supposed to be under the sovereignty of God. Rather, it gives a frightening picture of this world—a world gone awry. Imperial economics might prize a 100-percent return on investments, but an economy held to standards like those undergirding the Jubilee vision of the Bible would know that was unacceptable. To have traded with that result meant that someone was defrauded. The third servant is in fact the hero of the story if we follow the economic—and thus social, ethical, and religious—logic of God. That servant is portrayed as knowing the nature of those who claim to run the world, and refusing to play by their rules. Discipleship is costly, and by the world's standards it is absurd. Yet, in the background of the story we still hear the echoes of the words to Zacchaeus who dared to live into another reality, "Today salvation has come to this house, because this too is a child of Abraham."

According to Luke, once Jesus and those with him have arrived in the Holy City, events move quickly toward Jesus' crucifixion. He turns his attention from providing guidance to his followers, to confronting the authorities and their values one last time. From 19:29 to 21:38, we feel the tension mount as Jesus walks the fine line that keeps him just short of open defiance and indictable offense. He predicts the downfall of the powerful without openly advocating action to bring it about. He unmasks the sham of laws and formal practices without ever rejecting them outright. He practices the type of metaphorical speech that dismantles the plodding literalism of power. A good example of this style of (non)confrontation is found in the story of the widow's coins in 21:1-4. On the surface he seems to praise the generosity of this woman, who put her coins in the temple treasury even though she was poor. How many "stewardship" sermons have we heard urging us who have more to be equally generous! But just before this account Luke has presented an indictment of the religious leaders who curry honor while they disregard the basic teachings of their religion about justice and care of the poor—a group encompassed in the Hebrew Bible by the phrase "widows and orphans" (20:46-47). This is one of those widows whose houses have been devoured and who now is down to these two coins! Far from a hymn of praise to her, this is a song of lament that leaves the guilty to indict themselves. By the very religious tenets they profess, she should not be in this situation!

And indict themselves they do. On the surface, the narrative makes clear, Jesus is innocent of the charges that will be mounted against him on the long final day—from the evening at supper to the evening of burial. The hearings before the assembly (22:66-23:1), Pilate (23:1-5, 13-25), and Herod (23:6-12) are inconclusive on the question of guilt, but thanks finally to the intervention of mob rule (23:13-25), the death penalty is invoked anyway. Jesus is not a threat to the authorities who fulfill their proper responsibilities. When they do not, however, he holds a mirror before their faces and shows them their own true selves.

CONCLUSION

Luke's Gospel ends on an ambivalent note. Following the account of Jesus' crucifixion and burial, and the requisite wait until "the first day of the week, at early dawn" (24:1), we learn of the empty tomb and several reports that the crucified one has been encountered alive again in their midst. Knowing Luke's larger plan to include a second volume about the Holy Spirit's work among Jesus' followers and their heirs, we who are present-day heirs of the community around Jesus (in whatever age) hear a note of hope and joy. Something about the way the story was told, though, evokes uneasiness in those of us who share the privileged place of much of Luke's audience. As would-be disciples, we have been cheering Jesus on in his confrontations with the authorities and in the wise and astounding teachings with which he has left his followers. Those of us who are among the non-poor and even the highly privileged of our own societies and world, however, find ourselves and our commitments challenged along with those of the authorities of Jesus' day and in Luke's audience as well.

Luke does nothing to mitigate their discomfort or our own. The story of the two followers—Cleopas and his unnamed partner (perhaps his wife, since women often were not given the dignity of their own names in ancient narratives)—on the road to Emmaus (24:13-35) gives us Luke's model for how to sustain one's courage to return to "Jerusalem" (or Washington, or wherever our home base may be) to continue the ministry begun with Jesus. The pattern is that of the "hermeneutical circle" of Latin American liberation theology: (1) *See* one's own reality (24:19-26). (2) *Judge* through a rereading of the traditions that set forth God's project (24:27-29) and through the sustaining rituals of community—the broken bread (24:30-31). (3) *Act*, together with one's companions (24:32-35), to make known the divine will for abundant life for all people.

I encounter this Gospel from a place as ambivalent as that from which it appears to have been written, and I find its word more a challenge than a comfort. Like Luke, I am captivated by the vision of the reign of God, which promises a world of justice and peace, and I try to find the stories and the teachings that would convey that vision to the world in which I live. As a member of the dominant culture of the United States, as a tenured professor who is securely situated among the economically privileged of the world's people, and as an ordained minister, I read Luke's Gospel with considerable discomfort, because it makes me uneasy with the implications of that status in light of the project of God that, by faith, I espouse. Finally, as a woman and as someone in solidarity with persons who have been pushed to the precarious margins of life in Central America and in the cities and rural areas of North America, I am aware that even in the message that carries such a profound challenge to me as a person with power, there are dangerous compromises away from the radicality of the Gospel, which evoke equally profound suspicion. Perhaps the greatest challenge for me and people like me is to recognize in all the dimensions of that discomfort the message of "good news of great joy for all the people" of which the angels sing.

RESOURCES FOR FURTHER STUDY

Brown, Raymond E. *The Birth of the Messiah*. Garden City, N.Y.: Doubleday, 1977.

Craddock, Fred B. *Luke*. Interpretation. Louisville, Ky.: John Knox Press, 1990.

Neyrey, Jerome H., ed. *The Social World of Luke-Acts: Models for Interpretation*. Peabody, Mass.: Hendrickson, 1991.

Reid, Barbara E. *Choosing the Better Part? Women in the Gospel of Luke*. Collegeville, Minn.: Liturgical Press, 1996.

Ringe, Sharon H. *Luke*. Westminster Bible Companion. Louisville, Ky.: Westminster John Knox, 1995.

Schaberg, Jane. "Luke." In *Women's Bible Commentary*, expanded edition, edited by Carol A. Newsom and Sharon H. Ringe. Louisville, Ky.: Westminster John Knox, 1998.

Seim, Turid Karlsen. *The Double Message: Patterns of Gender in Luke-Acts*. Nashville: Abingdon, 1994.

Tannehill, Robert C. *The Narrative Unity of Luke-Acts: A Literary Interpretation*. 2 vols. Philadelphia/Minneapolis: Fortress, 1986, 1990.

5

John's Gospel's Call to Be Reborn of God

WES HOWARD-BROOK

IF ONE HAS READ MARK, MATTHEW, AND LUKE in succession, reading John's Gospel might lead people to feel that they have arrived suddenly in a foreign land. The rapid-fire sequence of healings and exorcisms is replaced by more reflective encounters between Jesus and representatives of particular viewpoints. Parables of God's reign are replaced by a series of metaphorical "I AM" statements, through which Jesus invites people to a deeper understanding of his identity and theirs too. A series of unique characters and events is portrayed, such as Nicodemus the Pharisee, the Samaritan woman at the well, Lazarus and his sisters, and the one identified only as "the disciple whom Jesus loved." Even Jesus' attitude toward his death is different: the psalmic cry of despair is replaced by a calm series of final ministerial acts. What is the relationship between this very different story of discipleship and the Synoptics? What social situation evoked such a narrative? What kind of discipleship community is John's Gospel[1] calling forth in its listeners?

Understanding John's Gospel requires stepping out of our dominant culture of individualism and privatized spirituality into the social world of the first-century Mediterranean basin. Like all the Gospels, John's is concerned not with a "personal relationship with Jesus" for its own sake but with a communal "conspiracy" to become children of God.

---

[1] For familiarity and convenience, I will continue to refer to the text by its common name of "John's Gospel." The facts are, however, that we have no idea who the actual person or persons were who wrote the narrative or where they lived.

Also like the other narratives of Jesus in the New Testament, John's Gospel must be read from start to finish rather than as a collection of short stories taken out of their larger context.

At the beginning of the journey on which this Gospel calls us, the author has given us a roadmap. The first eighteen verses comprise what is usually referred to as the "Prologue." Its poetic rhythms and structure introduce the themes and images which develop depth and resonance as one proceeds scene by scene. If you find yourself lost or confused in the Johannine landscape, the Prologue's guidance can help you find your bearings. To get started, then, let's take a look at the Gospel's overture.

"In the Beginning"

"In the beginning was the Word (*logos*), and the Word was with God, and the Word was God." While all the Gospels situate themselves within the framework of Scripture, John's takes this literally back to the beginning, consciously echoing the opening verse of Genesis. At the same time, it engages the Greco-Roman culture in which Jesus' first followers proclaimed the good news. The Greek word *logos* refers not simply to units of language (words), but to the rational principle of humanity extolled by the philosophers as the central distinguishing characteristic of human life. But John's Gospel is far from a paean to Hellenistic tradition. As it does with so many notions treasured by the elites of its world, John's Gospel introduces familiar ideas in order to *subvert* them. It is not the "rational principle" that is being celebrated in the opening sentence, but God's own power to bring forth light, life, and meaning to human existence.

The starting sentence also offers us a basic principle through which to interpret the Gospel. As with all biblical texts, John's chooses its words very carefully and specifically. It is not simply a matter of aesthetic crafting (although the text *is* a spectacular artistic creation), but of recognizing one of the central ways in which the God of Israel, and hence of Jesus, differs from the gods of neighboring peoples. Whereas the Babylonian Marduk, for instance, created the world out of a corpse generated through violent conflict, the biblical God creates by speaking a word into the chaos: "'Let there be . . .' . . . and there was." The Gospel both celebrates this affirmation and participates in it by "creating" Jesus out of words. Thus, our first principle of interpretation is:

Every word counts. Learning to read word by word can be a difficult task for those of us living in a world where "talk is cheap." We are so flooded by language that, practically speaking, many of us have forgotten how to read, choosing to skim texts for "the point" rather than meditating over each phrase and scene. Just as the long, leisurely meal has been replaced by fast food and on-the-run consumption, we have been tricked into losing one of our most important human capacities, that of careful, patient, wonder-filled attention to the details and nuances of life. John's Gospel offers healing medicine to enable our recovery of this capacity, if we are open to its call.

One way in which the Gospel invites us to this kind of reading is by structuring each of its scenes, including the Prologue, into word-shapes called *chiasms.* The term refers to the Greek letter *chi,* which is shaped like our *X.* What it means is that each text unit focuses on a central image or idea, with matching subunits of text surrounding the center like waves radiating out from a rock thrown into a still lake. To see how this works, here is the chiasm that makes up the Prologue:

A Vv. 1-5: Relationship of *logos* to God, creation, humanity
  B Vv. 6-8: Witness of John (the Baptist) (negative)
    C Vv. 9-11: Journey of light/*logos* (negative)
      D Vv. 12-13: Gift of authority to become children of God
    C' V. 14: Journey of *logos* (positive)
  B' V. 15: Witness of John (the Baptist) (positive)
A' Vv. 16-18: Relationship of *logos* to humanity, "re-creation," God

The chiastic structure calls us not simply to read in a linear fashion, but to *look at* the entire Prologue as a whole. This can feel strange at first for people trained to read the way one travels on a train, moving from point A to point B without considering the entire terrain as a whole. When we consider the whole "picture," however, two important things can happen. First, we learn to see not a series of "Bible verses" that can be pulled out as weapons in an ideological or moral battle, but a verbal icon or mandala that beckons us into its world. Second, we can discern the central message of any given passage not through the lens of our preexisting theology but through the text's own "rules of engagement."

In the case of the Prologue, many readers unaware of the importance of chiasm tend to focus their reading of the whole Gospel on *Christology*: "The Word became flesh" (1:14). But when seen through the chiastic structure, the focus shifts to *discipleship*: "he gave authority to become children of God" (1:12). In other words, chiasm shows us that the goal of John's Gospel is worship of Jesus not for its own sake, but for the sake of the empowering of communities of discipleship in Jesus' name. We will return to this theme in a moment when we look at the heart of the Prologue and hence, of the entire Gospel.

A final "mapping" function of the Prologue is to introduce many of the central images that recur throughout the narrative. In the first verses we hear not only of "Word" but of life, light/darkness, witness, trust (faith), world, children/Father flesh, and glory. Each of these terms is taken from the everyday context of the original audience, just as most of them remain ordinary words for us as well. But John's Gospel rarely uses its primary vocabulary in "ordinary" ways. Indeed, one of its basic invitations is to learn to see how the "ordinary" contains the sacred. Thus, rather than using specialized "theological" terms, John's Gospel paints its picture with repeated strokes of everyday colors. Its vocabulary is constrained, in pointed contrast to that of Luke/Acts, in which literally hundreds of words are used that are not found elsewhere in the New Testament. This constraint is a sign not of lack of learning but of a specific strategy through which it tries to inculcate a commitment to discipleship in Jesus' name. Only by engaging the text within its own terms of word-by-word reading, chiastic shaping, and ever-deepening meaning of specific words can we learn to hear the powerful message the Gospel seeks to communicate.

"AUTHORITY TO BECOME CHILDREN OF GOD"

The master metaphor through which John's Gospel speaks is that of *birth*. At the heart of John's use of the metaphor is the Prologue's centrally placed contrast between being born "of God" and three alternatives: being born "of blood(s)," of "the will of the flesh," or "of the will of a man." Passages from this Gospel selected since ancient times as lectionary readings for the church's Lenten journey invoke the three stories, each of which presents one of these contrasts. These stories make up the three "scrutinies," the close mutual look between the existing discipleship community and prospective members: the encounter between Jesus and a woman at a Samaritan well (chap. 4), the healing of a blind person and its consequences (chap. 9), and the struggle for faith around the tomb of Lazarus (chap. 11). A look at each of these stories, along with the Nicodemus narrative, will illustrate both the link between the Prologue and the wider narrative, and the message for discipleship which unfolds within these "birth" stories.

"NOT BORN OF THE WILL OF THE FLESH," PART 1: NICODEMUS

We risk misunderstanding the thrust of the whole Gospel if we read its individual passages out of context. Thus, to discern the meaning of the Nicodemus story in John 3, we must first look briefly at the text that precedes it. After the Prologue, we are told of "the witness of John" to those sent from Jerusalem with the question, "Who are you?" (1:19). John's witness takes place over three carefully delineated days, pointing away from himself and toward Jesus, whom he calls "the Lamb of God" (1:29, 36).

On the Gospel's fourth day, Jesus begins to gather a group of disciples. For those raised with the notion of religion generally and the Bible specifically as "serious business," it might be surprising to see the sometimes outrageous humor with which the Gospel—like so much of the Hebrew Bible—conveys its story. An early example of this humor is the encounter between Jesus and Nathanael, whom Jesus sees "under the fig tree" (1:48). Jesus' ability to discern Nathanael's simple honesty leads the latter to proclaim wildly, "Rabbi, you are the Son of God! You are the King of Israel!" Jesus' response suggests to the eager disciple, "You ain't seen nothing yet!" If the idea that the Gospel is funny seems strange, we should remember how hard it is to recall a serious political speech or church homily, and how easy it is to repeat a good joke one has picked up during the day. In addition to serving as a popular mnemonic device, the Gospel's wit works like a good editorial cartoon, puncturing pretension and falsity through caricature rather than through rational argument.

After proceeding slowly through its first four days, the Gospel then jumps in both time and space: "On the third day there was a wedding in Cana of Galilee . . ." (2:1). It is now the Gospel's seventh day, the day of Sabbath, of rest and re-creation after the busy work of generating a new narrative of God's presence amidst humanity. The wedding at Cana forms one half of a diptych (along with Jesus' visit to the Jerusalem temple which follows) that sets up the tension between the joyous celebration of God's presence in the world and the necessary confrontation with the dark forces that work against that celebration.

At Cana, we hear the fulfillment of numerous prophetic images of the overflowing joy of the messianic banquet (e.g., Amos 9:13; Isa. 62:4). John's Gospel shouts, "This is what God intends for you! May life be like a wedding banquet at which the choicest wine flows without end!"

Sadly, though, life for most people is not like this at all. The problem is not the lack of God's abundance, but the systemic injustice and oppression that have sated the few with luxuries while denying daily bread to the many. In Jesus' day, this system was nowhere more clearly visible than in the corrupt deal made between the Jerusalem temple elite and the Roman empire. Thus, Jesus' "mission statement" in John's Gospel involves not only his proclamation of messianic celebration but also his prophetic denunciation of the "world's" evil. He expresses this through the "sign" of overturning the tables of those who serve as the visible face of the unjust status quo, the Jerusalem money changers and sacrificial animal dealers.

This act and its aftermath establish a pattern frequent in the Gospel. Jesus offers a metaphorical double entendre which his would-be interpreters misunderstand by taking literally. This enables Jesus to offer more Johannine talk, which forces his dialogue partners into a "crisis," from the Greek *krisis*, meaning a "moment of decision." In this case, the metaphor is "temple": "Destroy this temple, and in three days I will raise it up" (2:19). His opponents think "building" but the narrator tells us he means "body" (2:20-21). Whether they understand or not, however, Jesus' action and words provoke the crisis from which "many trusted (*episteusan*) in his name because they saw the signs that he was doing" (2:23). Although many Bibles translate the Greek verb *pisteuō* as "to believe," in John's Gospel, it connotes not "faith" or "belief" as adherence to an idea or doctrine but *trust* in the name (person) of Jesus as the One who most fully reveals the will of "the Father." To trust in Jesus is to become his disciple, which in turn means to become a member of the "children of God."

It is out of this confrontational crisis that Nicodemus the Pharisee comes to Jesus "at night." The introduction to the story in John 3 reveals another pattern frequent in John's Gospel. The narrator provides a context for the encounter intended to shape readers' interpretation. Once again, every detail counts; readers who skip over these little narrative prologues run the risk of siding with those who misunderstand Jesus' metaphors. In this case, the focus is on Jesus' reaction to those who "trusted in his name because they saw the signs that he was doing" (2:23). The narrator tells us that Jesus "would not entrust himself to them, because he knew all people, and needed no one to testify about anyone; for he himself knew what was in each person. Now there was a person named Nicodemus, a Pharisee, a ruler of the Judeans" (2:24-3:1). In other words, to illustrate why Jesus does not entrust himself to persons who trust because of signs, let's bring one of those "persons" on stage: Nicodemus. Translations often fail to catch the crucial wordplay with which this scene is set up. For example, in the name of gender inclusivity, the NRSV offers "he himself knew what was in everyone. Now there was a Pharisee named Nicodemus. . . ." However, the Gospel itself is here, as almost always, gender inclusive, using the Greek *anthrōpos* ("human being" or "person") rather than *andros/anēr* ("male"). The point is not "men" versus "humans" but "persons who trust because of signs," of which Nicodemus is an important example.

We also learn that Nicodemus is a "Pharisee," that is, a member of the liberal reform group which attempted in its own way to reduce the suffering caused to the poor by the "strict constructionism" of the temple elite and its supporters. Further, he is a "ruler of the Judeans," that is, a member of the Jerusalem Sanhedrin, the ruling council upon whose cooperation the Roman colonial deal depended. Finally, he comes to Jesus "at night," which associates him with "darkness," the power that threatened but did not overcome the Word-made-flesh (1:5).

We should pause here to consider a crucial piece of Johannine terminology, the Greek *Ioudaioi*, usually translated "Jews" but rendered here "Judeans." Two thousand years of unwarranted Christian anti-Judaism has purported to find an ally in John's Gospel's supposed opposition to "Jews." However, the term refers first to "Judeans," that is, people from Judea, as opposed to Galileans or Samaritans. But more importantly, although the Gospel begins with this everyday meaning, like so many of its terms, it fills it with a special meaning that unfolds as the narrative proceeds. In this case, the "Judeans" are not simply residents of the southern province of Palestine, nor are they limited to the religious establishment. Rather, *they represent all those who identify with and defend the unjust status quo.* Just as folks in Washington, D.C., regardless of their political views, are largely glad the government's headquarters are in *their* city, the Judeans are those who profit from the Jerusalem temple and its system, which oppresses the poor. There is not the slightest basis for accusing the Gospel of "anti-Judaism"; practically everyone in the story except Pontius Pilate is a "Jew" of one form or another!

As with the Prologue, the story's chiastic structure sheds light on its focus:

A Vv. 1-2: Nicodemus calls Jesus a "teacher sent from God"
  B Vv. 3-4: Jesus speaks of birth *"anōthen"* and Nicodemus asks "How?"
    C Vv. 5-6: Jesus speaks of birth "of water and spirit"
  B' Vv. 7-9: Jesus speaks of birth *"anōthen"* and Nicodemus asks "How?"
A' V. 10: Jesus calls Nicodemus a "teacher of Israel"

The framing contrast in the A parts is between "teacher" as an authority given by God and as an official in an institutional religion. The B parts twice present Jesus' invitation to rebirth, to which the shocked Nicodemus responds "How is this possible?" And at the center of the scene is the contrast between "fleshly" birth and birth by "water and spirit," that is, baptism. Nicodemus, who, like almost every character in the Gospel, speaks in the first person plural on behalf of the social group and attitude he represents, cannot understand Jesus' invitation to rebirth. After all, he is not an evil person, but one who has apparently succeeded in becoming a religious leader in accordance with the rules and principles of his religion as they had been taught to him and practiced first by his own teachers and then by his peers. How can it be, he wonders, that God could be telling me to be born *anōthen* (a double entendre meaning both "from above" and "again")? What would it mean to start over like a baby after a lifetime of piety and faith according to the traditions of the ancestors?

Twice more the Gospel presents Nicodemus struggling with the crisis provoked by Jesus (7:45-52; 19:38-42), one of the only characters to make a multiple appearance. At the feast of Tabernacles, when the temple police sent to round up Jesus come back empty-handed, the Pharisees deride them and the "accursed crowd," who, unlike themselves, follow after would-be messiahs. Just when the situation calls for Nicodemus to confront his peers by revealing his own heretofore secret trust in Jesus, he offers instead impersonal "due process of law" (7:51). And at the foot of the cross where Jesus hangs dead, Nicodemus comes, along with Joseph of Arimathea, to anoint the body with a "royal" quantity of precious spices. While we may be tempted to applaud his courageous recognition of Jesus' true power, his act represents just the behavior that Jesus harshly critiques in Matthew: "Woe to you, scribes and Pharisees, hypocrites! For you build the tombs of the prophets and decorate the graves of the righteous!" (Matt. 23:29). Like those today who "love" Martin Luther King Jr. in death but despised and feared him in his lifetime, Nicodemus, despite his secret trust in Jesus, is a "grave decorator" rather than an open disciple. In Johannine terms, he remains born of "the will of the flesh" rather than "of God." The Gospel seeks disciples who, like John the Baptist, "witness" openly to who they are and who they are not. To illustrate "how this is possible," we must look at the story of "successful" witness portrayed in John 9.

"NOT BORN OF THE WILL OF THE FLESH," PART 2: THE ONE BORN BLIND

The immediate context of this popular story is the aftermath of Jesus' presence in Jerusalem for the feast of Tabernacles (chaps. 7-8). Tabernacles (also known as Booths or *Sukkot*) was one of three festivals that called faithful Jews back to Jerusalem. In the context of Roman occupation, it also served to arouse nationalistic fervor among the pilgrims. The Jerusalem authorities were torn between two competing forces: maintaining loyalty to the temple (and hence to them) and keeping the peace to maintain the puppet authority Rome had provided and the personal wealth that flowed to them from that authority. The feast was celebrated with two powerful symbols: a tremendous flow of water from the temple out into the dry streets and a dramatic procession of lights. At each of these key moments, Jesus cries out in opposition to the Jerusalem establishment: "Let anyone who is thirsty come to me and drink!" (7:37) and "I am the light of the world!" (8:12). These outrageous proclamations lead to a "paternity suit" between Jesus and the Judeans. Jesus claims that God is his Father (8:16ff.), while they assert that their father is Abraham (8:39). Jesus announces, however, that their real father is "the devil," who was a "murderer" and "liar" from the beginning! (8:44).

Thus, the scene is set. Our master metaphor of rebirth is fully at issue. Meanwhile, where are Jesus' own disciples during all this heated, public confrontation? The text does not say, but as chapter 9 starts, they are arguing over whose fault it is that a beggar has been born blind (9:1). It is a mirror in which they peer at their own blindness: Was it their parents who taught them to revere and obey the Jerusalem authorities whom Jesus condemns, or have they been complicit in their own oppression? Rather than get caught in this futile argument, Jesus goes about the business of healing. He mixes his saliva with the soil and anoints the blind one's eyes, telling him to "wash in the pool which means 'sent'" (9:7). It is a rebirthing process: saliva, "living water" from one's innermost parts, represents the spirit (7:38-39), which, when mixed with earth, recalls God's first creation of the ʾādām (earth creature) from a mixture of the ʾădāmâ (earth) and God's own spirit (Gen. 2:7). The story enacts the drama of discipleship, beginning with precisely the act of baptismal rebirth to which Nicodemus responds, "How is this possible?"

Once washed, the formerly blind one sees all: the doubt of his neighbors, the closed-mindedness of the Pharisees, the defensiveness of the Judeans, and, most sadly, the cowardice of his own parents. In this scene, we get the closest look at the life of the discipleship community that formed around this Gospel narrative. They had been touched by Jesus' spirit and healed of their blindness, only to be challenged relentlessly and threatened with expulsion if they dared to continue proclaiming their experience of God's power at work in his name. It was the very process of being challenged that backed them into the corner from which the Gospel's "high Christology" emerged. When push came to shove, either Jesus was indeed the One sent from God or they were risking all for a false prophet. Their discipleship was forged in the crucible of confessional witness; and rather than making them popular evangelists, it cost them their whole world.

But having been thrown out, Jesus found them "outside" (9:35). The one born blind, representative of Jesus' own disciples, had experienced the wrenching journey from the comforts of "home" (also known as "the will of the flesh") to the truth of God. Their insistence on sharing their experience of how God had touched their lives in a new way had put an end to the life that "the world" had to offer. They were indeed like little children, having been born anew in God.

"NOT BORN OF THE WILL OF A MAN": LIVING WATER IN SAMARIA

The Prologue's second dramatization of choosing a "false birth" is presented in the encounter between Jesus and the Samaritans in chapter 4. The narrator's introduction again sets the stage with the focus on Samaria's relationship with "Jacob," whom the woman claims on behalf of her people as "our father" (4:12). This passage has been repeatedly taken out of its historical and narrative context to serve as a spiritualized call to "those who thirst." However, the link with Jacob and the historical specificity of the Samaritans place this passage squarely in the midst of Jesus' Johannine mission: to call people away from commitments to man-made[2] systems of identity and into rebirth as children of God.

The central metaphor is "living water," a double entendre referring both to "flowing" water (as opposed to the stagnant well water) and to Jesus' own spirit. The woman Jesus meets gets it "wrong," but unlike her counterpart Nicodemus, she persists in challenging Jesus until more of his truth is revealed. On the surface, the conversation seems constantly to shift gears, from wells and water to husbands, to prophets, to places of worship, to the Messiah. But below that surface, the narrative thread is consistent. Jesus the "prophet" knows the Samaritans' history of oppression by empire and rejection by their Judean kin (cf. 2 Kgs. 17:24-41; Ezra 4). It was "necessary" for Jesus to go to Samaria (4:4) in order to offer an alternative to the endless struggle over ethnic identity and nationalism which was the truth of their past and their present. To the question, "Which mountain does God live on?" Jesus responds, "Neither!" (4:20-21). Just as he told Nicodemus that God's Spirit blows like the wind and hence can't be contained by religious institutions, so he tells her and her people that it cannot be contained by national or ethnic boundaries.

The woman responds by becoming the Gospel's first "apostle," meaning "one sent forth." She rushes back to town to bring the news that the Messiah might be at the well, and the people drop their work and follow. The numerous interpretations that denigrate this woman as an "outcast" overlook the fact that the townspeople would hardly chase after a Messiah whose herald was a tainted woman! The suspicion she carries (hence, her midday water drawing) is a result not of her personal sin (sexual or otherwise) but of the racism that has isolated her people (of whom she is a representative) from their rightful place at God's messianic banquet. Jesus heals the breach and is proclaimed "truly savior of the world" (4:42). This title is in direct opposition to the proclamation of the Roman emperor as "savior of the world." No longer will the Samaritans claim either Jacob or Caesar as their "father," but God alone.

In this context we can see how important the *metaphor* of God-the-Father is in John's Gospel. Like all of Jesus' "I AM" statements, which express metaphorically something of how Jesus is an expression of God (e.g., Vine, Good Shepherd, Light, etc.), calling the One who sent Jesus

---

[2] I have intentionally forgone using the gender-inclusive "human-made" because of the link with "will of a man" in this story.

"Father" is a statement of both political and theological commitment. In the midst of various pressures to root one's identity in human fathers (as Americans are urged to do through the image of the "Founding Fathers" or Germans under Hitler were through the image of the "fatherland"), Jesus calls would-be disciples to claim no "father" except God alone. This is the meaning of the Prologue's warning not to be born "of the will of a man" (1:13). John's Gospel's frequent use of "Father" for God (136 times; 137 in all three Synoptics combined) is an expression not of the "nature" of the divine (i.e., as opposed to "Mother") but of God's exclusive power to create and name us as God's own "children." The Johannine discipleship call makes penultimate all claims to belong to a "chosen people" grounded in land or genetics.

"NOT BORN OF BLOOD(S)": CONFRONTING DEATH WITH THE POWER OF RESURRECTION

The final external challenge to discipleship which John's Gospel confronts is the paralyzing fear of death itself. Although there was no systematic Roman persecution of Jesus' disciples at the time of the Gospel, there was always the local threat of violence against those who dared to trust in unofficial powers, whether via the "civilized" violence of empire or the more raw power of the mob. All who would claim to be followers of Jesus must deal with our own often enshadowed attitudes toward the final threat. John's Gospel does this through the story of two women's struggle to trust in John 11.

The passage begins in the familiar style, with the narrator offering an interpretive "clue." "Mary was the one who anointed the Lord with perfume and wiped his feet with her hair; her brother Lazarus was ill" (11:2). The key here is that this anointing does not take place until the next chapter, where Jesus affirms her act as preparation for his burial (12:7). By introducing Mary and Martha in this way, we are asked to read the entire episode in light of Jesus' impending death, and, possibly, our own.

The story presents every conceivable attitude toward death. Mary *prepares* for it, while the disciples *avoid* and *deny* it (11:8, 12). Thomas, in one of the most multivoiced lines in the Gospel, offers, "Let us also go, that we may die with him" (11:16). Whether this expresses courage, resignation, despair, or dark humor is left to readers to decide. Meanwhile, the Judeans join the sisters as professional mourners, part of the business of death as familiar then as it is now. Amidst all of this, Jesus arrives secretly outside the village, where he challenges Martha to trust in him who is "the resurrection and the life" (11:25). Martha's "Yes, Lord" is followed by a sequence of holy titles for Jesus, correct answers to a question other than the one Jesus asked her. Her rapid exit speaks volumes; Jesus' own beloved friends have not put their trust completely in him.

Jesus' deepest emotions are aroused by this lack of trust, feelings for which the Greek language can only grope (11:33; compare English translations). "For the sake of the crowd" (11:42) he calls the dead Lazarus from the tomb, in confirmation of the authority he has been given by God (5:25-29). It is an authority meant not to place Jesus on the pedestal but to empower trust in those who hear and see him. It is a trust so powerful that death and those who threaten to cause it cannot take that trust away. Once disciples overcome their fear of death, the "world" can have no further power in their lives. This is the paradox at the heart of the passion and of the life of discipleship. It is precisely because disciples reject the threats of empire that they are found to be most threatening *by* empire, and therefore, most in need of destruction.

This is the reaction of the quickly gathered Sanhedrin, who meet in emergency session to decide what to do about this Jesus. Caiaphas, the only level-headed one in their midst, enunciates clearly the "scapegoat principle" upon which so much of civilization is based: "You know nothing at all! You do not understand that it is better for you to have one man die for the people than to have the whole nation destroyed" (11:49-50). Yet by taking us into the Sanhedrin's secret deliberations, the Gospel unmasks their plan to pull the "nation" together through the sacrifice of an innocent victim upon whom they can cast their rage. They fear that political instability will arouse the Romans to renege on the colonial collaboration. But, of course, they did kill Jesus and the Romans came and destroyed Jerusalem anyway! The Gospel's insight into the nature of political authority is great and calls disciples to withdraw their allegiance from a system birthed through "blood(s)"—an ancient euphemism for political violence—and commit instead to the community birthed through the gift of *agapē*, as we will see in the next section of the narrative.

THE CONSPIRACY TO BE CHURCH

The first twelve chapters of John's Gospel, in which Jesus challenges the status quo and its defenders, are often referred to as the Book of

Signs. Starting with the overturning of tables in the temple, Jesus provokes the crisis that forces people to take sides in a battle they may have been unaware was raging in their midst between "the light" and "the darkness." The narrator says, however, that people "loved darkness rather than light because their works were evil" (3:19). Why would people insist on practicing evil when offered a choice? Because, the narrator adds, "they loved human glory more than the glory that comes from God" (12:43). This is indeed the crux of the matter. To follow Jesus is to choose God's "glory" over the glory people offer to each other. And so, with this statement, the Book of Signs ends and the Book of Glory (chaps. 13-21) begins.

As with its imagery of God as Father, John's Gospel uses the language of "glory" more than the Synoptics combined. The Greek *doxa* is a term from the domain of honor and shame: to give someone "glory" is to honor them with acts that enhance their public standing. Yet Jesus' glory, as we shall see, is most visible, according to this Gospel, on the cross. How can we comprehend this paradoxical, even apocalyptic, idea? More importantly, how can we *witness* to it not only in the life of Jesus but in the life of all those who suffer in the name of God's love? It is this challenge that leads the Gospel to spend five full chapters (13-17) on Jesus' preparation of his frightened and confused disciples for his death and possibly their own.

The so-called Last Supper Discourse (or Farewell Discourse) begins with an action central to the Gospel's notion of discipleship. Jesus gets up from the meal and washes his disciples' feet, then tells them to become washers of one another's feet. In my years of teaching John's Gospel to church groups, I have found no text to produce a more "doctrinal" response than the footwashing. It is a call to "humble service," people say. And yet, contained within the story is this interpretation, and Jesus says it is wrong! It is Peter who expresses it in his vehement objection to Jesus' washing of his feet. Jesus' response is equally strong: "Unless I wash you, you have no part in my inheritance." In other words, the footwashing is so important that if Peter will not participate in it, Jesus will cut him out of his will! For a "last will and testament" is what these chapters present, modeled deliberately on Moses' own departure speech in Deuteronomy. Jesus offers his disciples a Way to live through Good Friday, and footwashing is a step in the initiation into this Way. Peter, seeing his master acting like a humble servant, is shocked. But Jesus says to him, "You do not know now what I am doing, but later you will understand" (13:7). It is *not* about humble service, Peter, but about something that will enable you to face the suffering that the world will offer in "thanks" for your witness to and against it.

Jesus tells them that "servants are not greater than their master" (13:16, again at 15:20), and hence they cannot avoid the duty of becoming footwashers. As anyone who has ever washed someone's feet knows, the invitation is not simply to service but to *intimacy*. This is clearly what is lacking amidst the fledgling discipleship community, as is revealed when Jesus tells them ominously, "One of you will betray me" (13:21). But not one of them has a clue who the betrayer is! The problem is that they have been so focused on Jesus that they have forgotten to pay attention to one another. With Jesus' imminent departure, they are wholly unprepared to continue the discipleship journey.

Footwashing is the remedy to this problem. John's Gospel places this episode where the Synoptic and Pauline traditions recall Jesus' identification of himself with the bread and wine. In replacing the link between Eucharist and Last Supper (the question of "munching my flesh and drinking my blood" is addressed in John 6 after the wilderness feeding) with footwashing, the narrative signals its view that this ritual is key to the life of discipleship. For indeed, without deep intimacy among its members, any would-be faith community is destined to fail during hard times. Footwashing is the ritual that begins and strengthens the process of "conspiring" to be church.

It is right at this darkest place on the discipleship journey that John's Gospel introduces one of its central characters: the anonymous figure referred to as "the disciple whom Jesus loved" or the Beloved Disciple. Many interpreters have tried to crack the puzzle of his identity, attempting to link him with various named figures within the narrative. But this effort misses the powerful choice made by the author to leave some of the story's most important persons unnamed, including the Samaritan woman, the one born blind, and even Jesus' mother. Anonymity provides readers with more room imaginatively to identify with those characters. The Beloved Disciple, who sits in the same position of intimacy in relation to Jesus as Jesus does in relation to the Father (13:23; 1:18), is the embodiment of the Johannine community, especially as it stands in tension with a different emerging model of discipleship community, embodied in Simon Peter. From this point on, the two become representatives of Spirit-driven church and apostolic church. This tension is made even clearer in the Gospel's final scene.

As the Last Supper Discourse continues, Jesus provides numerous images that attempt to reinforce the process of becoming the kind of church that continues his mission after his departure. He warns them that they will be persecuted and hated as he has been (15:18-20). The transformation that results from this suffering will be like "birth pangs" (16:21). But if they remain in union with Jesus the Vine, the One from whom their life flows, their suffering will be turned into joy (16:22). To protect them along the Way, Jesus promises them "another Advocate, to be with you forever. This is the Spirit of truth whom the world cannot receive" (14:16). The uniquely Johannine description of the Holy Spirit is the Greek *paraklētos*, variously translated as "Advocate," "Comforter," or "Paraclete." The term conveys both one who speaks on behalf of another in court—that is, a defense attorney—and one who offers comfort amidst suffering. The life of discipleship will be, as it was for the one born blind, a continuous courtroom drama, a battle between the "Satan" (i.e., the accuser or prosecuting attorney [13:27, cf. 17:15]) and the Paraclete. The only way to keep the faith amidst this kind of daily struggle is by sharing in a community of intimacy in which one's pains can be poured out and compassionately received and healed, enabling the return to the world in further witness. This rhythm of "breathing in" (receiving Holy Spirit through community prayer, celebration, and Bible study) and "breathing out" (witnessing to the world) is the conspiracy, the "breathing together" that is intended to be church.

And holding this together is *agapē*, the love that knows nothing greater than to lay itself down for friends (10:15-18; 15:12-13). Of the forty-four uses of a form of the word *agapē* in John's Gospel, thirty-two are in chapters 13-17. But the love that disciples are to share bears no resemblance to the cheapened use of the word familiar to us, which can be applied equally to pizza or cars. *Agapē* is the fruit of intimacy in the Spirit, the "glue" that binds all things together (cf. 1 Corinthians 13). Jesus implores his disciples to have this love for one another not for their own sake but as a witness to the world of what a community of people "born of God" looks and lives like (13:34-35; 15:7-9). This conspiratorial community is called not to transform the "world" but to walk the tightrope of being "in" but not "of" it (15:19; 17:13-16). John's Gospel resists the twin options of trying to beat empire at its own game (i.e., to fight it with scapegoating violence or political compromise) and walking away altogether into some imagined "pure" realm "outside" the world. Instead, it beckons disciples into the more painful but paradoxically more joyous conspiracy that offers the light of God's love, lived right in the midst of the world's darkness. To show them, and us, how this is possible, Jesus' next move is to place himself at the heart of darkness as he undergoes his passion.

THE PASSION ACCORDING TO JOHN

Despite their many differences, each of the four Gospels knows that the passion narrative is at the heart of the call to discipleship. John's version is structured chiastically to emphasize that it is the world, not Jesus, that is truly on trial. Jesus is not a fugitive finally nabbed by the authorities, but a model of *agapē*, the Good Shepherd who puts his life on the line for his friends. Furthermore, Jesus is both "high priest," offering the ultimate sacrifice, and "king," reigning in judgment, exercising the authority given to him by God.

A 18:1-12 Jesus' arrest: a garden, Jesus is bound; Simon Peter treats Jesus as a "worldly" king

    B 18:13-27 Judean interrogation: Jesus as "high priest"; Beloved Disciple witnesses (with Simon Peter, who denies his discipleship)

        C 18:28-19:16 The "world" (Judeans and Roman empire) on trial before Jesus the king

    B' 19:17-30 Jesus' crucifixion: Jesus as "high priest"; Beloved Disciple witnesses (with Jesus' mother, who begins her discipleship)

A' 19:31-42 Jesus' burial: a garden; Jesus is bound; Nicodemus and Joseph treat Jesus as a "worldly" king

A key point in the drama of John's passion story is the portrayal of the Judeans and Roman authorities as collaborators in Jesus' execution. We misread the narrative if we see Pontius Pilate as a "neutral" figure suddenly confronted with the "problem" of Jesus, or even, as some have described him, as sympathetic to Jesus' release. Pilate's imperial fingerprints are evident from the beginning, when we are told that Judas the betrayer is accompanied by "a cohort (*speiran*) of soldiers together with police from the chief priests and the Pharisees" (18:3). The *speiran* was the detachment of soldiers under the command of the procurator Pilate, the local Roman official in charge of the province of Judea. It would consist of two hundred to six hundred soldiers. There is no way that these Roman troops could be part of the arresting mob without Pilate's express authorization. Thus, throughout the passion, we are called to see the Judeans—the local collaborators—and Pilate—

the power of empire—as representatives of "the world" unified in resistance to the One sent from God.

Once arrested, Jesus is taken before the high priest. This scene is not a trial. No charges are proffered and no witnesses are called. Rather, it is a nighttime interrogation designed to get Jesus to "name names," which, of course, Jesus refuses to do (18:19-21). Meanwhile, Peter, who rashly promised to lay down his life for Jesus, is being interrogated by the high priest's *servant girl*, a bit of dark humor which underscores the diametric contrast between the would-be disciple and his teacher. Whereas Jesus is the great "I AM" (*egō eimi* [6:35; 8:12; 8:24; etc.]), Peter is the great "I am not" (*ouk eimi* [18:17, 25]).

With this we reach the centerpiece of the passion story. It is itself a seven-part chiasm, dividing easily between scenes "inside" and "outside" Pilate's praetorium. On the inside, we find an arrogant Roman official whose imperial confidence is gradually eroded by Jesus' courageous witness. On the outside, we hear the cries of a Judean mob possessed by the spirit of empire, expressed through the terrifying confession, "We have no king but Caesar" (19:15). Amidst the Passover frenzy of nationalistic pilgrims in Jerusalem, the Judean authorities and their collaborators call on the oppressor's power to crucify one of their own people, following Caiaphas's advice. Once Pilate tires of the game of toying with the Judeans and the mystery of Jesus becomes too much for him, he gives in to the inevitable and hands Jesus over to the executioners.

Where do we stand amidst this power struggle? The Gospel attempts to keep us focused by beginning a series of Scripture fulfillment notices (18:32; 19:24, 28, 36). As we watch the seeming defeat of Jesus at the hands of the powers, we are called to interpret events from a "heavenly" perspective. As the "world" sees it, Jesus dies a humiliating and painful death. But from God's viewpoint—and ours?—Jesus has been "lifted up" in fulfillment of his own predictions (3:14; 8:28; 12:32), declared a "king" by the representative of Rome (19:14, 19).

An important Johannine piece of the picture is the witness to the "blood and water" released from Jesus "side" (*pleuran*) at the soldier's swordstroke (19:34-35). It is the completion of the birth imagery with which the Gospel began. Just as God separated the original "earth creature" into male and female humans by taking from the *pleuran* ("rib," Gen. 2:22) of the *ʾādām*, so now Jesus "gives birth" (the natural context of flowing blood and water) to the Spirit (7:38-39), which animates the newly born community of discipleship. Among those who witness to this process are two anonymous figures, the Beloved Disciple and Jesus' mother, whom the dying but still royal Jesus commends to one another (19:26-27). The old and the new, tradition and Spirit, one generation and the next, are joined together as God's people. The fleshly Jesus of Nazareth has come and gone, but the God who sent him and who was in the beginning remains.

RESURRECTION

Many scholars have seen the stories of Jesus' risen presence in John's Gospel divided into two parts, calling those in John 21 an "epilogue." However, all available ancient manuscripts contain the final chapter. There appears to be no good reason to tear apart the text without evidence. As it is, John 20-21 forms a seamless garment of stories, each of which serves to solidify and clarify the trust upon which the discipleship community is formed.

A consistent element of all the Gospel accounts of the first Easter is that Mary Magdalene was the first witness to the empty tomb. Like the Samaritan woman, she is often wrongfully assumed to be tainted by sexual sin, but there is not the slightest support for such a conclusion. Similarly, common lectionary divisions of John 20 place her witness outside what they see to be the central scene, the discovery of the empty tomb by Peter and the Beloved Disciple. However, when seen both chiastically and in the context of the narrative plot, the emphasis is the other way around: it is the two men who serve as "legal" witnesses to Mary's experience. She is the one who encounters the risen Jesus first and is the one "sent" by him to share the good news. Like the Samaritan woman, Mary is an "apostle." It is key to the Gospel's sense of church and ministry that "apostle" throughout is used as a verb (*apostellō*) rather than as a noun. This act of "being sent" rather than the institutional office of "apostle" is key.

This tension, between the Spirit-driven command to be sent and the emerging structure of ecclesial ministry, is a core question in the resurrection stories. Late on that long Easter day, the disciples are found "behind locked doors for fear of the Judeans" (20:19). Yet in the midst of their fears and doubts, they find Jesus "in their midst." He is not a ghost, but an empowering presence, breathing the Spirit on them and sending them just as the Father has sent him (20:21). The commission is not to specific, named persons, nor to "the Twelve," but to "the disciples," that is, to the gathered community as a whole.

This kind of empowerment was very different, however, from the attempt to limit ministry to "authorized" individuals who partake in officially granted ministries. By the end of the first century, this tension was beginning to stretch the early Christian communities. Some, like the Montanists, broke off from the network of churches to attempt to live "pure" Spirit-driven lives. Others, faced with public confusion about what it meant to be baptized and to live the Gospel, leaned toward development of creeds and power positions that could define and control such questions. John's Gospel offered a third way: to discern the Spirit's call without losing connection with communities coalescing around the "Petrine" and "Pauline" traditions.

Thus, after the comic race to the tomb between Peter and the Beloved Disciple, we find them in tension again in the Gospel's final scene. Jesus solemnly asks Peter, "Do you love (*agapē*) me?" (21:15). Peter's answer is yes, but in terms of *philia*—love among friends—rather than *agapē*. In the end, Jesus changes his own terms to meet Peter where he is (using *philia* in the third query), but links Peter's role as leader to his eventual laying down of his life, willing or not (21:18). After this, for the first time in the narrative, Jesus says to Peter, "follow me" (21:19).

Meanwhile, the Beloved Disciple waits in the wings, and a seemingly resentful Peter turns and asks Jesus, "What about him?" Jesus' final teaching is for Peter simply to be trusting in the call *he* has received and not to be concerned with another's call. John's Gospel calls for love that is *willing* to lay down its life, but does not make "martyrdom" a measure of fidelity. It trusts, as does Paul, that the one Spirit animates all its gifts within the discipleship community, with all working toward the common good.

LIVING JOHN'S GOSPEL TODAY

The Fourth Gospel is enormously concerned with generating loving relationships that incarnate God's love for humanity. Perhaps even more than in Jesus' day, we in Western societies are confronted with a milieu that rewards seeing others as competitors rather than as co-conspirators. Furthermore, despite our enormous hunger for intimacy, we flee from it more often than embracing it when it is offered. Having been wounded in love, we are reticent to risk trusting in the love of others, and thus, in the love of God.

I have found this challenge to be an acute one. As a Roman Catholic working ecumenically, I know that the proclaiming of a call to be a church which seeks the Spirit's guidance above all can lead to painful confrontation. There are many who, like the Judeans, are more invested in defending the status quo than in listening for the whispering sound of the Spirit in our midst. But the truth of the Gospel continues to sound joyous music in my heart, as I look out at a world continually torn by ethnic, racial, and national divisions. In our small house community of discipleship, my wife, Maggie, and I have found a place in which deep drafts of the Spirit can be breathed in, empowering us to take that energy into the darkness where it is not always welcome. And when I am centered enough to put aside my ego and allow the One who sends me to speak, I feel the great joy and honor of allowing life to be breathed back into the sometimes dry bones of Scripture, like living water poured out into the dry and dusty desert of our culture and sometimes of our church.

POSTSCRIPT: THE JOHANNINE LETTERS

Scholars have long debated the perhaps unanswerable question of the specific relationship between the author and audience of the Fourth Gospel and that of the letters known as 1, 2, and 3 John. While the first letter is narrated in the first person plural by an unnamed voice, the second is between "the elder" and "the elect lady" (*eklektē kyria*, the latter word only in this letter in the New Testament) while the third is between "the elder" and "the beloved Gaius," an otherwise unknown figure.

Their inclusion in the literary corpus known as "Johannine literature" stems from the familiar language of love that runs throughout all three. First John is also the source of a famous epithet hurled at some former community members who have left: "Antichrist" (1 John 2:18, 22; 4:3; 2 John 1:7). Far from the supernatural embodiment of evil imagined by some popular prophecy writers over the years, the term refers simply to those whose teaching and practice is contrary to the authentic gospel and threatens to lead disciples astray (cf. Mark 13:22). This tension between the joy and peace of discipleship lived within loving community and the dangerous possibility of the infiltration of evil is at the heart of 1 John.

This tension underscores the challenge of a church life grounded not in formal structure of ministerial office but in what the letter calls "discernment of spirits" (*dokimazete ta pneumata*, 1 John 4:1ff.). The specific struggle within the writer's community took on theological and practical form. The theological question centered on whether Jesus was truly incarnate or was simply masquerading as a human, a heresy known later as *docetism* and refuted vigorously by such writers as Tertullian and Augustine: "By this you know the Spirit of God: every spirit that confesses that Jesus Christ has come in the flesh is from God" (1 John 4:2).

The practical question focused on the love of sisters and brothers:

> The children of God and the children of the devil are revealed in this way: all who do not do what is right are not from God, nor are those who do not love their brothers and sisters. (1 John 3:10)

> Those who say, "I love God," and hate their brothers or sisters, are liars; for those who do not love a brother or sister whom they have seen, cannot love God whom they have not seen. The commandment we have from him is this: those who love God must love their brothers and sisters also. (1 John 4:20-21)

Thus, as in the Fourth Gospel, this letter tightly links the validity of one's verbal confession of faith to the life of discipleship one lives in community with others. It appears that this led to a bitter split within the community, causing the author to revile those who "went out from us" as Antichrists (1 John 2:19). Within this painful situation, the author, like the Jesus of the Gospel, calls his community to the challenging but joyous path of life lived not according to "the world" but according to God's will alone (e.g., 1 John 2:15-17; *kosmos* is used 23 times in this letter). This means showing the very kind of love for sisters and brothers that Jesus showed for them: "We know love by this, that he laid down his life for us—and we ought to lay down our lives for one another" (1 John 3:16). This love is not a mere theological platitude but a very practical condition of discipleship:

> How does God's love abide in anyone who has the world's goods and sees a brother or sister in need and yet refuses help? Little children, let us love, not in word or speech, but in truth and action. (1 John 3:17-18)

The brief second letter from "the elder" continues in this tradition: "And this is love, that we walk according to his commandments; this is the commandment just as you have heard it from the beginning—you must walk in it" (2 John 1:6). The metaphor of "walking" is taken up again in the third letter: "I have no greater joy than this, to hear that my children are walking in the truth." So, regardless of whether these letters are authored by the same or different persons from each other or from the Fourth Gospel, they clearly share a core message. To be a disciple of Jesus is to continue to walk only in the truth of *agapē*-love that is shown by one's love for sisters and brothers in Christ, not for its own sake, but as a witness to the evil-enshrouded world of the ongoing presence of the love of God, beckoning followers to travel together on the Way.

RESOURCES FOR FURTHER STUDY

Brown, Raymond E. *Community of the Beloved Disciple*. New York: Paulist, 1979.

Crosby, Michael H. *Do You Love Me? Jesus Questions the Church*. Maryknoll, N.Y.: Orbis, 2000.

Howard-Brook, Wes. *Becoming Children of God: John's Gospel and Radical Discipleship*. Maryknoll, N.Y.: Orbis, 1994.

———. *John's Gospel and the Renewal of the Church*. Maryknoll, N.Y.: Orbis, 1997.

Koester, Craig R. *Symbolism in the Fourth Gospel: Meaning, Mystery, Community*. Philadelphia: Fortress, 1995.

Ringe, Sharon H. *Wisdom's Friends: Community and Christology in the Fourth Gospel*. Louisville: Westminster John Knox, 1999.

Schneiders, Sandra. *Written That You May Believe: Encountering Jesus in the Fourth Gospel*. New York: Crossroad, 1999.

Segovia, Fernando, ed. *"What Is John?" Readers and Readings of the Fourth Gospel*. Atlanta: Scholars Press, 1996.

Staley, Jeffrey L. *Reading with a Passion: Rhetoric, Autobiography and the American West in the Gospel of John*. New York: Continuum, 1995.

Stibbe, Mark W. G. *John as Storyteller: Narrative Criticism and the Fourth Gospel*. Cambridge: Cambridge University Press, 1992.

6

Acts of the Apostles

Also Known as Acts of the Holy Spirit

Justo L. González

Acts and the Gospel of Luke

Luke is the only Gospel that does not end with the resurrection but goes on to the ascension (Luke 24:50-53). That in itself gives us a hint of Luke's interest in the events linking the Gospel narrative with the existing community of his time.[1] That hint is confirmed in that the Gospel of Luke is the only one with a sequel: Acts. Unfortunately, since the present ordering of the books in the New Testament places the Fourth Gospel between Luke and Acts, that connection is sometimes obscured. However, even a quick reading of the first verses of the two books (Luke 1:1-4; Acts 1:1-5) should suffice to show that connection—a connection further ascertained by similarities in style, vocabulary, and so on.

Acts, however, raises another interesting issue connected with authorship. Toward the end of the book, part of the narrative is in the *first* person plural: "we." (Apart from a doubtful reading in 11:28, the passages in question, often called the "we passages," are 16:10-17; 20:5-15; 21:1-18; 27:1-28:16.) Some scholars suggest that here Luke

---

[1] The question of the identity of the author of these two books has already been discussed in the introduction to the Gospel. For the sake of convenience, I call him (or perhaps her) Luke.

was employing someone else's travel account, written in the first person plural. Others suggest that Luke does this for special effect. It seems best, until a better explanation appears, simply to take the text as it stands, as meaning that "Luke"—whoever that may have been—was actually present on those occasions.

READING ACTS TODAY:
LUKE'S AGENDA AND OURS

How should we read this book? Clearly, the title is a misnomer. Like other such titles, this one was not the work of the author but was added later, as a quick way to identify a particular book. In this case, someone in the second century apparently decided that, since the first of Luke's books was about Jesus, the next should be about the apostles, and so dubbed the book "Acts of the Apostles."

That the book is not really about the apostles should be clear to any careful reader. Although there is a list of the eleven—the twelve minus Judas—in 1:13, hardly anything more is said about them. Matthias, who is chosen to take Judas's place, disappears as soon as he is elected. James is not mentioned again until 12:2, where we are told that Herod had him killed. (The "James" in 12:17; 15:13; and 21:18 is not the apostle but the "brother of Jesus.") John appears as Peter's companion in chapters 3, 4, and 8, but nothing more is said of him. Peter plays a central role in chapters 1-6, and then again in 7-12. After that he disappears and makes only one more appearance, in chapter 15. Some would say that the reason for this is that in the latter part of the book Paul becomes the central apostle. But the book does not even tell us what became of Paul!

As a historian, I know that history is never the mere chronicling of past events. History may be about the past, but it is written in the present, by historians who cannot help but read the past from the perspective of their present situation and concerns. In the brief span of my own life and career, my own reading (and writing) of the history of the church has changed considerably, as new issues have come to the fore. Two examples should suffice. First, when I first studied church history, there were three towering personalities called the "three great Cappadocians"—Basil of Caesarea, his brother Gregory of Nyssa, and their friend Gregory of Nazianzus. Today, for reasons obvious to any who know of events in the second half of the twentieth century, I speak of the "four great Cappadocians"—making place for Macrina, the often forgotten sister and teacher of Basil and Gregory. Second, when I first read the writings of Basil of Caesarea, I read him as the great theologian of the Holy Spirit and therefore found in his writings much about the Third Person of the Trinity. Today, again for reasons having to do with events in my own lifetime, I read Basil as the great advocate of the poor and of social justice. The writing of history involves a process of selection and interpretation.

In this sense, Luke is a historian, and Acts is indeed a history of the early church. It is not a chronicle. It is a selection and interpretation of events from a certain perspective and with certain agendas.

The matter is further complicated because we also have our perspectives and our agendas, which both help and hinder us in the process of trying to discover Luke's agendas. It is for this reason that I must explain that I read this book as someone who has had the experience of being both a religious and an ethnic minority. I grew up as a Protestant in a predominantly Catholic country, long before the Second Vatican Council. Then I came to live in this country, where I again became a minority, although now for ethnic and cultural reasons rather than for religious ones. In each of those circumstances, I have belonged to a community which, while still being part of the greater whole, is the object of marginalization and discrimination. This leads to an ambiguous situation in which, while being profoundly loyal to the whole, one also feels the need to question it and even to subvert it. As a Protestant in my native Cuba, in pre-Castro and pre-Vatican II times, I was part of a minority community which, while supporting much of the wider culture and tradition of the larger community, still found it necessary to question it. Today in the United States, as a Latino in a predominantly white denomination, I again find myself at once supporting and seeking to subvert the church to which I belong. In both cases, I could define my own perspective and agenda as one of "moderate subversion"—or, as some of my more radical critics would say, of "ambivalent subversion."

For these reasons—and because I believe that the text itself supports such a reading—I tend to read Acts as at once supportive and subversive of both the church and the wider society. This in turn means that it is possible to read Acts as a fairly conservative book, supporting the existing order, and also to read it as a rather subversive piece of literature. Most of the traditional readings of Acts underscore its more conservative elements.

This was the case already in the second century, when some unknown person decided to call this the "Acts *of the Apostles*." When faced by such a title, one tends to approach the book expecting it to be about how the early church was structured, and about how the church must now continue to be structured. The result of this sort of reading is that for many Christians Acts has become a sort of early canon law, book of discipline, or form of government—depending on whether one is Roman Catholic, United Methodist, or Presbyterian.

Reading the book from my perspective and circumstances outlined above, I venture to suggest that Acts is written with the double agenda of supporting the church in its moderate subversion of the society around it, and of moderately subverting the church itself.

There are many indications in the history of the early centuries of Christianity that the Roman authorities, and society in general, saw the new faith as somewhat subversive. It was not only a matter of insisting that Jesus is Lord—*Kyrios*, a title the rulers claimed for themselves. It was also a matter of opposing many of the common practices of society, of rejecting violence, of criticizing the generally accepted mores of the time, of meeting for worship in apparently secretive ways, of violating the laws against the formation of private clubs, and even of promoting riots. Acts was written at a time when the first conflicts with the state had already taken place, but had not yet risen to the fever-pitch level that we find, for instance, in the book of Revelation. At least, Luke clearly does not belong to the radical school of John of Patmos, who saw Rome as the great whore drunk with the blood of the martyrs.

In this regard, Luke's "moderately subversive" agenda is to present and promote a form of Christianity that stands firm in its conflicts with the surrounding society, but does not seek such conflicts, and even sees much good in that society.

This, however, is grounded on an agenda within the church. In Luke's time, there was the beginning of a movement within the church to make it more "respectable." This involved, among other things, putting women "back in their place" by limiting their leadership in the church.

There are many indications that toward the end of the first century, and certainly during the second, there was a strong current in the church to curtail the leadership of women. Luke is writing Acts precisely at the time when this movement is beginning. He is aware that there are deep roots for such sentiments in the various cultures of the Mediterranean as well as in his own religious tradition. Yet both of his books seem to be challenging the increasingly antiwoman sentiments of the time. That is clearly the case in his Gospel, where stories about women often parallel stories about men, and where we are told that it was the women who paid the bills for Jesus and his followers. The same is true, although perhaps in more subtle ways, in Acts.

The quote from Joel that Peter uses to interpret what is taking place at Pentecost sets the stage for the important role of women in Acts: sons and daughters shall prophesy, and slaves, women as well as men, shall receive the Spirit (2:17-18). Throughout the book, then, women play an important role—often one of leadership—even though, in order to note this, one has to be aware that this was beginning to be an issue in the church of Luke's time.

Then, the emerging mood in the church also involved establishing patterns of church government that would guarantee orderly procedures. Both of these trends would become dominant in the second century. Luke, however, witnessed their early manifestations, and before them his agenda is, once again, one of moderate subversion. He writes a treatise in which he shows the action of the Spirit bringing women to positions of leadership in the church, and the action of the same Spirit at once affirming and correcting the decisions and actions of the apostles and other leaders.

Luke attempted his "moderate subversion" by writing a sequel to his Gospel—which was also moderately subversive—focusing on the actions of the Spirit. His first book had dealt with the acts of Jesus. Now this second book would deal with the acts of the Spirit—indeed, a much more appropriate title for it would have been "Acts of the Spirit"!

How Subversion Has Been Subverted

Unfortunately, from a very early date ways were found to read and interpret Acts in ways that hid its subversive agenda. A striking example of an attempt to subvert the message of Acts is found in its "Western" text. As we compare ancient manuscripts of Acts, it is evident that they belong to two large families, one reflecting what is usually called the Egyptian or Common text, and another the Western text. Scholars generally agree that the Egyptian text is closer to the original and that the Western text is a very early revision. Many of the differences between the two texts are minor. Others appear to be attempts to spell out something that was not altogether clear in the original. But amidst hundreds of apparently innocuous variants, there are several that show a markedly antifeminine bias. The earlier text, and the entire New Testament, consistently refers to the couple that befriended Paul as "Priscilla and Aquila" or "Prisca and Aquila" (except in Acts 18:18, where the grammar requires that Aquila be named first). In contrast, the Western text of Acts equally consistently calls them "Aquila and Priscilla." In 17:21, where Luke says that "not a few women of high standing" believed, the Western text changes the order of the words, so that the adjective applies not to the women but to the men. (In this regard, the NRSV falls into the same trap: "not a few Greek women and men of high standing." The Jerusalem Bible does a better job: "many Greek women from the upper classes and a number of men.") Finally, in 17:34 the Western text simply omits any mention of Damaris.

From that point on, as the church has become more settled within society, as interpreters have become more comfortable, and as Christianity has become more acceptable, even the moderate subversion of Acts has been radically subverted—to the point that some can even read it as an attempt to show Roman authorities that Christianity was not subversive at all!

SUBVERSIVE HUMOR

One of the subtle ways in which Acts subverts a church order that is tempted to take itself too seriously is by means of humor. Although Acts is a serious book with a serious agenda, this does not preclude the use of humor to further that agenda. Unfortunately, most of us have been taught that humor has little place in religious matters—certainly not in the Bible!—and therefore when we come to some of the passages or phrases that may be intended as a touch of humor, we miss the point—even though the same words or similar events in any other context would be understood as somewhat humorous. To some of these I shall refer as we study specific passages. However, there are many more.

In Acts 2, when Peter rises to explain what is happening, he says: "These are not drunk, as you suppose, for it is only nine o'clock in the morning." The clear implication is: Come back this afternoon, and they'll really be drunk!

In Acts 10:28, Peter says to Cornelius and his friends: "You yourselves know that it is unlawful for a Jew to associate with or to visit a Gentile; but God has shown me that I should not call anyone profane or unclean." In other words, if it were up to me, that is precisely what I would call you!

In Acts 12, Peter is in prison, presumably awaiting execution, while the church prays for his release. An angel pokes (the NRSV makes this milder by saying "tapped") Peter, who more or less wakes up, but still needs detailed instructions as to how to dress, and then follows the angel in a sort of daze. When he finally arrives at the house where the church is praying, the maid (whose name, "Rhode," is something like "Rosey") thinks she sees a ghost. She runs to those who are praying, and they think she is crazy. Meanwhile, Peter is left outside, where he keeps knocking at the door . . . .

In Acts 19:15, when people who are not Christians try to expel a demon by means of the formula "I adjure you by the Jesus whom Paul proclaims," the demon sarcastically replies: "Jesus I know, and Paul I know; but who [the devil] are you?"

The episode in Lystra (14:8-20) reminds me of many a joke about misunderstandings when Latinos immigrate to the United States. Paul and Barnabas speak Greek. The locals speak Lycaonian, but they worship gods that have been brought to them by Greek and Roman expansion. The result is that while Paul and Barnabas believe they have had great success, the local residents, who speak a different language, decide that these visitors are Zeus and Hermes and get ready to offer sacrifices to them. In the end, the preachers have to hightail it out of town.

In Troas (20:7-12), Paul preaches such a long sermon that a young man goes to sleep, falls out of a window, and is killed. Paul says he is not really dead and the service continues as if nothing had happened.

In Malta (28:1-10), in the episode of the snake bite, it is clear that the Maltese simply can't get it. First they think Paul must be a terrible sinner. Then they decide he must be a god.

Many other such cases could be cited—and indeed we shall see others later on. The point is that one of the ways in which Luke subverts both a society and a church that tend to take themselves too seriously is by means of humor, and that therefore we would gain by being ready to perceive such humor as we read his book.

INSIDERS AND OUTSIDERS: THE ELECTION OF MATTHIAS

There was a struggle taking place when Luke wrote his book: The first disciples of Jesus were passing away, and a new generation was coming to the forefront, perhaps not always with the blessing of the older leadership. In addition, the Christian community, originally almost exclusively Jewish, was attracting ever growing numbers of

Gentiles. Thus, the normal generational conflicts that the passing of time always brings were being compounded by cultural conflicts. We see this throughout the letters of Paul, and Acts will deal with it again in chapter 15. In the later books of the New Testament, the Pastoral Epistles deal with it. The same subject appears in early Christian literature of approximately the same time.

This struggle may well be the background against which to understand the election of Matthias. After the verses where Luke introduces the book and reminds the reader of the end of his Gospel, Acts begins with the strange episode of the election of Matthias. (Actually, it is in the *mise en scène* of that election that the eleven are listed, thus leading to the obvious but misleading title "Acts of the Apostles.")

Although Luke offers no comment, the very act of this election is rather questionable. Jesus had commanded the disciples to go to Jerusalem and wait there for "the promise of the Father"—that is, the power of the Holy Spirit (1:4). But Peter is not content to wait and decides to take matters into his own hands. He stands and gives a speech in which he describes the death of Judas with words that include a certain morbid humor (he burst open in the middle and spilled his guts [1:18]), and then he sets a standard of eligibility for this position. Significantly, Jesus had said nothing about such standards. Given some of my experiences with church organizations, I am not surprised at those who are "in" setting new requirements for others to join them. Apparently this is what Peter is doing, and he is doing it, as we still do today, covering his claim with theological sanctions. Indeed, twice he speaks of a "necessity": it was necessary that Judas betray Jesus, and it is equally necessary now that someone be named in his place. Furthermore, Peter's argument is essentially that of the structural conservative: we were twelve; therefore, we must continue being twelve. (Here Peter reminds us of those members, present in every church, whose motto seems to be: "But we've never done it that way before!")

With a very eloquent silence that has repeatedly been noted by commentators, Luke simply ignores Matthias in the rest of his narrative. Rather, he turns immediately to the outpouring of the Spirit at Pentecost. If, as I believe, the book is not so much about the acts of the apostles as about the acts of the Spirit, it would appear that the election of Matthias, rather than an example to be followed or a pattern for the election of further successors to the apostles, is a word of caution, that the leadership of the church can easily err if it does not wait for the guidance of the Holy Spirit. The joke is on Peter and the rest of the disciples, who attempted to shortcut the workings of the Spirit!

INSIDERS AND OUTSIDERS:
THE OUTPOURING OF THE SPIRIT

The central narrative of the book actually begins in chapter 2, with the fulfillment of the promise Jesus had made to his disciples. This is the event of Pentecost.

We usually think of Pentecost as the act whereby the Spirit empowers the apostles for their special ministry and for leadership in the church. Look, however, at the text itself, and this interpretation becomes questionable.

First of all, Luke does not say, as we often surmise, that only the apostles received the gift of the Spirit. On the contrary, he says that they were "all" together—probably meaning at least the hundred and twenty mentioned earlier (1:15), and certainly the women, for otherwise Peter's application of the passage from Joel would make no sense (2:17-18). The empowerment by the Spirit is not the exclusive gift of the Twelve.

Then Luke makes it very clear that the miracle of Pentecost did not consist in all sorts of different people being able to understand the language of the Twelve. Rather, they are made to hear "each of us in our own native language" (2:8). The significance of this is enormous. If the message is to be spoken and heard only in the language of the apostles, they and others like them will always be in control. Others must become like them. That, however, is not the case. Those present at Pentecost hear in their own native tongues. Parthians, Medes, Elamites, and all the rest, come into this community with no disadvantage because they are foreigners or because they belong to a culture different from that of the apostles. The Twelve have no advantage even though their culture is the original one in which the gospel first appeared. Significantly, the rest of the book tells the story of how the leadership passes from the original Aramaic-speaking group to others.

Similar issues of language and culture, usually overlooked by interpreters who are not sufficiently sensitive to such matters, appear repeatedly in Acts. In Lystra, the missionaries do not take into account the culture of the place, and their attempt to communicate only in the language of empire results in dismal and even ludicrous failure (14:8-18). Later in Jerusalem, a Roman tribune does not respect Paul until he hears him speaking in cultured Greek and realizes he is a Roman citizen (22:23-29)—an episode that resonates with the experience of many an immigrant in the United States.

SUBVERSIVE SHARING

Twice in the early chapters of Acts we are told that believers shared their resources (2:44-45; 4:32-35). Even though to many today this might seem subversive enough because of its communistic flavor, the subversive nature of such a statement was even deeper in ancient society, where the patronage system meant that the fabric of society was woven around relationships of dependence between patron and client. While this normally protected the client from extreme want, it also solidified and guaranteed the patron's control over the client. Thus, in providing an alternative means to respond to need the early church was profoundly subverting the established economic and social order.

This subversion too has been subverted by interpreters. Thus we are told that the commonality of goods was only an ephemeral experiment, which soon was abandoned, when in fact there are Christian texts that show that the practice continued at least until the end of the second century. Likewise, we are told that such an ephemeral experiment was the reason why the church in Jerusalem became poor, believers having spent all their resources and then having to depend on collections from other churches, when in fact there is ample evidence that this was a time of poor crops and even famine in the region. Third, the text has been subverted by interpreting it as if the early believers had simply sold all their goods, and then lived off the common coffer, when in fact the verbs—all in the imperfect tense—indicate that this was a continuing action, in the sense that the "would sell," or "used to sell" their properties as this was made necessary by the needs of the community.

A MESSAGE FOR THE PEOPLE

As one reads the first chapters of Acts—until 6:12—it appears that the followers of Jesus and their followers are quite popular. Indeed, in those early chapters there is a clear contrast between the "people," who favor the disciples, and the religious elite, who oppose them and their preaching. Almost immediately after Pentecost (2:47), we are told that the disciples were "having the goodwill of all the people." When the lame man was healed at the gate of the temple, "all the people saw him walking and praising God . . . and they were filled with wonder and amazement . . ." (3:9-10). Then Peter addressed "the people" (3:12). When Peter and John are "speaking to the people" (4:1), the opponents come in. They are "the priests, the captain of the temple, and the Sad-ducees." These are "much annoyed because they were teaching the peo-ple" (4:1-2). The next day there is an assembly of the "rulers, elders, and scribes," with "Annas the high priest, Caiaphas, John, and Alexan-der, and all who were of the high priestly family" (4:5-6). Peter addresses them correctly as "rulers of the people" (4:8).

The concern of these important people is "to keep it from spreading further among the people" (4:17)—which reminds us of the many ways in which even today those in power seek to control information, or at least to give it their own "spin."

If the "rulers" do not punish Peter and John, it is "because of the people, for they all praised God for what had happened" (4:21).

In chapter 5, much the same thing happens. Many "signs and won-ders were done among the people through the apostles," and although others would not join them, "the people held them in high esteem" (5:12-13). "Then the high priest took action; he and all who were with him (that is, the sect of the Sadducees), being filled with jealousy, arrested the apostles" (5:17-18). When they are miraculously freed, the "apostles" (Peter and John) go back to the temple to "tell the people" (5:20). Again, the powerful intervene, and it is now the captain of the temple and the temple police that arrest the apostles and bring them before the rulers, "but without violence, for they were afraid of being stoned by the people" (5:26).

What we have here is the reaction of the powerful, who resent the teaching of the apostles, and in particular the implication that the man whom they had turned over to Roman authority to be crucified had been sent by God, and that they, the powerful, were responsible for his death (5:28).

On their part, the disciples are quite ready to resist any order silenc-ing them. Indeed, in 4:13 Luke tells us that what struck the rulers was that Peter and John spoke "with boldness," and then, after they have been ordered not to speak, he uses the same word in the prayer of the church after they receive the apostles' report: "Grant to your servants to speak your word with all boldness" (4:29). This request is granted, and they "spoke the word of God with boldness" (4:31).

Thus, from his early chapters, Luke depicts a church that, while not seeking the enmity of those in power, is certainly not willing to obey them if this means disobeying God—in other words, a moderately sub-versive church. This moderately subversive church has a message that is primarily for the people, and which the powerful seek to suppress both because it puts them in a bad light ("you are determined to bring this man's blood upon us") and because they resent their loss of leadership ("being filled with jealousy").

JUSTICE BEYOND WHAT WAS INTENDED

In Acts 6 the early church has to face a matter of justice. There are in the community two groups, both Jewish, but one rooted in Palestine and its traditions (the "Hebrews"), and another more adapted to the life and culture of the Hellenistic world (the "Hellenists"). The community is providing support for its widows, as is the custom in synagogues throughout the world. In this case, however, the widows of the Hellenists do not seem to be getting their fair share. This is a common enough situation, where those who do not speak the language or follow the customs of the dominant groups are excluded or marginalized. The Twelve decide to remedy the situation by asking that seven men be elected to manage the distribution. This will allow them—the Twelve— to devote themselves to preaching. The election takes place, and the seven who are given this responsibility appear to have been all Hellenists—at least, all have Greek names.

The response of the Twelve and of the congregation to what appears to be an unjust situation is commendable. The Twelve are giving up control of the distribution. The entire congregation seems willing to give positions of leadership to the "Hellenists," even though this could hurt their own prestige and acceptance in the society at large. Indeed, it is now, when the Hellenists take positions of leadership, that for the first time "the people" turn against the disciples and take the side of "the elders and the scribes" (6:12).

It is on the basis of this action of the apostles, and of the division of labor that they suggest, that many churches have defined the respective roles of elders and deacons. In the text, the Twelve decide that the newly elected seven will have the *diakonia*—that is, the service—of the tables, and for that reason it has traditionally been thought that these seven were the first deacons. (Although the Twelve also say that they will reserve for themselves the *diakonia* of the word.)

However, even this forward-looking action is not enough for the Spirit. In a turn of events that has a marked touch of humor, the very next thing that happens in Acts is that Stephen, one of the seven, starts preaching. Actually, Stephen, who is supposed to be managing the distribution and leaving the preaching to the Twelve, preaches the longest sermon in the entire book! Then, after he is martyred, Luke turns to another of the seven, Philip, and to his preaching and teaching (chap. 8). Thus, in a moderately subversive manner, the Spirit both affirms and supersedes what the leadership had determined.

The difference between this reading and the one that makes Acts a sort of Book of Discipline is crucial. If Acts is a guidebook whose procedures have to be imitated and whose prescriptions have to be followed, then the injunction of the Twelve, that seven *men* be elected, would exclude women from positions of leadership in the church. If, on the other hand, we read this passage as affirming the quest for justice on the part of the Twelve and the early church and moving beyond the limits set by them, then it is possible to argue, for instance, that the same Spirit who moved beyond the limited expectations of the apostles is the Spirit who is calling the church beyond the notion that those named to such offices must be men.

A God Who Speaks at the Margins

The episode of Peter and Cornelius (chap. 10), and its sequel when Peter returns to Jerusalem (11:1-18), is illustrative of the manner in which Acts subverts our religious and ecclesiastical expectations.

This is the story of two visions and an encounter: the vision of Cornelius at Caesarea, the vision of Peter at Joppa, and the meeting between Peter and Cornelius. In the matter of visions, we would expect Peter to take the lead. After all, he had taken the lead in confessing Jesus as the Christ, then at Pentecost; later in healing the lame man at the gate of the temple, he took the lead in speaking before the council, and he took the lead in spreading the word of Jesus throughout Judea.

But that is not what happens. The vision comes to Cornelius almost twenty-four hours before it comes to Peter. Before Peter even has his vision, the messengers from Cornelius are already well on their way to the house where Peter is staying.

Furthermore, the text says that Cornelius's vision was clear: "He saw *clearly* in a vision an angel of God coming in" (10:3). The angel told him exactly what he was to do, including the precise address where Peter could be found: "Send men to Joppa, and bring one Simon who is called Peter; he is lodging with Simon, a tanner, whose house is by the seaside" (10:5-6). (Just about the only thing lacking was the zip code!)

In contrast, Peter's vision is not clear. He sees "*something* descending, like a great sheet" (10:11). There is a dialogue in which Peter stubbornly resists the voice that comes to him. According to the text, the voice speaks three times, and still Peter will not budge. Then, when "the thing" (that is what the text calls it) is finally taken up to heaven, "Peter was greatly puzzled about what to make of the vision that he had seen" (10:10-17).

This entire story is usually called the conversion of Cornelius. But read carefully, it is the conversion of Peter just as much as of Cornelius.

Then, in chapter 11, Peter has to report to the church in Jerusalem. They are not too thrilled about what he has been doing, visiting the uncircumcised and eating with them. But eventually, after Peter tells them of his vision and of events in Caesarea, they too are converted—converted from a narrow understanding of the gospel to one that recognizes that this message is for all people, including the supposedly unclean Gentiles.

As I read this passage, it seems clear to me that at least part of what Luke is telling us is that the Holy Spirit uses those outside the church to call both the church and its leaders to a fuller understanding of the gospel—a subversive notion indeed!

THE SUBVERSION OF PAUL

The story of Paul's conversion is well known. Paul was from Tarsus, the capital of Cilicia, and therefore his synagogue—and perhaps Paul himself—was among those who arranged for the trial and condemnation of Stephen (6:9). He then became a persecutor of the Christian community. Thus, in some ways, his conversion was a signal success of subversion.

Yet this does not mean that Paul himself is exempt from subversion by the Spirit. Again, because we have been taught not to look for humor in Scripture, we often miss the subtle ironies with which Luke depicts such subversion.

A case in point is the famous vision of the "man of Macedonia," which leads Paul to cross over to Macedonia, and therefore to Europe. From our much too triumphalistic perspective, we see in this one more step in the process by which the gospel spreads to new areas, eventually to conquer them all. For Paul, as for Luke, there was not such a clear distinction as there is for us between Europe and Asia, and therefore all this could have meant, as far as the expansion of Christianity, was its spread into a new province.

But there is more to the story. Luke makes it very clear that the person in the vision is a male. Although in many other places our English versions insert words such as "man" or "he" where the subject is not clear, that is not the case here, where Luke uses the word *anēr* (16:9), which means male.

It is on the basis of the call of this man—"Come over to Macedonia and help us"—that Paul decides to go to Philippi, in Macedonia. As is his custom, he begins his mission there by attempting to visit a synagogue on the Sabbath. The expectation to find a synagogue there would seem to have been confirmed by the vision of the Macedonian man calling for help in the plural: "Help us." On that basis, Paul would have reason to think that he has been called to help the synagogue—whose leadership was all men, and whose very act of meeting required a number of men to be present. He and his companions go to where "we supposed there was a place of prayer" (16:13). The word used here, *proseuchē*, meant both a formal synagogue and simply a place where people gathered to pray. Thus, apparently the missionaries went thinking they would find a synagogue. The expected synagogue was "outside the gate by the river"—in itself a discouraging circumstance. When they reach the place, what they find instead of a synagogue is a group of women.

There is irony here. Could it be that the Spirit presented Paul with a vision of a Macedonian *man* because, had Paul known that all he would find at Philippi was a group of women meeting outside the city gates he would have decided not to go? And, as a further irony, this mission, which begins with a gathering of women outside the gates, becomes one of the most important and most supportive churches founded by Paul—a church whose main leader is the woman Lydia of Thyatira.

ECONOMIC SUBVERSION

The notion that the preaching of the gospel may have a negative economic impact on some circles, and that this in turn may cause a reaction against such preaching, is not, as many would have us think, a recent discovery. On the contrary, it appears repeatedly in Acts.

Most people who are acquainted with the story of Paul know something about the story in Acts, that he and Silas were jailed in Philippi, that they were freed by an earthquake, and that the jailer asked: "What must I do to be saved?" (16:25-30).

What few people know, because it is not preached as often, is the reason why Paul and Silas were jailed in the first place. They were not jailed simply for preaching, but because Paul had exorcised a "spirit of divination" from a slave girl. When she was possessed, this girl "brought her owners a great deal of money by fortune-telling" (16:16). The result is that the girl's owners, seeing their profit lost, seized Paul and Silas and accused them before the magistrates, not of curing the girl—which would hardly have been a crime—but of "advocating customs that it is not lawful for us Romans to adopt or observe" (16:21). Another interesting feature in this passage and its sequel is that these accusers call themselves "Romans." As is often the case to this day, economic interests present themselves as moral and patriotic concerns, and in so doing subvert the very laws and principles they claim to defend.

Another similar case occurs in Ephesus (19:21-41). Demetrius and apparently many others made their money by producing and selling small silver replicas of the great temple. (It is interesting to note that the Greek word employed here, which the NRSV translates as "business," *ergasia,* is the same word used to refer to the business of the men in Philippi who owned a slave girl with divining powers, and who made a business, an *ergasia,* out of her divination.) Demetrius is in the business of religious tourism. But now, because of the preaching of Paul and other Christians, his business is threatened. So, he calls a meeting of others who are equally threatened and gives them an interesting harangue.

He begins talking only about their business and the threat to it: "You know that we get our wealth from this business. You also see and hear that not only in Ephesus but in almost the whole of Asia this Paul has persuaded and drawn away a considerable number of people by saying that gods made with hands are not gods" (19:25-26). So far, the economic interest is clear. "Hey, fellows, this Paul is wrecking our business."

But then the plot thickens, for Demetrius subtly connects the economic interests of his hearers with religious issues: "And there is danger not only that this trade of ours may come into disrepute, but also that the temple of the great goddess Artemis will be scorned, and she will be deprived of her majesty that brought all of Asia and the world to worship her" (19:27). The mixture of themes is subtle and is left to the preferences of the hearers.

The cry, "Great is Artemis of the Ephesians!" is economic and patriotic as well as religious. Eventually, as the text depicts the situation with masterly strokes, "some were shouting one thing, some another; for the assembly was in confusion, and most of them did not know why they had come together" (19:32).

Finally the town clerk intervenes. The clerk, like Demetrius before him, but now in reverse order, moves from the patriotic and religious motivations of the Ephesians to their more material interests: "You ought to be quiet and do nothing rash. You have brought these men here who are neither temple robbers nor blasphemers of our goddess. If therefore Demetrius and the artisans with him have a complaint against anyone, the courts are open. . . . If there is anything further you want to know, it must be settled in the regular assembly. For we are in danger of being charged with rioting today, since there is no cause to justify this commotion" (19:36-40). The word that the clerk uses here to describe the commotion, *stasis,* would immediately provoke fear among any who lived in the Roman empire. This was the technical term employed for a riot, usually against the empire or its officers, and it was punishable by death. Furthermore, since such a crime was difficult to ascribe to particular individuals, it could also bring general and harsh punishment upon the entire city.

Thus, in brief, what the clerk is saying is, first, that they should not be worried about the good name of Artemis or of the city, for all know how great she is, and that her famous temple is in Ephesus. Second, they should worry rather about their own conduct, which could bring upon them the wrath of the empire. Thus, while Demetrius's speech moves from self-interest to religiosity and patriotism, the speech of the town clerk moves in the opposite direction, from religiosity and patriotism to self-interest.

This text, although referring to a goddess long forgotten, is strikingly modern. No one, as far as I can tell, worships Artemis anymore. Yet, today, just as in the time of Demetrius and the silversmiths, self-interest is often clothed in the garb of religion and patriotism.

An Imperfect Government

Those who seek to subvert Luke's subversion claim that he is trying to gain the sympathy of Roman authorities. If so, he does it in a strange way, for he does not hesitate to show the imperfections and corruption of Roman government. Although this appears in other places in Acts—for instance, in Philippi, where the magistrates beat Paul and Silas without much inquiry—it becomes clearer in the last chapters of the book, where Paul is arrested and has to appear before an entire series of people in authority.

His arrest itself is described as a mistake. There is a riot in the temple, because some mistakenly accuse Paul of having brought a Gentile into the holy enclosure. The Roman tribune Claudius Lysias intervenes and arrests Paul under the false impression that he is "the Egyptian who recently stirred up a revolt and led the four thousand assassins into the wilderness" (21:38). Paul clearly proves to him that this is not the case. What is more, he is a Roman citizen. Eventually, because he learns that there is a plot to kill Paul—and not because he really has a reason to keep him under arrest—Claudius Lysias decides to rid himself of the problem by passing it on to Governor Felix in Caesarea. In so doing, however, he misrepresents the course of events, in order to place himself in a better light: "This man was seized by the Jews and was about to be killed by them, but when I learned that he was a Roman citizen, I came with the guard and rescued him" (23:27).

Felix is no better. He conducts a trial, but withholds any decision. Luke tells us that when Paul began speaking of "justice, self-control and the coming judgment, Felix became frightened" (24:25). A contemporary reader would have understood the allusion to the well-known cruelty and debauchery of Felix. At any rate, the governor simply keeps Paul under arrest, because "he hoped that money would be given him by Paul" (24:26).

Two years later, when Felix is succeeded by Porcius Festus, Paul is still in prison. Here Luke uses the term *dietia*, which was the technical term for the two years that were the maximum time for preventive imprisonment. Thus, what Luke tells us is that Felix disobeyed the law in order to ingratiate himself with the Jewish leadership who opposed Paul.

Festus acts more promptly. Almost immediately he takes up the case of Paul. He too, however, is eager to ingratiate himself with the leaders who seek to destroy Paul, and therefore suggests transferring him back to Jerusalem. It is at this point that Paul appeals to Caesar.

It is difficult to see how this entire narrative could be intended as a way to gain the sympathy of Roman authorities, who are repeatedly depicted as self-seeking, corrupt, and pusillanimous.

NO FINAL WORD

We come now to the final puzzle—or, perhaps better, the final joke—of the book of Acts: the book does not end. It simply quits. Someone reading the book for the first time, without warning, would come to the end of chapter 28, where Paul is preaching in Rome while he awaits trial and turn the page confident that the story will continue. But it does not. The reader is left, so to speak, hanging in midair.

There are many explanations for this. A traditional one is that when Luke wrote his book, Paul was still in Rome awaiting trial by Caesar. This would require dating the book exceedingly early—at least some twenty years before its first possible date of composition. Another explanation is that "Theophilus"—the reader to whom the book is addressed—already knew the rest of the story and did not need to be told. A third explanation is that the book is intended to present Christianity in the best possible light before Roman authorities and that in this case it would not do to have Paul killed by order of the emperor. Still others suggest that Luke intended to write a third book.

All of these explanations are too cut-and-dried. They miss the openness—the "moderate subversion"—of the entire book. We want the book to be, if not the story of the apostles, at least the story of Paul. We want the story to end. We want to know what happened. But that is precisely what Luke does not want us to have. He does not want us to have a book that we can close and move to something else. He does not want us to say—as Christians have too often said—that the "apostolic age" was the time when the Spirit acted as Acts says, but that now we live in a different time. He wants his readers—and, in a sense, us—to be part of the story. If his book were the "Acts of the Apostles," we could not be part of the story. But since it is the "Acts of the Spirit," we are either part of the story or we cannot claim any of it. Luke does not finish his book, because his story is not finished. That is his final subversive word!

7

Paul's Letters

God's Justice against Empire

Neil Elliott

NORTH AMERICANS OFTEN READ Paul's letters with specific assumptions about the narrow band of inner experience that our society calls "religion." Because Paul's so-called conversion figures so prominently in the Acts of the Apostles (9:1-22; 22:6-16; 26:9-23), and because in Romans 7 Paul himself offers a meditation on being able to will the good but not to do it (7:14-24), we are tempted to think Paul was as preoccupied with the anguished "inner life" as our own Puritan and revivalist heritage has trained many of us to be. As a consequence, we may approach Paul's letters expecting a guide to inner peace, rather than a challenge to endure hardship, distress, persecution, famine, nakedness, peril, and the lethal power of the state ("the sword" [Rom. 8:35-39]). How much less do we turn to Paul seeking encouragement to defy the rulers and powers that set themselves against the justice of God (1 Cor. 2:8)! To the contrary, to the extent that we are aware of the apostle having a "political" stance, we are used to thinking of him as indifferent, at best, to social inequalities. At worst, we regard him as encouraging the oppressed to accept their condition as God-ordained.

The preoccupation with the inner life is *ours,* of course—not Paul's. So too is the acquired habit of regarding concern for social injustice as somehow separate from the religious life. Over the last quarter century, careful readings have offered a dramatically different understanding of the apostle's vision. We have begun to recognize the true political and cosmic horizon of Paul's hope, as well as the vital connection between that hope and the defiance of Roman imperial authority to which it led him, and to which he very deliberately called attention (Phlm. 1, 9, 13; Phil. 1:7, 12-14, 16; 4:14; 1 Thess. 2:2; 1 Cor. 4:9; 2 Cor. 1:8-9; 6:4; 11:23).

THE "GOSPEL" OF EMPIRE

There are deep and enduring similarities between our world and the world Paul called "the present evil age," awash in idolatry and injustice. Grinding poverty, the rule for most of his urban contemporaries, was aggravated by frequent famines—like the one in Judea, to which Paul was first "sent out" (the meaning of *apostle*) to organize relief (Acts 11:27-29)—and by a globalizing economy which its Roman architects themselves described as parasitic. Heavy taxation and steep loan policies had put most of the best land in Egypt and Palestine into the hands of absentee landlords and brokers, who diverted the produce to international markets, to their very great profit.

Most of the wealth in the Mediterranean world was created by peasant sharecroppers and urban slaves, who often received only enough in return to keep them alive and producing. Wars of conquest and containment and policies of economic exploitation displaced millions of refugees, who choked the slums of cities like Rome and drew the contempt of the elite. As powerful as iron chains, the constraints of the patronage system precluded most efforts by the poor to work together in their own interest, convincing them instead that their own needs could be met only by serving the needs of their superiors first. When crowds spontaneously gathered to protest taxes or other imperial impositions, they were often answered by massacre (as in Samaria in the 30s, Alexandria in the 40s, and in following years, Puteoli and Rome itself). On the rare occasion when a city dared to resist the empire's grip, it was destroyed, its population put to the sword or enslaved, then rebuilt as a Roman colony (the legendary fate of Corinth and, in Paul's lifetime, Sepphoris). Increasingly brutal spectacles offered up for entertainment in the arena gave a false sense that terrible death was reserved only for the empire's enemies, criminals, and subversives.

Meanwhile, poet-propagandists such as Virgil rhapsodized the nostalgic fantasy of the free Roman farmer. The wealthy and privileged elite in every province vied with one another for the most conspicuous places in imperial cult and civic ceremonial, daily rehearsing the official "good news" in the public square. (The Greek word *euangelion,* "gospel," was a fixed feature of imperial rhetoric before Paul turned the word to a startling new use.)

According to this imperial gospel, a golden age of prosperity, of "peace and security," had dawned (compare 1 Thess. 5:3!). Heaven's own justice had come to earth in the person of the sole ruler, who alone had caused warfare to cease and ushered in a new world order of harmony and international "friendship" (as proclaimed by the *Res Gestae* of Augustus). In the person of the emperor, perfect piety, the dutiful and humble worship pleasing to heaven, had been realized. So, at least, testified the monumental "Altar of Augustan Peace" in the Roman forum, and the mass-produced images and public ceremonies in every colony. Nor were the court poets slow to take up the theme. Augustus's triumph and the increasingly consolidated rule of his successors were no merely private or dynastic victories. To the contrary, the ascendant supremacy of the Roman people over all the nations of the earth was their divine birthright, their manifest destiny.

NEGOTIATING THE CURRENTS OF IMPERIALISM

Paul, on the other hand, was a Jew from the Diaspora, a member of a people regarded by Roman aristocrats such as Cicero or Tacitus as "born for servitude." Like other ethnic and religious minorities living under the pressures of Romanization, often excluded from citizenship in the cities they inhabited, Diaspora Jews were forced constantly to negotiate the delicate balance between accommodation to the customs and laws of their Gentile neighbors and maintenance of their own ancestral customs in family life and in the synagogue. In the midst of an overwhelming and often hostile environment, Jews were anxious about the civic privileges they had won through careful diplomacy. Jewish apologetic writers such as Philo of Alexandria and Flavius Josephus were eager to present the Jewish way of life as embodying the best Hellenistic and Roman ideals of justice, moderation, and self-control. (That those arguments rarely found a sympathetic hearing among the Roman elite is clear enough from the policies of Gaius, Claudius, and Nero—the emperors during Paul's apostolic work—and from a tradition of harsh anti-Jewish prejudice stretching from Cicero to Suetonius.)

While his letters show his fluency in Hellenistic Greek and his considerable rhetorical skill (even the protest of being a poor speaker [1 Cor. 2:1-5], is a common rhetorical technique), Paul's own sense of pride as a Jew and of "zeal for the traditions of the ancestors" is clear (Gal. 1:14; Phil. 3:4-6). So is his enduring concern for the welfare of his people and his unwavering conviction that God will ultimately save them (Rom. 9:1-4; 11:25-27). (According to Acts, Paul was named after his ancestor in the tribe of Benjamin, Israel's first king, Saul. The Greek name *Paulos* represents the Latin Paulus, suggesting to some—but not proving—that Paul held Roman citizenship, as Acts 21:39 indicates.)

Paul's loyalty to his people undoubtedly shaped his decision as a young man to come to Jerusalem, to study as a Pharisee (with the rabbi Gamaliel II, according to Acts 22:3) and, if Acts 9:1-2 is accurate, to seek a specific commission from the high priest to attack the early communities of believers in Jesus. Paul first appears in the narrative of Acts, and he evidently introduced himself to congregations in Christ (Gal. 1:13) as a persecutor of the Judean "assemblies" (*ekklēsiai*—the Greek term had political connotations that we normally do not associate with the English translation "churches").

It is crucially important to understand the motives of this persecuting activity. It is often assumed that, as an ultra-pious Pharisee, Paul was enraged by the affront to the Torah presented by Jews and Gentiles sitting down to common meals. There is no evidence, however, that the small communities of Christ-followers had decided to abandon Jewish custom. Nor would the inclusion of Gentile men and women alongside Jews necessarily have implied a suspension of Torah. (We should be hard pressed to explain why Paul should work so hard later to negotiate the issue of common meals, as in Rom. 14:1–15:13, if the requirements of *kashrut* had already been relinquished!) Jews and Gentiles regularly associated together. Indeed, synagogues such as the one in Antioch cultivated a following among sympathetic Gentiles who found the ritual austerity and moral rigor of Jewish life attractive (compare Acts 13). Further, so long as the Torah's prohibitions of blood and meat offered to idols were observed, Jews and Gentiles apparently could and did share meals. (An agreement like the so-called Apostolic Letter in Acts 15:23-29 would simply have formalized this state of affairs.)

Paul's motives for persecuting the Judean *ekklēsiai* are rather to be sought in the field of social and political tensions under which he lived. Judea had been subjected to Roman imperial expansion for more than a century, and after 6 C.E., to direct military rule.

Other Jewish writings from the time give ample evidence that many Jews walked a razor-thin line of public acquiescence to Roman power.

Throughout the period from Rome's entry into Judea up to the cata-strophic Jewish revolt (63 B.C.E.—66 C.E.), sporadic uprisings revealed a tremendous undercurrent of Judean resistance to Roman rule. Most of the time, however, most Jews were constrained to recognize the brute fact of Rome's supremacy and to suppress whatever impulses toward defiance they felt. We have a few tantalizing glimpses of this "hidden transcript." In a few oblique paragraphs in a rather esoteric commen-tary on Genesis, Philo of Alexandria discusses the "caution" Jews must constantly exercise in public, keeping their true thoughts regarding their rulers to themselves (*On Dreams* 2:83-98). The author of 4 Mac-cabees rehearses the bold defiance of the Maccabean martyrs under the guise of a philosophical treatise on "patience." The author of the com-mentary on Habakkuk found among the Dead Sea Scrolls—the so-called *pesher* on Habakkuk (1QpHab)—bitterly derides the Romans under an archaic Hebrew codename, *Kittim*. Even decades later, in the wake of the disastrous rebellion, that renegade and consummate politi-cian Josephus told his Roman readers that the rebels had filled the air with eloquent anti-Roman speeches—but he is careful not to leave a record of their views (*War* 2.348-50). Intimately acquainted with the ancient biblical prophecies of messianic deliverance, Josephus was still shrewd enough to assure his readers that these prophecies really pointed to the worldwide dominion of *Rome*. Josephus would not risk describing the hope of his ancestors in its traditional contours!

Although an extreme example, and from a time somewhat later than Paul's, Josephus illustrates a pattern of Jewish hypervigilance toward Roman power. This constant perception of threat, and of the need to conceal the true nature of Israel's prophetic hope from outsiders, was pervasive in the volatile decades that led up to the revolt as well. It informed Paul's persecution of the Judean assemblies of Jesus-followers, as well. The bold and public announcement that Israel's traditional hopes were coming to fruition *now*, in the person of Jesus, would have threatened to expose the messianic transcript that so many Jews endeavored to keep hidden. For the sake of the Jewish community under Roman rule, Paul knew, the messianic hotheads would have to be stopped.

THE APOCALYPSE OF THE CRUCIFIED MESSIAH

What happened instead stopped Saul the persecutor in his tracks. In three different passages, and in colorful detail, Acts tells the dramatic story of Paul's vision of a blinding light on the road to Damascus (9:1-22; 22:6-16; 26:9-23). Paul himself is much more reticent, declaring only that "God was pleased to reveal his son to me" (using the Greek verb *apokalyptein* [Gal. 1:16]). In what may well be a cryptic reference to the same event, however, in 2 Corinthians 12 Paul describes "visions" and "revelations in the Lord" (using the related word *apokalypseis*). Fourteen years earlier, Paul says, "a person in Christ"—apparently referring, obliquely, to himself—was "caught up into the third heaven," into "paradise," and "heard things that are not to be told, that no mortal is permitted to repeat" (12:2-4).

This language bears strong resemblance to the way other Jews, known to us from the apocalyptic writings of the time, would describe a visionary's ascent into heaven. From a political perspective, apocalyptic faith—as we see it most vividly in the Apocalypse to John, for example—provided an extensive "hidden transcript" of hope and defiance, encoded as *heavenly* revelations that God is about to restore the perfect order of creation *here on earth*. Apocalyptic writings sustained hope and cautioned patient endurance among communities suffering the humiliation and recurrent brutality of first Hellenistic, and then Roman rule. One of the most compelling insights of modern scholarship is that Paul had drunk deeply from the wells of this powerful apocalyptic tradition.

But the *apokalypsis,* the "revelation," given to Paul was also breathtakingly different. The book of Daniel had traditionally assured the persecuted that their endurance *now,* during the time when power and dominion were given into the hands of foreign empires, would *eventually* be rewarded in the glorious resurrection of the righteous, at the end of days (12:2-3). Paul declares, however, that he has *already* seen the risen Lord (1 Cor. 9:1; 15:8), the "firstfruits" of the resurrection (15:20). Apocalyptic logic led to a single brilliant consequence, for Paul as for those mostly anonymous visionaries who had seen the risen Jesus before him (e.g., 1 Cor. 15:6): *The time of Rome's sovereignty had drawn to an end.* When Paul addresses his letters to the "holy ones" (or "saints") in various Roman cities, he is using the apocalyptic language of the book of Daniel to salute the "holy ones of the Most High" who have lived to see the dawning of God's reign on earth (compare Dan. 7:18, 22). It is clear from the first of his letters to the last that Paul expected to be present, with the company of the elect, at "the coming of the Lord" (1 Thess. 4:15). He insisted, to the last, that "the day is at hand" (Rom. 13:12). He believed—as did the ardent souls who penned the scrolls found at the Dead Sea—that the quickening Spirit of God was already poured out on human flesh, not only to sustain the righteous but to trouble them with the constant, groaning yearning for God's imminent redemption (Rom. 8:23).

Paul could speak of God simply as the God "who gives life to the dead" (Rom. 4:17, 24). It was God's life-giving power, manifested in the raising of Jesus, that would ultimately redeem all of Israel (Rom. 11:11-15). Furthermore, Paul solemnly proclaimed that all who had joined the *ekklēsia* of the holy ones through baptism had been joined to Jesus' death and burial. They had come, through the same divine power that had raised Jesus from the dead, to a "newness of life." This new life was to be characterized by service to justice (or "righteousness," in good sixteenth-century English [Rom. 6:1-23]). The baptized were "alive to God" and empowered to walk "according to the Spirit" of God, fulfilling the good that the Torah required (8:4).

Since the one revealed to Paul as risen Lord had suffered, first, as an example of Roman terror through crucifixion, the *political* consequences of Paul's revelation were unmistakable. Indeed, Paul's gospel can be described as a "politics of resurrection." In Paul's view, the "rulers of this age" had been exposed as empty frauds (1 Cor. 2:8). It is hardly an accident, then, that the apostle should come to understand his own subjection to state authority—in arrests, trials, beatings, imprisonments—not as a series of embarrassments or misunderstandings but as signs of his genuine, apostolic conformity to Christ (2 Cor. 11:23-27; compare 1 Cor. 4:8-13; Gal. 6:17).

THE GOD OF THE HAVE-NOTS

That conviction would have wider *social* consequences in the congregations Paul helped to organize. Paul writes to the *ekklēsia* in Corinth, for example—a prosperous city that Rome had razed and left in ruins for a century until rebuilding it as a Roman colony, more than a century before Paul's arrival. As the apostle sees it, the *ekklēsia* is now troubled by factions that divide along lines of class. Ambitious members of the city's elite have apparently been drawn into the *ekklēsia* by the inspiring erudition of Paul's colleague, Apollos. Perhaps they have come to regard "their" church as experiencing phenomenal, even God-given growth and prosperity. But Paul reminds the Corinthian Christians that his "planting" or "fathering" of the congregation was the definitive act of God:

Consider your own call, brothers and sisters: not many of you were wise by human standards, not many were powerful, not many were of noble birth. But God chose what is weak in the world to shame the strong; God chose what is low and despised in the world, things that are not, to reduce to nothing things that are, so that no one might boast in the presence of God. He is the source of your life in Christ Jesus. . . . (1 Cor. 1:26-30)

Whatever their subsequent growth in per capita wealth or prestige, according to Paul it was their initial makeup as a congregation largely of the poor, the unimportant, the "low and despised," the "nothings," that revealed God's power and purpose. It is precisely among those the world has discarded as irrelevant that God acts, to put to shame worldly privilege, to expose as foolish the world's wisdom, to bring to nothing the vaunted accomplishments of human power.

This claim, at the heart of Paul's proclamation, has an irreducibly social and political dimension. The Corinthian congregation risks forfeiting their call from Christ, Paul warns, because they have simply reproduced in their own midst the social stratification of Roman society. They even tolerate hunger in their congregation while some have the means to become fabulously sated—and they have the audacity to speak of the "Lord's supper" (1 Cor. 11:17-34)!

This letter shows the precise symmetry Paul perceives between God's raising the crucified Jesus from the dead—the core story to which Paul constantly refers by terms such as "the power of the cross" or "the word of the cross"—and God's creation of congregations of "holy ones" out of "have-nothings"(1 Cor. 11:22) and "are-nothings" (1:28). Both actions expose the fraudulent claims of imperial society, the "rulers of this age," to define power, truth, and worth. With good reason, theologians of liberation have found in this letter the earliest Christian articulation of the "preferential option for the poor."

This election of "the low and despised" must not be sentimentalized, however, either romantically, as if God sympathized with the poor but was tragically impotent to change their plight, or moralistically, as if Paul were always reminding the privileged to be charitable to the less fortunate. (Even our English phrase "the lowly"—used in Rom. 12:16, for example—has a moralistic tinge inappropriate to the Greek word *tapeinoi*. That word should be translated, as it usually is in writings outside the New Testament, in terms of social class, not disposition: "the oppressed.") God's "preferential option" for the crucified Jesus was, in Paul's eyes, far more than sympathy: God raised Jesus from the dead as a manifestation of power (Rom. 1:4). Nor were the Corinthians called upon to memorialize Jesus' death with the solemnity of a funeral. Paul told them to live out the life of the crucified, in the power of the God who raised Jesus from the dead (1 Cor. 11:26; compare Rom. 6:1-14).

For Paul, the small base communities of the oppressed (for such they are—always meeting "house by house"), were fully and completely established as the assemblies, *ekklēsiai,* of God's elect. In these base communities and among them, the poor shared their resources, skills, and wisdom in a deliberate mutuality. Because this mutuality of the poor defied the codes of patronage in the wider imperial society, it regularly attracted the suspicion and resentment of the well-to-do. Paul was compelled, for example, to write 2 Corinthians as a bitingly ironic defense of his decision not to accept "support" from a wealthy few in Corinth, a move that would have put him in the position of a client obligated to serve his patrons' interests.

On the other hand, in the letter to the Philippians—a congregation who have freely shared what they had with other base communities in their region—Paul speaks with unfeigned intimacy and affection. Interpreters in developed countries often remark on what seems to them the disproportionate attention Paul devotes in his letters to maintaining community ties. They routinely characterize his letters as instruments through which Paul seeks support for "his" mission. But this rather misses the point. Paul and the forty-odd "co-workers" whom he routinely names form a network of contacts among neighborhood communities in and among cities and towns, who choose to share their gifts with each other (1 Thess. 4:9-12; Phil. 4:15-16; 2 Cor. 8:1-7). *Paul's* "gift," or "commission" (*charis* is routinely translated both ways), is to be present at the birthing of these communities (1 Thess. 2:1-12) and to encourage and facilitate their reciprocal generosity.

The point is the sharing of resources in order to meet human need. Paul finds he must explain this at greater length when he addresses the more prosperous in Corinth, who have balked, thinking they are being asked to give disproportionately more than others. "I do not mean that there should be relief for others and pressure on you, but it is a question of a fair balance between your present abundance and their need, so that their abundance may be for your need, in order that there may be a fair balance" (2 Cor. 8:13-14). Paul leaves it to the rich Christians in Corinth to puzzle out what the poor of Judea may have in "abundance": generosity of spirit, perhaps (2 Cor. 9:14)?

The mutuality Paul advocates is both material and international. The collection for the "poor among the saints" in Jerusalem expresses solidarity with the hard-pressed Judean churches (Rom. 15:25-26; 1 Cor. 16:1-3; 2 Cor. 9:1-15; Gal. 2:10). Paul is not above playing on the competitive pretensions of the rich (2 Cor. 8:8; 9:3-5; compare Rom. 12:10, "outdo one another in showing honor"). But his core motive—beyond the fundamental Jewish principle of "remembering the poor" (Gal. 2:10)—is to conform his congregations to the example of the Lord, who "though he was rich, yet for your sakes . . . became poor, so that by his poverty you might become rich" (2 Cor. 8:9). Similarly he calls on the Philippian community to imitate Jesus, who "humbled himself and became obedient to the point of death, even death on a cross" (Phil. 2:8). We see that the cross of Jesus, which is never far from Paul's mind, fundamentally symbolizes the renunciation of privilege on behalf of others. Not accidentally, it comes to the fore of Paul's rhetoric when he addresses congregations where the material and social privilege enjoyed by some are obstacles to the genuine community (koinōnia) of all.

A POLITICAL AND MATERIAL READING OF PAUL'S THEOLOGY

Archbishop Oscar Romero of El Salvador dedicated much of his pastoral work to articulating the church's "preferential option for the poor" and defending it against misunderstanding and misrepresentation. If, as suggested above, the option for the poor finds its New Testament roots in Paul's letters, we should not be surprised to find that on this point Paul, too, has often been misunderstood.

Over the last century, European and American scholarship on the social status of the Pauline communities has routinely generalized Paul's social ethic as a "love patriarchalism." Onto waters troubled by revolutionary currents, we have been told, Paul poured the soothing oil of fellow-feeling, without questioning the social institutions and practices that perpetuated injustice and inequality. In the last thirty years, sociological interpretations of Paul's churches insisted that to speak only of tremendous social stratification in Paul's day—to emphasize the "steep pyramid" of privilege and power—is too simplistic. Rather than the stark differences between rich and poor that characterized the Mediterranean economy, we are told we should locate Paul's communities amid a healthy middle class of merchants and independent craftspeople who were relatively comfortable, if also anxious about their perceived "status ambivalence." According to this interpretation, most of Paul's urban contemporaries were more worried about the great social contest for prestige and honor than about the hard necessities of survival. Paul himself was less concerned with the living conditions of slaves or poor freedpersons in his churches, than that "his" churches should survive as models of harmonious integration, where poor and rich could sit together—at least for an evening—and share a modest, if largely symbolic, meal.

Where has this widespread understanding of Paul's "love patriarchalism" come from? In part, these common generalizations are based on the complex picture of status and conflict in the Corinthian correspondence. Paul's repeated allusions to "one body" (e.g., 1 Corinthians 12) suggest to many that the harmonious *unity* of the church is Paul's chief concern. But it is a mistake to generalize to all Paul's churches the situation in Corinth. And it is a mistake to read Paul's demand for unity in the face of clear social stratification as a strategy of superficial inclusiveness and acquiescence in the face of supposedly unchangeable social realities.

The Corinthian letters give evidence of social stratification—of rich and poor mixing together in the *ekklēsia*—because growing social inequities in that congregation had provoked Paul's vigorous response. From the first chapters of 1 Corinthians, *Paul reminds the church of their origins*—when they were more clearly a "church of the poor," when they more clearly embodied God's preferential option in Christ, and *before* they succumbed to the illusion that God's work among them was represented by the property and prestige that *some* in their midst enjoyed. The bite of Paul's ironic rebukes of the wealthy (in 1 Corinthians 4 and 11), like his command to the "powerful" to defer to the needs of the "weak" (in Romans 14), send a clear message: Those with wealth and power are to practice renunciation for the sake of the needy, both in their midst and around them. To be sure, there are protests throughout 1 Corinthians that "all things are permissible" and that "food doesn't matter," but these are rightly recognized as Paul's ironic quotation of the slogans spouted by the wealthy members of the Corinthian assembly. It becomes apparent, then, that the *"love patriarchalism" evident in 1 Corinthians is that of the Corinthian elite: it is not Paul's.*

Generalizations about Paul's social ethic of the "status quo" also rely on the sustained "pedagogy *to* the oppressed" that appear in later writings in our New Testament. The anonymous authors of the "letters" Colossians, Ephesians, 1 Timothy, and Titus insist that slaves and others in subordinate positions must accept their lot as God-given and live out their discipleship to Jesus by obeying those who dominate them.

For centuries, this ethic of subordination has been read as Paul's own view—and even allowed to control the interpretation of the letters Paul unquestionably wrote. Modern interpreters increasingly describe these letters as efforts, made after Paul's death, to "adapt" or "accommodate" the memory of the apostle to the pressures Christian communities felt in Roman society. These letters can also be seen, however, as *deviations* from Paul's own policy in the assemblies he served. As we shall see, *Paul's own letters show him struggling for the mutuality of the poor against powerful social codes that legitimized inequality, subordination, and exploitation.*

LIVING IN SOLIDARITY WITH THE OPPRESSED

From Paul's earliest letter, written to the assembly in Thessalonike, the contours of his apostolic praxis among the assemblies he served are evident. His letters are instruments—as are his own personal presence or the presence of co-workers—to "strengthen and encourage" the assemblies to "stand firm" in lives of holiness and patience, despite persecution. Paul reminds the Thessalonians that they "turned to God from idols"—from the imagery of Roman power and privilege that surrounded them—and encourages them as they wait for the advent—the *parousia*—of Jesus (1 Thess. 1:9-10; 4:15). (This language derives from the diplomatic sphere: Just as cities were often warned to prepare for the arrival in force of a powerful king or general, so the Thessalonian assembly must await Jesus' "cry of command" and the trumpet signal of his *parousia*.) Paul's message is subversive, however. The lord *he* expects will arrive "as a thief in the night" (5:2), at the very moment when "they" proclaim "peace and security" (5:3)—the very watchwords of Roman propaganda (*pax et securitas*). Rather than pursuing the elusive "peace" promised by the patronage of the provincial elite, the "saints" are to practice mutual love (3:11-13) and refuse to defraud one another (4:3-8), preferring to build a quiet community life of economic self-sufficiency, "dependent on no one" (4:9-12), seeking always the common good (5:12-15) as it is discerned in community (5:19-22).

Although Paul writes to the assembly in Philippi in difficult circumstances (Roman imprisonment: 1:12-14), he strikes many of the same themes. He commends the assembly for their faithfulness to him (and their gift to him, 4:10-19), to God, and to their life together (1:1-11). He charges them with discerning together the common good (1:9-10) and standing fast in the face of persecution (1:27-30) so as to be ready for the "Day of Christ" (1:10; 2:16). He reminds them of their constitution as a community of mutual support (2:1-4), where they are charged to realize the model of renunciation given by Jesus himself (2:5-11). And he holds out (as in 1 Thessalonians) the expectation that the assembly will be vindicated in their "heavenly citizenship" by the Lord, who will transform their "bodies of humiliation" into glory (3:20-21).

What would this language about mutuality and "heavenly citizenship" mean for concrete, day-to-day social relationships in a Roman city? We get a dramatic answer in the brief letter we call "Philemon." That name is misleading: the letter is actually addressed to "Philemon our dear friend and coworker, to Apphia our sister, to Archippus our fellow soldier, and to the *ekklēsia* in your house" (1-2). We cannot be sure which of these members of the *ekklēsia* was the owner of the slave Onesimus: Even that relationship is hinted at fairly late in the letter, in the subtlest of terms (16). Neither can we tell exactly what the "duty" was to which Paul said he could "command" that individual (8): merely to accept the slave back without punishing him? to "lend" the slave to Paul for an indefinite period? We *can* tell that Paul intended his request to be the subject of discernment by the whole assembly, not the slave-owner alone!

Because Paul never explicitly calls on the slaveholder to grant freedom to Onesimus by the legal act of manumission, interpreters have almost always agreed that Paul never challenged the institution of slavery. Especially in the slaveholding South, Paul's suggestion that Onesimus be accepted "no longer as a slave but more than a slave, a beloved brother" (16) was seized upon as evidence that whatever Christian "brotherhood" entailed, it was not incompatible with chattel slavery. (Of course, the specific instructions to Christian slaveowners in the pseudo-Pauline writings reinforced this conclusion.)

Only in the last twenty years have these conclusions been exploded, and the real force of Paul's rhetoric recognized. Contemporary evidence (for example, letters from the moralist and imperial advisor Seneca) shows that in the Roman era, requests for a master to release a slave through manumission or to accept a returned runaway without harsh punishment were normal enough within the slave system. After all, manumission relieved the master of responsibility for feeding, clothing, and housing a slave who was no longer profitable, and the promise of eventual manumission—like gentler treatment accorded the runaway—presumably gave the slave an incentive to devote more years in obedient service. Contrary to modern assumptions, a frank request for Onesimus to be manumitted would only have reinforced the sovereign legal right of master over slave, just as much as a polite request for lighter punishment for a returned runaway.

This letter does none of that. Paul never pleads the slave's contrite repentance or appeals to the master's mercy. Rather he makes a single, solemn offer to "repay" the master if the slave has "wronged" him (18-19)—which, of course, a runaway slave would have done simply by depriving his master of his labor. An outright offer to buy the slave would have fit comfortably enough within a slave system. But Paul so construes the situation that the master will be put to shame if he presumes his place within that system. He will have failed to do his "duty," to obey the apostle's implicit "command" (8), to have shown proper respect for the apostle as an equal (17) or gratitude for the apostle's giving him his very life (19). How much greater will his failure be to live, out of his own good will, and in the presence of the assembly, the communality and "love for all the saints" for which Paul has already congratulated him (4-5)!

The act of manumission is irrelevant to what is, for Paul, the crucial issue: the fundamental equality of all in the community of the *ekklēsia*. Whether or not Paul imagined that human effort could bring the Roman slave system to an end—he had no doubt, of course, that at "the end," Christ would destroy "every ruler and every authority and power" (1 Cor. 15:24)—it is clear enough that for *this* assembly, it could no longer be imagined that one man might wield over his brother "in the Lord" the power of a master over a slave. We do not know the master's response to Paul's letter; we do not know how the two men, no longer slave and master but more, brothers, worked out a new life of brotherhood within the assembly. We *do* know that, by seeking out Paul, Onesimus—the first Christian-owned slave of whom we have knowledge—staked his very life on the vision of a true community of equals and thus brought an end to the "love patriarchalism" still tolerated within his master's *ekklēsia*.

As we have seen, Corinth proved a far more difficult case simply because of the greater preponderance of well-off Christians like Onesimus's master. While earlier scholarship imagined that some alien religious ideas had infiltrated the Corinthian church, we can clearly recognize today that *the heart of the problem is the rationalization, in Christian terms, of wealth and privilege.*

More than any other letter, 1 Corinthians allows us to hear echoes of this theology of prosperity. Surely "food is meant for the stomach and the stomach for food" (6:13); "all things are lawful for me" (6:12; 10:23); "an idol has no real existence" (8:4). So why shouldn't we continue to participate with our neighbors (and business partners) in sacred meals at the temples of other gods? Of course some of the "weaker" members of the *ekklēsia* are offended—they're not skilled in the etiquette required to ignore the sacred associations of the meat in front of them. But shouldn't the poor be satisfied that they are allowed to participate in our own sacred meals to Christ, so long as they keep their place? (11:17-24). Shouldn't some of these old-timers recognize that they are inferior in Christ's eyes, simply because they have remained in their marriages to nonbelievers? (7:1-40). Of course, we can forgive the occasional indiscretion among our own, especially if it keeps an old, honored family name intact (5:1-2). We are, after all, a community of tolerance and inclusion; we can embrace the people of Paul and the people of Apollos alike (1:12). Why, we even include people who are suing each other in court! (6:1-8). And we are rightly proud that some of our own men hold high positions in the city, even being invited to officiate in civic prayers, drawing their togas over their heads in proper imitation of the emperor himself (11:2-16). Grateful as we are to Apollos, we can take pride in the skill of some of our own young men to move us with wise words. But that is another sore point: Shouldn't the poorer among us yield the disorderly noise of *their* worship—"tongues of angels," indeed!—to the eloquence of fine speakers? (chaps. 12–14).

If the elite had in fact adopted such a rationale, we can see that Paul opposes it whenever it touches on practical matters of community life. Sexual immorality and lawsuits against brothers are not to be tolerated (chaps. 5–6). On the other hand, it is holy and peaceful living that sanctifies the baptized—not one's relative freedom from social constraints. Those "called" into the community (i.e., baptized into Christ) while engaged or married to others, even to unbelieving spouses, are not somehow less holy and need not strive to be "free" of the marriage (though Paul expects separations may nonetheless take place [7:10-11]). The spouses and the children in such families are no less sanctified (7:12-16). Nor need the betrothed fear that they will "sin" by consummating a marriage (although Paul would prefer that anyone remain "as he is," that is, celibate [7:8-10, 25-31]). Slaves should not fear that their status somehow makes them less than their freeborn peers, though by all means they should "avail yourselves of the opportunity" for freedom (7:21, NRSV variant). Despite a common tendency in many modern translations, Paul never says that marriage, or celibacy, or slavery, or any social position is a "calling" to *which* God has "called" people. Rather, God calls people, *in* whatever situation they find themselves, to "peace" (7:15) and to obedience (7:19).

Paul's repudiation of an ideology of privilege is sustained and bitter. His insistence that the individuals in the Corinthian congregation are members of "one body" (11:29; 12:12-31) echoes a commonplace of Roman and Greek political philosophy, but the pundits of the age usually urged the *poor* to subordinate their interests to those of the larger "body politic." Paul, however, repeatedly curtails the vaunted freedom of the Corinthian elite. All things are permitted me—"*but* not all things are beneficial" (6:12). All of us have knowledge—*but* "knowledge puffs up; . . . love builds up" (8:1). Idols are not real, "*but* watch out: do not let your freedom somehow present a scandal to the weak" (8:4, 9). The "knowledge" claimed by the powerful (1:26) is a smokescreen for indifference and contempt toward "the foolish," "the vulnerable," "the ill-born," "the nothings," "the have-nots" (1:27-28; 11:22). They have become bloated—"puffed up"—with boasting, the self-satisfaction of the well-off. Paul mocks their boast: "Who sees anything distinctive about you? What do you have that you were not given? If you were given it, why do you boast as if it were not a gift? Already you have all you want! Already you have become rich! Quite apart from us you have become kings!" (4:7-8).

If rich members of the Corinthian church have justified themselves in crossing the boundary of the *ekklēsia* and communing with their social equals in the city square, they apparently have not managed to accept members of their own assembly as equals. Rather the community meal, the "Lord's supper," still reflects the sharp social stratification that prevails in the wider society. There it is quite appropriate for the honored and significant to be offered the best seats, the best food, the best wine, and for the poor to fend for themselves. There everyone knows his or her place in relation to one's fellows and conducts oneself accordingly. To Paul's eyes, such distinctions forfeit the very character of the common meal as a Lord's supper. He not only rebukes the Corinthians; he recommends that if they cannot share in the meal as equals, they may as well "eat at home—so you do not come together to be condemned!" (11:21). But that would only mean that the assembly of the holy disintegrate into self-contained households, ordered by rank and wealth.

Clearly, for Paul, the *ekklēsia* is constituted by the practice of a radical equality, which will cost the elite dearly. They must give up the privileges to which their social status entitles them, and do so publicly —excluding a sexual offender from the assembly, withdrawing from any civic function where food consecrated to the city's gods might be served, declining to offer prayers at these same functions. The natural consequence of such changes in behavior will be social ostracism, or worse.

We know from the strained protests of 2 Corinthians that Paul's appeal was not well received. Indeed his very legitimacy as an apostle was apparently called into question, given the sordid details of his arrest record (and an apparent sentence to death [1:9]!). Clearly some Corinthians preferred their leaders to be paragons of civic virtue, unsullied by the public humiliation of a criminal conviction (beatings, imprisonments [6:5]). They also prefer their leaders to accept financial support, something Paul refused to do—apparently only too aware that such an offer would seem to obligate him more to the rich than to the poor (chaps. 11–13). Not for a moment does Paul protest that this is an accident, that there has been some misunderstanding. Rather, in the moment of what seems the deepest civic shame, he has been "led in triumphal procession" by Christ, spreading "the fragrance that comes from knowing him"—though the unperceiving smell only "a fragrance from death to death" (2:14-17). In their very painful and very public degradation the apostles are "always carrying in the body the death of Jesus" (4:10), just as the acolytes of Caesar carry about the images of imperial power and glory. Paul's use of language evocative of imperial ritual is more than satire. He speaks to a very real contest of power in the public square, between the ambassadors of a crucified Lord and the ministers of an age that is "passing away" (1 Cor. 7:31). The choice he finally lays before the rich of Corinth is just as clear. They can avoid terrible humiliation by responding to this, his third request, and matching the generosity of much poorer assemblies (2 Cor. 8:2) who have already extended generous support for "the needs of the saints" in Jerusalem (9:1-5).

REMOVING THE REFUGE OF RELIGION

If in Corinth Paul confronted an ideology of comfortable complacency, he seems in other letters to address a more clearly religious opposition. In Philippians 3, he warns against "the dogs, . . . the evil workers, . . . those who mutilate the flesh," apparently referring to a campaign by some to encourage men in the assembly to accept circumcision (3:2-3). His letter to the Galatians is written in a much harsher tone of recrimination and rebuke: A similar campaign has been successful in persuading some in the Galatian assemblies. In both places—and, significantly, *only* in these places—Paul provides the few autobiographical details of which we can be certain. He was "circumcised on the eighth day, a member of the people of Israel, of the tribe of

Benjamin, a Hebrew born of Hebrews; as to the Law, a Pharisee; as to zeal, a persecutor of the church; as to righteousness under the Law, blameless" (Phil. 3:5-6). Regarding his "earlier life in Judaism"—*ioudaismos*—he tells the Galatians he had "advanced beyond many" of his fellow Jews, "for I was far more zealous for the traditions of my ancestors," going so far as to persecute the *ekklēsiai* (Gal. 1:13-14). He tells the Philippians that he has come to regard these "gains" as "loss because of the surpassing value of knowing Christ Jesus my Lord" (3:7-8).

Because of the strident tone of these warnings against accepting circumcision; because here, and in Romans, Paul speaks in negative terms of life "under the Law"; and because he looks back at his previous life "in Judaism" as something he has surrendered, Christian interpreters have been swift to conclude that Paul was a "convert" from Judaism to a new religion, Christianity. Jewish interpreters, for their part, have often labeled him an "apostate" or "renegade" from Torah observance. Even today—*especially* today—learned attempts to unravel the Gordian knots concerning Paul, the Jews, and the Law multiply. Ironically, much of the modern discussion ignores a simple but profoundly important observation: *Paul writes all of his letters to congregations made up predominantly of Gentiles.* Although generations of Christian interpreters have been more interested in describing one or another form of "Jewish opposition" to Paul, usually in order to highlight the superiority of his views over "Jewish" views, a much more central question has long been neglected: *What would motivate Gentile adherents to Paul's assemblies to seek circumcision?*

The answer runs like a fault line from Paul's earliest letter to the latest. Paul says he warned the assemblies clearly enough that those who have "turned to God from idols" should expect to face "distress and persecution" as something they "are destined for" (1 Thess. 1:6-10; 3:1-4). They are now called to see the world around them as full of "darkness" and "impurity," destined for "wrath," and their neighbors, even their own family, as "asleep," "drunk"—as "Gentiles" (4:5). But they themselves have not become Jews and thus cannot turn for support or shelter to the synagogue community. Nor can they offer the ancient heritage of the Jews as explanation of their own sudden and inexplicable withdrawal from the sacred routines of everyday life in the Roman city. How tempting a ritual like circumcision must have seemed; after all, it signaled a clear transition to a publicly recognized, officially sanctioned (if often vilified) ethnic identity, promising shelter from scorn and abuse. It is clear enough from Galatians that the baptized are con-

templating circumcision not as an entrance into a life of Torah observance within the bosom of the synagogue—for then Paul's solemn
warning would be meaningless: "every man who lets himself be circumcised . . . is obliged to obey the entire Law" (5:3). Rather, those
accepting circumcision themselves, and encouraging it in the assemblies, do so "that they may not be persecuted for the cross of Christ"
(6:12). Instead of allowing the Gentile believers to adopt a protective
religious alias—to "judaize"—Paul offers only the assurance of the new
way of life they have discovered in community: the "gifts of the Spirit"
are all found in mutual regard, support, and encouragement, the bearing of one another's burdens (5:22–6:6).

We should note that in none of his letters does Paul provide a full
"diagnosis" of "the Jewish condition," let alone a "critique" or "attack"
on "the Jew." Even in Romans 2—where such an "attack" has routinely been perceived—Paul's call-and-response style is meant to draw
"the Jew" to his side as he addresses Gentile readers. If the Jew, to
whom the glorious privileges of the covenant have been given (3:2; 9:1-
4), nevertheless stands fully accountable to God, without recourse to
religious belief or identity as a defense or "excuse," then surely no one
can (3:9; 19-20). "The Jew" is not the target, but the example that
proves Paul's point. How much less should *Gentiles* who have come to
Christ presume upon their baptism to shield them from judgment
according to works! (2:1-16; 6:1-23).

THE OBEDIENCE OF THE NATIONS

Romans—the latest and the most intricate of Paul's letters—shows
the urgency with which Paul confronted all the assemblies with the
demand of just and holy living. This is no theological testament, no
essay on a theme—however useful that assumption has been to the history of Christian doctrine. As much as any of Paul's letters, Romans is
built upon the fundamental change in life that baptism has meant for
his readers. The idolatry, immorality, injustice, and dishonor of the
Roman world (1:18-32) have been left behind in baptism; sin is no
longer to "rule" in the bodies of believers (6:1-23). Now they are to
present the bodies as a "living sacrifice, holy and acceptable to God,
which is your spiritual worship. Do not be conformed to this world"
(12:1-2). Their positive response to Paul's letter will make them part of
the "offering of the Gentiles" that is his apostolic responsibility to

gather (15:14-16). That is, Romans is as much directed toward the "turning to God from idols" as 1 Thessalonians is!

The climax of the letter is Paul's impassioned plea in chapters 9–11, a plea rooted in Paul's indelible ethnic identity (9:1-4) and God's irreversible commitment to Israel (11:1-2, 25-27). He admonishes the Gentiles in the Roman assemblies not to "boast" over their Jewish neighbors (11:13-21) or "claim to be wiser than you are" (11:25). As with the Corinthian letters, so here the turns of Paul's argument and information from other, roughly contemporary sources allow us to reconstruct the situation he addresses with some confidence. Jewish believers in Jesus—such as Prisca and Aquila (16:3-4) or the other "relatives" that Paul identifies only here (Andronicus and Julia [16:7]; Herodion [16:11]; compare 16:21)—have probably returned to the city after being expelled by the emperor Claudius (so Acts 18:2; compare Suetonius, *Life of Claudius* 25.3). The miserable plight of Jewish refugees and the contempt shown them by members of the Roman aristocracy are evident from later Roman writings and from the strident anti-Judaism of the counselors on whom Nero relied. When Paul addresses "the powerful" (or "strong") and "the weak" in relation to questions of unclean foods (14:1–15:13; see 14:14), he uses a common Roman vocabulary of honor and contempt for those of higher and lower status. Throughout these later chapters of the letter, his concern is that the relatively comfortable Gentiles in the Roman assemblies ("the strong" [15:1]) should not provoke or challenge "the weak" but should seek to build them up and satisfy their needs (the pejorative NRSV translation at 15:1, "put up with" their "failings," is unfortunate).

If Paul's purpose here is to encourage holy living among Gentile believers, as in every other assembly he addressed, in Romans he also faces a new and unprecedented challenge. The rhetorical questions that punctuate the letter reveal the central issue: the perception among the Gentile assemblies that the "faithlessness" of some Jews will "nullify the faithfulness of God" (3:3-9), that the Law works death (7:1-25), that the disinclination of many Jews to accept the message about Jesus means that "the word of God had failed" (9:6), that God has "rejected his people" (11:1). Efforts to derive these questions as more or less natural conclusions from Paul's own theology have proved unconvincing. Rather Paul here confronts a virulent new form of the generalized contempt for Jews that swirled in the Roman air, especially among the aristocracy, now given new purchase as a theological "fact" in the

Gentile church. Surely the miserable plight of the Jews is evidence of God's judgment! Surely "branches were broken off" of the holy root of Israel, and the Gentiles were "grafted in their place" (11:17)! We know that within fifty years of this letter, just this theology of Israel's "replacement" by Gentile Christianity would become the settled, "orthodox" view—only to come again into question in the last half of the twentieth century. In Romans, we see Paul striving mightily against its first appearance.

Throughout the tortured chapters 9–11 Paul struggles to explain that what now appears as Israel's fate is nothing of the sort. Rather God has "hardened" Israel, just as God "hardened" Pharaoh (9:16-18; 11:7-10). This "hardening" is not permanent, however. It is God's mysterious strategy for provoking Israel to jealousy through the success of the Gentile mission—*of Paul's own work, that is*—so as to win them back: "and so," in this way, "all Israel will be saved" (11:25-32). The proper response of the Gentile church is humility—"not to think of yourself more highly than you ought to think" (12:3); genuine love, "mutual affection," and contributing to "the needs of the saints" (12:9-13); and especially consideration for "the weak" (15:1-2), meaning apparently the circumcised of Rome, whose servant Christ became (15:8), and the "saints" of Jerusalem (15:25-29).

Of course this will require a change of heart, a genuine transformation "through the renewing of your minds" that will put the Gentile church at odds with "this world" (12:1-2). Though the early chapters of Romans have often been read as an abstract essay on salvation in Christ, Paul meant them to achieve the very alienation from the standards of "the world"—more specifically, the standards of imperial Roman culture—that he appeals for in later chapters. Roman ears could not have missed the implied contrast between Jesus, the genuine Son of God, "descended from David according to the flesh" and confirmed "with power according to the spirit of holiness by resurrection from the dead" (1:3-4), and the claims of the reigning emperor, Nero, to be Son of God through descent from Julius Caesar and the late, but recently deified, Claudius. (Indeed Nero's self-serving claims to descent from the Roman hero Aeneas and his deification of his uncle Claudius, whose death Nero's own mother was widely believed to have achieved through poison, were ridiculed in graffiti and even a satire written by Nero's own advisor, Seneca.) Nor would Roman ears have missed the clear judgment expressed against those whose arrogance, idolatry, and abuse of the bodies of others led to utter depravity and murder (1:18-32). Similar judgments of Nero's crimes were made by contemporaries even in the Roman aristocracy. Paul's purpose is not to vilify a wicked ruler, however, but to bring home to his readers the tremendous disparity between what the world calls "justice" and the justice of God (1:15-17).

In Romans, the pretensions of the imperial house, and the presumption of the God-ordained superiority of the Roman people over subject peoples like the Jews, are exploded. The justice of God—divine wrath against wickedness and divine faithfulness to the covenant with Israel—may still appear a "mystery." But it is a mystery already being "revealed" to those with eyes to see (1:17-18; 11:25-36), in the depravity to which God has abandoned the wicked (1:18-24) and in the preservation of a "remnant" in Israel (11:1-7). Paul asks his Gentile readers for simple changes: mutual respect, deference to "the weak," regard for Israel, the avoidance of civil unrest (13:1-7). But in his sweeping vision, their obedience will mean nothing less than participation in the glorious day that Israel's prophets foretold, when the nations would join with Israel in the holy worship of Israel's God (15:6-13).

PAUL'S LEGACY

History has not been kind to Paul's vision. We do not know how the Roman church responded to Paul's letter. The book of Acts tells us that the mission Paul described to them in Romans 15:22-32—his delivery of the collection, and his presentation of a delegation of holy Gentiles, to the temple authorities in Jerusalem—ended in disaster. Paul was accused—wrongly, Luke insists—of violating the sanctity of the temple by bringing Gentiles into its inner court (Acts 21:27-36). He escaped death only by appeal to the Roman garrison for protection (21:37–22:29). A series of hearings followed, before Jewish and Roman authorities alike, until Paul made an appeal to Caesar, that is, Nero (25:1-12). Acts concludes without telling us the final disposition of Paul's case. Later Christian writings recall his execution in Rome, however, the victim of the Roman sword that he had warned the Roman congregation was no empty threat (Rom. 13:4).

Death spared Paul the disappointments that would rock the churches over the next few decades: Rome's brutal suppression of the Judean revolt and with it the apparent demise of the Jerusalem church; the ascendancy of Gentiles and the deepening divide between church and synagogue; increased vulnerability to persecution as the Christian movement gained public notoriety. Paul anticipated none of this. Nor could he have imagined how his own memory would be appropriated and reshaped to meet the perceived needs of later Christians. Some remembered him as an itinerant radical, preaching a gospel of withdrawal from civic obligations and of equality between men and women (as in the early-third-century *Acts of Paul and Thecla*). A more defensive reaction to the pressures of the social environment produced a more conservative, patriarchal Paul, the champion of household subordination who now appears in our New Testament (Ephesians, 1 Timothy, Titus). The Acts of the Apostles did much to consolidate Paul's reputation as the founder of the Gentile church. The encyclical we call Ephesians avoided the complex arguments of Romans and Galatians and simply declared that Christ "has abolished the Law with its commandments and ordinances" (2:15), a view hard to reconcile with Paul's own (compare Romans 3:31), but welcome to the emerging Gentile church. By the mid-second century, when Marcion and other Gnostic Christians replaced the apocalyptic prophet of Israel's redemption with Paul the Gnostic, the transformation was near complete.

We stand at a tremendous distance from the events that inspired Paul's irrepressible hope. Paul is not the only New Testament writer to confront us with the apocalyptic matrix in which the Christian faith was born, but his letters make the confrontation unavoidable. One modern response is to seek to refurbish first-century apocalyptic beliefs so as to recapture some of the certainty of imminence that Paul expresses in his letters. But this is like trying to move into a house built for others, long, long ago.

Other aspects of Paul's vision may prove more compelling and challenging for our own day. Paul saw the cross as the unmistakable sign of the implacable hostility of the powers of this world to God (1 Cor. 2:8), and the resurrection as the sure sign of God's eventual triumph over those powers (1 Cor. 15:20-28). In the long twilight before that dawn—a time filled with hardship, distress, persecution, famine, nakedness, peril, the sword—Paul heard the groans of a captive creation, the cries of men and women yearning for "the glorious freedom of the children of God," as the moving of the very Spirit of God through our world (Rom. 8:18-25). Such themes have caught fire throughout parts of the world where struggles for the most basic human needs have shaped powerful and flourishing theologies of liberation. If these theologies still strike many North American believers as somehow "foreign" to our faith, the reasons may lie in just the sorts of material and ideological obstacles to genuine mutuality and solidarity with the oppressed that Paul faced in first-century Roman culture.

The tremendous individualism of U.S. culture—due more to the forces of industrial capitalism and the saturation of our lives by the electronic media than to any stoic heroism on the part of our pioneer forebears—is corrosive of community and compassion alike. We need to hear Paul's exhortations to awaken from slumber and live out our responsibilities to our neighbors. We need to feel the bite of his anger at spiritual complacency and the arrogance that baptizes privilege as God-given. And when we find ourselves at a safe distance from the risks of genuine discipleship, we need to hear Paul's burning insistence that it is nowhere else than in the hunger, persecution, imprisonment, torture, and deaths of those who dare to build a new humanity in the shadow of an unjust world order that the dying of Jesus, and the power of his resurrection, appear in the world around us.

RESOURCES FOR FURTHER STUDY

I have made more detailed arguments for some of the interpretations presented here in *Liberating Paul: The Justice of God and the Politics of the Apostle* (Maryknoll, N.Y.: Orbis; Sheffield: Sheffield Academic Press, 1994). Justin L. Meggitt presents a sober picture of the poverty of Paul's age and points to the importance of the "ethic of mutuality" in Paul's churches, in *Paul, Poverty and Survival*, Studies of the New Testament and Its World (Edinburgh: T. & T. Clark, 1998). Dieter Georgi, *Remembering the Poor: The History of Paul's Collection for Jerusalem* (Nashville: Abingdon, 1965, 1992) and David Horrell, *The Social Ethic of the Corinthian Correspondence* (Edinburgh: T. & T. Clark, 1996) offer valuable appreciations of the material aspects of Paul's work.

Important recent scholarship on imperial culture and ideology and its implications for the study of Paul's letters are well represented by the essays gathered in Richard A. Horsley, ed., *Paul and Empire: Religion and Power in Roman Imperial Society* (Philadelphia: Trinity Press International, 1996). James C. Scott develops the notion of "hidden" and "public transcripts" in *Domination and the Arts of Resistance: Hidden Transcripts* (New Haven: Yale University Press, 1990). For the challenges facing Jewish identity under Roman imperialism, see John Barclay, *Jews in the Mediterranean Diaspora from Alexander to Trajan (323 BCE–117 CE)* (Edinburgh: T. & T. Clark, 1996); for a judicious application of these insights to Paul, see Calvin J. Roetzel, *Paul: The Man and the Myth* (Columbia: University of South Carolina Press, 1998).

On questions surrounding Paul's early persecution of the Judean churches and his subsequent reversal of course (the term "conversion" carries unfortunate baggage today) I have relied on insights and arguments by Paula Fredriksen, *From Jesus to Christ: The Origins of the New Testament Images of*

Jesus (New Haven: Yale University Press, 1988) and Alan F. Segal, *Paul the Convert: The Apostolate and Apostasy of Saul the Pharisee* (New Haven: Yale University Press, 1990). The apocalyptic interpretation of Paul's thought has an impressive heritage, from Albert Schweitzer's seminal *The Mysticism of Paul the Apostle,* trans. William Montgomery (London: Adam & Charles Black, 1967; first English translation 1931), through more recent landmark works by Ernst Käsemann (*Commentary on Romans,* trans. G. Bromiley [Grand Rapids: Eerdmans, 1980]), J. Christiaan Beker (*Paul the Apostle: The Triumph of God in Life and Thought* [Philadelphia: Fortress, 1980]), and E. P. Sanders (*Paul and Palestinian Judaism: A Comparison of Patterns of Religion* [Philadelphia: Fortress, 1977]).

The literature on Paul's attitude to the Torah is vast and complex. There is probably no more accessible introduction to the questions—and to the difference it makes to read Paul's letters as addressed *to Gentiles!*—than John G. Gager, *Reinventing Paul* (Princeton: Princeton University Press, 2000). I owe much to Paula Fredriksen's succinct and lucid discussion of these questions in *From Jesus to Christ.*

My reading of the Corinthian correspondence in terms of social and political tensions depends in part on Peter Marshall, *Enmity in Corinth: Social Conventions in Paul's Relations with the Corinthians* (Tübingen: Mohr/Siebeck, 1987), John K. Chow, *Patronage and Power: A Study of Social Networks in Corinth* (Sheffield: JSOT Press, 1992), and Dale B. Martin, *The Corinthian Body* (New Haven: Yale University Press, 1995). I have profited much from Antoinette Clark Wire, *The Corinthian Women Prophets: A Reconstruction through Paul's Rhetoric* (Philadelphia: Fortress, 1990), though I do not share her assessment that the whole of the letter is directed to—and partly against—a strong group of women in the Corinthian church.

Mark Reasoner has provided crucial insights into the political context of the "weak" and "strong" language in Romans—and to my knowledge, introduced the notion of *Roman* "ethnocentrism" behind the letter—in *The Strong and the Weak: Romans 14.1–15.13 in Context* (Cambridge: Cambridge University Press, 1999). The character of this letter continues to vex interpreters. Karl P. Donfried's valuable collection of essays, *The Romans Debate,* appeared in a second, much-expanded edition almost a decade ago (Peabody, Mass.: Hendrickson, 1991), and much has happened since then. The approach along traditional theological categories (God, Anthropology, Soteriology) persists, notably in James D. G. Dunn's monumental *The Theology of Paul the Apostle* (Grand Rapids: Eerdmans; Cambridge: Cambridge University Press, 1998). This approach is seriously challenged from recent efforts to understand the letter in the context of Stoic, Cynic, and Augustan ideological currents: see Stanley K. Stowers, *A Rereading of Romans: Gentiles, Jews* (New Haven: Yale University Press, 1994), F. Gerald Downing, *Cynics, Paul, and the Pauline Churches* (London and New York: Routledge, 1998), and John L. White, *The Apostle of God* (Peabody, Mass.: Hendrickson, 1999).

The insight that from Romans 1:18 onward Paul is criticizing the ideological constructions of an unjust social order in light of the justice of God hails almost exclusively from Latin American interpretation: Juan Luis Segundo, *The Humanist Christology of Paul*, trans. John Drury (Maryknoll, N.Y.: Orbis, 1986); and José Miranda, *Marx and the Bible: A Critique of the Philosophy of Oppression*, trans. John Eagleson (Maryknoll, N.Y.: Orbis, 1974). As to specific contrasts with imperial propaganda, I have followed suggestions made by Dieter Georgi in an essay appearing in Horsley, *Paul and Empire* (see above) in a more extensive essay on Romans in *A Postcolonial Commentary on the Bible*, ed. R. S. Sugirtharajah (Sheffield: Sheffield Academic Press, forthcoming).

8

Deutero-Pauline Letters

Colossians, Ephesians, and the Pastoral Epistles

A. KATHERINE GRIEB

THE INTERPRETER OF COLOSSIANS, Ephesians, and the so-called Pastoral Epistles (1 and 2 Timothy, and Titus) immediately faces an important decision: What is the relationship of these Deutero-Pauline letters to the seven uncontested letters of Paul? Are they to be described primarily in terms of authorship, assessing their continuity (letters in the Pauline tradition) or discontinuity (letters that Paul did not write) with Paul's letters? Or should the question of authorship be minimized or bracketed entirely (by describing the Pastorals as letters to Paul's delegates)? After all (unlike some other New Testament texts), these letters were accepted and cited as Pauline by the early church and were accepted easily into the canon. They were not challenged by Luther. Only in the last several hundred years has their authenticity been questioned and the canonization process itself been studied with attention to the intersection of theology and politics. I write assuming that the authorship question is central to interpretation and that Paul (the historical first-century apostle and theologian) wrote none of these letters, although there may be fragments of Paul's writings in some of them and there are "Pauline" ideas in all of them. Ignatius of Antioch (writing about 110) knew Ephesians, which leads scholars to date both it and Colossians, on which it depends, anywhere from 70-100. The Pastoral Epistles may be even later (90-110?). They are all "post-Pauline," then, or "Pauline" in a secondary sense ("Deutero-Pauline").

The close relationship between the words "authorship" and "authority" suggests the next logical question: How shall we read these letters written in Paul's name and preserved in the church's canon largely because of their attribution to the apostle Paul? The historical and literary question becomes also a theological and political one. The term "pseudonymous" (literally "falsely named") is not helpful. It was common in antiquity to write in the name of another person; no deliberate deception need be assumed. For example, the sixth-century B.C.E. writer of so-called Second Isaiah wrote in the name of Isaiah, presumably to honor the great eighth-century B.C.E. Judean prophet Isaiah of Jerusalem and to suggest continuity between Isaiah's work and the writer's own. It is because there are interesting and important *differences* between them (as well as major similarities) that later readers wish to understand both writers more clearly by distinguishing between them. The assumption that Second Isaiah intended to continue the work of Isaiah does not excuse later readers from the task of assessing the extent to which they actually agree.

Something similar is true of the relationship between the apostle Paul, who wrote his letters between 50 and 58 C.E. and the later (70-110?) writers of Colossians, Ephesians, and the Pastorals, but with two additional complicating factors. First, as far as we know, Second Isaiah could write unhindered by theological disputes about what Isaiah had said and meant: we know of no rival schools of interpretation arguing among themselves about how Isaiah should be interpreted or competing to be identified as the rightful inheritors of the prophetic tradition associated with him. In Paul's case, things were (and still are) otherwise: Paul was problematic for the early church! Raymond Brown has shown that much of the New Testament was written to agree or disagree with Paul, or to correct some (mis)understanding of Paul. For example, the author of 2 Peter warns at the close of the letter:

> So also our beloved brother Paul wrote to you, according to the wisdom given him, speaking of this [eschatological holiness] as he does in all his letters. There are some things in them hard to understand, which the ignorant and unstable twist to their own destruction, as they do the other scriptures. (2 Pet. 3:15-16)

This later writer may himself be questioning the extent of Paul's wisdom. If not, he is clearly concerned to head off possible misunderstandings of Paul's letters, which are already being read as "Scriptures," sacred writings meant to instruct Christian communities. What Paul said and how it was interpreted evidently mattered greatly to this writer and to many others, both because Paul had been controversial and because his theology was highly respected. The tradition of Paul's martyrdom under the emperor Nero (about 64/65) only increased the weight of his influence.

Moreover, as 2 Peter concedes and as every student of Paul's letters knows well, "there are some things in them hard to understand." Paul's subtle and brilliant dialectical theology is in constant danger of being reduced to the level of the interpreter's understanding. Sometimes what Paul said was not difficult, but how he could say such an offensive thing (e.g., his comments about the Mosaic Law in Galatians) was hard for later writers (whose work also became "Scriptures") to understand. Finally, there are areas of Paul's thought that are genuinely ambiguous, such as his discussions of slavery and of women. Scholars still argue about whether in 1 Corinthians 7:21 Paul is urging slaves to gain their freedom if they can or advising them to make the most of their slavery. Probably the same confusion existed when the Deutero-Pauline letters were written.

Paul on the subject of women is even more complicated; he can logically be interpreted in several different ways. Dennis MacDonald has shown that very early there were rival schools of interpretation of Paul on just this point. The extracanonical *Acts of Paul and Thecla* portrays Paul as an evangelist preaching freedom in Christ for women as well as for men and urging unmarried women not to marry, but to become celibate disciples of Jesus. Thecla hears his preaching, abandons her fiancé, follows Paul, and finally dies a martyr's death. The radical Paul described here cares less about the order of the household (the basic social, political, and economic unit of Greco-Roman society) than about following Christ. This would have been highly problematic for conservative Christians trying to blend in with the surrounding culture. MacDonald argues that the Deutero-Pauline authors wrote precisely to counter this interpretation of Paul and to invalidate ideas about Paul as a promoter of powerful, independent women. Since only one side of the debate found its way into the Christian Bible, most readers are unaware of these other early traditions about Paul.

The second complicating factor is the "placement" of the Deutero-Pauline writings within the canon, the collection of early Christian sacred writings which became the New Testament. The Deutero-Pauline letters are not placed separately, but are blended with Paul's own letters. Because they were written in his name (each one begins by identifying the author as Paul, an apostle of Jesus Christ), their historical and political function of interpreting Paul to a later generation is hidden. The canonical structure itself reflects the custody fight over the body of Paul in the early church.

C. K. Barrett has identified three distinct strains of post-Pauline interpretation endorsed by the process of canonization: Luke-Acts, Colossians and Ephesians, and the Pastorals, respectively. Acts idealizes *Paul the missionary*, dividing early Christian history into two halves, represented by Peter and Paul. Because Acts precedes Paul's letters, before we hear a word from Paul himself, we are already programmed to see Paul in the framework of the missionary journeys described in Acts. The "Paul" of Acts is God's chosen instrument to move Christianity from Jerusalem to "the ends of the earth." This "Paul" is not the author of the controversial letters written by the historical Paul: his letters are not mentioned and Acts shows no knowledge of their contents. Paul the problem has been domesticated in favor of the Law-obedient "Paul" in harmony with the leadership of the Jerusalem church. Colossians and Ephesians honor *Paul the apostle*, who authoritatively addresses the church (built on the foundations of the prophets and the apostles [Eph 2:20]). The "Paul" of these letters idealizes the church, adapting the historical Paul's image of the body (1 Cor. 12; Rom. 12) and developing it into a corporate structure with Christ as Lord over his church body (Eph. 4:4-5), now personified as Christ's "bride," and even identified with the kingdom of God's Son. The Pastoral Epistles value *Paul the elder*, who advises and orders the community. The "Paul" of these letters writes from prison at the end of his career with pastoral advice for two younger pastors (Timothy and Titus) about the importance of church structure and the need to guard the church from false teachings.

Because it is crucial for the interpretation of both the historical Paul and his post-Pauline interpreters to distinguish their voices, I will follow the convention of referring to "Paul" when I speak of the implied authors of Colossians, Ephesians, and the Pastorals. This reminds us that although the self-presentation of these letters is that they are authored by Paul, the figure who speaks in them is not the historical apostle Paul but a literary construction of later writers for their own purposes. After summarizing the contents of each writing and describing its theological and ethical vision, I will raise some questions about these writings as a group and about issues of discipleship for Christians struggling with the apparent endorsement of slavery, patriarchal assumptions about women, and church structures modeled on the empire, which were a part of their worldview and are now a part of the Christian Bible.

THE LETTER TO THE COLOSSIANS

Colossians appears to be the earliest surviving letter written in the name of Paul, and therefore the first step in the creation of the literary "Paul" of the Deutero-Pauline letters. Colossians both underlines "Paul's" authority and reshapes his theological vision into terms more attractive to the later writer. This is particularly evident in the interrelated doctrines of Christ, salvation, last things, the church, and ethics.

Doctrine of Jesus Christ (Christology)

At the center of the worldview of Colossians is a christological controversy about whether what God has already accomplished through Christ has actually released believers from the powers and principalities of the cosmos and provided them with the necessary relationship to God. The author warns against an opposing point of view, a "philosophy and empty deceit" (2:8), which is threatening members of the church. "Paul" uses metaphors of light and darkness to describe God's work in Christ: believers "share in the inheritance of the saints in the light" because the Father "has rescued us from the power of darkness and transferred us into the kingdom of his beloved Son, in whom we have redemption, the forgiveness of sins" (1:12-14). The letter's clearest statements of Christology are found in a hymn about Christ (1:15-20) and a description of baptism into Christ (2:9-15).

The Christ hymn (1:15-20) uses traditions about the role of Wisdom at creation (Wis. 7:25-27) to describe the preeminence of Jesus Christ in the cosmos. He is the invisible God's image, the firstborn of creation, by whom all things were made and in whom all things hold together. As head of the church, he has preeminence in everything. "For in him all the fullness of God was pleased to dwell, and through him God was pleased to reconcile to himself all things, whether on earth or in heaven, by making peace through the blood of his cross" (1:19-20). This vivid and powerful imagery continues in the description of Christian baptism (2:9-15). "For in him the whole fullness of deity dwells bodily, and you have come to fullness in him, who is the head of every ruler and authority" (2:9-10). Baptism is redescribed as the circumcision of Christ, "who disarmed the rulers and authorities and made a public example of them, triumphing over them" in his cross (2:15). The cosmic victorious Christ has taken revenge upon all his enemies in the power of God. Gone is the "power that is made perfect in weakness" of which the historical Paul wrote. The "Paul" of Colossians substitutes the power of the imperial Christ.

Doctrine of Salvation (Soteriology)

Although the apostle Paul saw Sin as an enslaving power (Rom. 5:12; Gal. 3:22) that traps the unwary through the weakness of the flesh (Rom. 8:3) and the commandments of the Mosaic Law (Rom. 7:11-13), the "Paul" of Colossians stresses that through Christ there is "forgiveness of sins" in the sense of "trespasses" or "complaints" (1:14; 2:13; 3:13), an important conceptual shift that lowers the stakes of redemption considerably. And while Paul spoke of wisdom, especially the wisdom of the cross in 1 Corinthians 1-2, humanity's problem was not ignorance but slavery to the powers of Sin and Death. The continuous use of wisdom language in Colossians (1:9-10, 28; 2:2-3, 23; 3:10) reflects the christological controversy described above and this author's different assessment of the human situation. Since Christ is the one "in whom are hidden all the treasures of wisdom and knowledge" (2:3), "Paul" describes his own work as "warning everyone and teaching everyone in all wisdom, so that we may present everyone mature in Christ" (1:28). His wish for the church at Laodicea is "that they may have all the riches of assured understanding and have the knowledge of God's mystery, that is, Christ himself" (2:2). For the "Paul" of Colossians, the soteriological solution to the human predicament is more education: the community needs to be taught and their faith firmly established (2:5-7).

Doctrine of Last Things (Eschatology)

Paul (Rom. 6:3-5) speaks of baptism into the death of Christ and "walking in newness of life" through the power of the Holy Spirit, but speaks only of the hope of sharing in Christ's resurrection. Moreover, Paul speaks so consistently of salvation as a future event that it is common to speak of the "already" and the "not yet" held in tension in

Paul's theology. But in Colossians, the author's already realized eschatology allows "Paul" to say of believers that they have already died, been raised (2:12), and are even exalted with Christ (3:1-4). When Christ is revealed, believers "also will be revealed with him in glory" (3:4). There remains a "hope laid up for you in heaven" (1:5), but the clear stress is on presently realized life in Christ.

Doctrine of the Church (Ecclesiology)

Paul's metaphor of the body of Christ and its members (1 Cor. 12:12-27; Rom. 12:4-5) has been transformed significantly by the statement that Christ "is the head of the body, the church" (1:18). This change probably both reflects a more centralized and hierarchical ecclesial structure and reinforces that tendency. The apostle Paul usually applied the term *ekklēsia* to the local community (1 Cor. 1:2). The author of Colossians sometimes does that (4:15-16) but also has "Paul" speak of the church in universal or even cosmic terms (1:18, 24). When this idea is combined with that of Christ as the head of his ecclesial body, the church is no longer just one social assembly among many others, but ruler of the world. If Christ is the head of the church and the church is the created world, then Christ's lordship is the universal dominion of empire. An additional complication is the tendency in Colossians to stress the fatherhood of God (1:2; 1:12; 3:17) and Christ as the Father's Son (cf. "the kingdom of his beloved Son" [1:13]) suggesting dynastic succession and the *paterfamilias* (father as head of the family) model of church government familiar to early readers of this letter from the household, the basic social unit of the Roman empire.

Ethics

After warning about the dangers of "philosophy and empty deceit," which reflect human tradition and the assumption that power resides in "the elemental spirits of the universe" (2:8), the "Paul" of Colossians further warns: "Therefore, do not let anyone condemn you in matters of food and drink or of observing festivals, new moons, or sabbaths" (2:16), describing these required Jewish observances (Ezek. 45:17) as only a shadow of what is to come (the reality is Christ). "Do not let anyone disqualify you, insisting on self-abasement, and worship of angels, dwelling on visions . . ." (2:18). Here it is more difficult to see what behaviors are being opposed. It is unlikely that the Colossians worshiped angels; this probably refers to "worship of the kind angels do" or "worshiping with angels" (without more information it is hard to know precisely). For "Paul" these are all symptoms of "not holding fast to the head, from whom the whole body, nourished and held together by its ligaments and sinews, grows with a growth that is from God" (2:19). (The number of organic metaphors is striking in Colossians; see 1:6, 10; 2:7; and the references to maturity in 1:28 and 4:12.)

Also opposed are "regulations" ("Do not handle. Do not taste. Do not touch" [2:21]) which seem to reflect an asceticism (self-denial) that is unnecessary from "Paul's" point of view. He calls them "an appearance of wisdom in promoting self-imposed piety, humility, and severe treatment of the body," which "are of no value in checking self-indulgence" (2:23). If the same opponents are in view in each of these three descriptions of their teachings (2:8; 2:16-18; and 2:21-23), they may represent some syncretistic religion (a combination of ideas) loosely based on Judaism. Again, without a more precise description from the author, our best guesses (about what behaviors are being criticized and the reasons why they are being required by someone and opposed by "Paul") can remain only that.

With respect to positive injunctions, Colossians appears to be the earliest New Testament text to include a "household code" (3:18-4:1), the structure of exhortation that urges the obedient subordination of wives to husbands (two verses, 3:18-19), children to parents (two verses, 3:20-21), and especially slaves to masters (five verses, 3:22-4:1). Although the household code is the literary climax of the letter, nevertheless it takes the reader by surprise. Moreover, since the prescribed political arrangements are in the context of the holiness that results from new life in Christ, there is no suggestion that these arrangements are either negotiable or capable of change. This is truly surprising, given the logic of the discussion about baptism near the beginning of the section.

There "Paul" urges the community, now raised with Christ, to seek the things above (where Christ is), not the things on earth (3:1-2). They are to put to death earthly things within them. A vice list of impure passions (including greed, which is equated with idolatry), impure emotions, and impure speech follows (3:5-8). Then comes powerful language of baptismal liberation: "Do not lie to one another, seeing that you have stripped off the old self with its practices and have clothed yourselves with the new self, which is being renewed in knowledge according to the image of its creator. In that renewal, there is no longer

Greek and Jew, circumcised and uncircumcised, barbarian, Scythian, *slave and free*; but Christ is all and in all!" (3:9-11, emphasis mine). A list of virtuous practices follows: humility, patience, forgiveness, especially love, all of which build to a vision of the community, filled with the word of Christ, engaged in mutual admonition, singing grateful hymns of praise to God through Christ. "And whatever you do, in word or deed, do everything in the name of the Lord Jesus, giving thanks to God the Father through him" (3:12-17).

While the community is worshiping God and loving one another, then suddenly, in what looks like a rhetorical sleight of hand, comes the household code: "Wives, be subject to your husbands, as is fitting in the Lord. Husbands, love your wives and never treat them harshly. Children, obey your parents in everything. . . . Fathers, do not provoke your children. . . ." But a disproportionate majority of the code urges slaves to obey their masters, as if they were obeying the Lord Jesus Christ. At the end, masters are also urged to treat their slaves fairly, since both of them share a Master in heaven (3:18-4:1). Whatever the author speaking as "Paul" meant by "no longer slave and free" (words echoing Paul's own baptismal language in Gal. 3:28), no transformation of the prevailing social structures seems to have been intended. The section concludes with injunctions to prayer, including prayer for "Paul" in prison (a well-placed element of pathos that would have functioned to short-circuit any protest of injustice on the part of wives, children, or especially slaves), and an exhortation to gracious speech. The letter closes with news of "Paul" and his associates, an exchange of greetings, and one last emotional appeal: "I, Paul, write this greeting with my own hand. Remember my chains. Grace be with you" (4:18).

THE LETTER TO THE EPHESIANS

Although traditionally addressed to the saints in Ephesus (1:1), the absence of the words "in Ephesus" in the best ancient manuscripts has suggested to some scholars that Ephesians once functioned as a general letter intended for many different congregations or, much less likely, as a cover letter for a collection of Paul's letters. There are no clues in either Colossians or Ephesians about place of composition. Both letters reflect a situation where women's roles were diminished and where household relationships were once again accommodated to the wider culture.

The Fatherhood of God

Much of the discussion about Colossians applies also to Ephesians, which is almost certainly modeled on that earlier text. Its beginning is identical to that of Colossians except Timothy is absent, and "and the Lord Jesus Christ" is added to the expression of grace and peace from God the Father. The fatherhood of God is even more pronounced in Ephesians (1:2, 3, 17; 2:18; 3:14 and 15, where the word translated "family" in NRSV is literally "fatherhood" 4:6; 5:20; 6:23 and 6:4, which refers to human fathers in the household, imitating the fatherhood of God at the level of the cosmic household). Church members are addressed as "citizens of the saints and members of the household of God" (2:19), a phrase that expresses precisely the political theology of Ephesians. "Paul" bows the knee "before the Father from whom every fatherhood in heaven and on earth takes its name" (3:14-15), so that in Ephesians (in contrast to Colossians) the household code (5:21-6:4), once again the rhetorical climax of the letter, does not surprise the attentive reader. Although the same subtle move from communal worship to household ethic in Colossians reappears in Ephesians, it is not entirely unexpected from what has come before.

The Unity of the Church

Part of that preparation is "Paul's" stress on "the will of God" (1:5, 9, 11; 5:17; 6:6), on the predestined plan of God (1:4-5, 10-11), and on the unity of the church, expressed in powerful (almost liturgical) language near the beginning of the section on proper Christian behavior: "There is one body and one Spirit, just as you were called to the one hope of your calling, one Lord, one faith, one baptism, one God and Father of all, who is above all and through all and in all" (4:4-6).

An important aspect of church unity in Ephesians is the reconciliation of Jews and Gentiles in Christ. The author has "Paul" speak as part of a group of Jewish Christians ("we who were the first to set our hope on Christ" [1:12]) to the Gentile recipients of the letter ("you also, when you had heard the word of truth, the gospel of your salvation" [1:13]). They are directly addressed as Gentiles twice more: first to be reminded that before God's action in Christ they were "without Christ, being aliens from the commonwealth of Israel, and strangers to the

covenants of promise, having no hope and without God in the world"
(2:12); second, to be exhorted not to live like Gentiles anymore ("you
must no longer live as the Gentiles live, in the futility of their minds"
[4:17]). The unity of Jews and Gentiles is the work of God in Christ on
the cross:

> For he is our peace; in his flesh he has made both groups into one
> and has broken down the dividing wall, that is, the hostility
> between us. He has abolished the law with its commandments and
> ordinances, that he might create in himself one new humanity in
> place of the two, thus making peace, and might reconcile both
> groups to God in one body through the cross. (2:14-16)

The author subtly interweaves language of mutuality ("he has made
both groups into one," "reconcile both groups to God in one body")
with a narrative of Gentile inclusion that stresses their total inadequacy
(compared to Israel) before God's reconciling action in Christ ("aliens,"
"strangers," "having no hope and without God"). He also suggests that
the reconciliation of the two groups is like the marriage of a man and
a woman ("one new humanity in place of the two") echoing Genesis
2:24 ("the two will become one flesh").

Simultaneously, the author has "Paul" make derogatory claims
about Israel that it is difficult to attribute to the historical Paul subsequent to the composition of Romans, his mature and most thorough
treatment of the subject. After telling the Gentile hearers, "You were
dead through your trespasses and sins in which you once lived, following the course of this world, following the ruler of the power of the air,
the spirit that is now at work among those who are disobedient"
(2:1-2), the author has "Paul" make a surprising statement about Jewish Christians: "All of us once lived among them in the passions of our
flesh, following the desires of flesh and senses, and *we were by nature
children of wrath*, like everyone else" (2:3, emphasis mine). Similarly,
the author's description of the work of Christ ("He has abolished the
law with its commandments and ordinances" [2:15]) is harsher than
anything the historical Paul ever said about Israel's Torah, even in the
polemical context of Galatians.

This language stands in some tension with the author's apparent
rhetorical strategy of comparing the Gentiles unfavorably with the people of Israel. Possibly it reflects a later period when the issues of the
temporal priority (1:12) and covenant privileges of membership in the

commonwealth of Israel (2:12) are still remembered from the time of
the historical Paul, but when the (now entirely?) Gentile church no
longer recognizes its indebtedness to the rich traditions and high ethical
standards of Israel. Alternatively, as Kittredge has suggested, language
about the unity of Jews and Gentiles does not reflect a historical situation concerned with that issue at all, but functions rhetorically to set up
the language about the subordination of slaves, and especially wives, in
the household code by comparing it to the remembered symbol of Jew-
ish/Gentile unity. In any event, after 3:13 discussion of the unity of Jews
and Gentiles virtually disappears, suggesting that it is not the author's
primary concern with respect to church unity.

The unity of the church is related to the exaltation of Jesus Christ
over the powers (as in Col. 1:16-18). Ephesians speaks of the "great
power" of God (1:19) which is manifested in the cosmic imperial
Christ:

> God put this power to work in Christ when he raised him from the
> dead and seated him at his right hand in the heavenly places, far
> above all rule and authority and power and dominion, and above
> every name that is to be named, not only in this age but also in the
> age to come. And he has put all things under his feet and has made
> him the *head* over all things for the church, which is his body, the
> fullness of him who fills all in all. (1:20-23, emphasis mine)

The Headship of Christ

The unity of the church is also tied to the "headship" of Christ, part
of God's predestined plan for the fullness of time, that he should "head
up" all things in himself (1:10; the NRSV translation "gather up"
obscures the author's patriarchal logic). Moreover, the headship of
Christ functions as the standard and goal of Christian growth, "until all
of us come to the unity of the faith and of the knowledge of the Son of
God, to mature manhood, to the measure of the full stature of Christ"
(4:13; the NRSV obscures the androcentric language by translating
"mature manhood" as "maturity"). Ephesians develops organic growth
metaphors from Colossians to relate Christian love and Christian unity:

> But speaking the truth in love, we must grow up in every way into
> him who is the head, into Christ, from whom the whole body,

joined and knit together by every ligament with which it is equipped, as each part is working properly, promotes the body's growth in building itself up in love. (4:15-16)

Finally, the headship of Christ is the dominant theme of the household code: "Wives, be subject to your husbands as you are to the Lord. For the husband is the head of the wife just as Christ is the head of the church, the body of which he is the Savior. Just as the church is subject to Christ, so also wives ought to be, in everything, to their husbands" (5:22-24).

If Colossians was particularly interested in the subjection of slaves to masters, Ephesians is primarily concerned with the subjection of wives to husbands. Indeed, in Colossians, "Paul" sends greetings "to Nympha and the church in her house" (Col. 4:15). Nympha, the only woman mentioned in Colossians, may be mentioned precisely because she is the head of a house church there or in nearby Laodicea. That no women are named in Ephesians tells us little since "Paul" mentions only one person, Tychicus in 6:21 (another reason why it is extremely unlikely that Paul wrote Ephesians; he knew many people in Ephesus). But the intended rhetorical audience of the household code is clearly men: "Each of you, however, should love his wife as himself, and a wife should respect her husband" (5:33).

The same rhetorical move used earlier to describe the unity of Jews and Gentiles reappears here to describe the unity of husbands and wives in Christian marriage. (For an alternative reading that contrasts the rhetoric of these two passages, see Kittredge.) The stated language of mutuality in 5:21 ("Be subject to one another out of reverence for Christ") is subtly but entirely subverted when it is combined with an analogy between the husband's headship of the wife and Christ's headship of the church, together with a narrative description of the total inadequacy of the church before the action of God in Christ:

Husbands, love your wives, just as Christ loved the church and gave himself up for her, in order to make her holy by cleansing her with the washing of water by the word, so as to present the church to himself in splendor, without a spot or wrinkle or anything of the kind—yes, so that she may be holy and without blemish. (5:25-27)

The analogy is underlined by the (explicit this time) quotation of Genesis 2:24, "For this reason, a man will leave his father and mother and be joined to his wife and the two will become one flesh," which the author describes as "a great mystery, and I am applying it to Christ and the church" (5:32). Unlike 1 Peter 3:1, 5-6, where wives are commanded to obey their husbands for the pragmatic purpose of winning Gentiles (and the example cited is Sarah's obedience to Abraham), Ephesians warrants the command christologically: the obedience of wives to husbands is grounded in the ontology (structure of being) of the body to the head, identified with the church's obedience to Christ.

The subjection of wives to husbands is the author's primary interest in Ephesians, but the other two pairs mentioned in Colossians are also exhorted: children must obey their parents; fathers must not provoke their children to anger; slaves must obey their earthly masters "with fear and trembling, in singleness of heart, as you obey Christ" (6:5) and masters must stop threatening them, "for you know that both of you have the same Master in heaven, and with him there is no partiality" (6:9). Ephesians ends with an extended metaphor exhorting the entire community to "put on the whole armor of God" to withstand the spiritual forces of evil, and with injunctions to pray, including prayers for Paul, "an ambassador in chains" (6:20). Once again (as in Colossians), the powerfully moving portrait of "Paul" in prison is the rhetorical capital behind commandments to one half of the community to subject themselves to the other half for the sake of Christian unity.

THE LETTERS TO TIMOTHY AND TITUS

Since the eighteenth century, the two letters to Timothy and the letter to Titus have been called the "Pastoral Epistles" because their stated purpose (at the surface level of the texts) is encouragement and instruction for Paul's delegates, who look to him as a mentor. They fit the standard Greco-Roman paraenetic letter form, giving practical advice and offering an example for imitation. The literary authority of the elderly "Paul" writing to his younger pastor-disciples is particularly enhanced by the convention of framing this advice letter from prison as his "last will and testament," final instructions for the community before his martyrdom. This is less pronounced in 1 Timothy and Titus, where "Paul" still travels freely, but 2 Timothy describes "Paul" as near death, having completed his work: "The time of my departure has come. I have fought the good fight, I have finished the race, I have kept the faith. From now on there is reserved for me the crown of righteousness"

(2 Tim. 4:6-8). Today's readers will appreciate the force of this rhetorical move: just as we value the last words of our loved ones and our final conversations with those who have taught us, so early readers of these letters would have been deeply moved by the portrait of an aged apostle passing on precious tradition to a younger successor shortly before his death.

The distance from "Paul" (far away, in prison, close to death) in the letters simplifies for contemporary readers a shift in interpretation from the time of "Paul" to the present time. Already in the text, "Timothy" and "Titus" have become symbols of general church leadership, at least for male readers of the text, who are invited to identify with them as they carry on "the good fight" that Paul, now imprisoned and close to martyrdom, will no longer be able to do. For women readers, that task is complicated by "Paul's" evident hostility to women and his recommendations about how to disable (or at least control) women church leaders, who are evidently much too powerful in the mind of the writer. Women readers can read "as men" for at least part of the time in the Pastorals, but since the patriarchal household provides the controlling metaphor for the church and its leadership, and since the letters focus on the apparently problematic situation of women in leadership (1 Tim. 2:8-15; 5:3-16; 2 Tim. 3:6-7; Titus 1:11; 2:3-5), many women will inevitably find themselves in the role of "resisting readers."

Personal Piety

The clearly stated themes of these three letters are personal piety ("godliness"), sound teaching, stable church order, and good works. Timothy and Titus are encouraged to continue in their preaching and teaching in spite of opposition, following the example of "Paul," who commissioned them: "Let no one despise your youth, but set the believers an example in speech and conduct, in love, in faith, in purity" (1 Tim. 4:12). "But as for you, man of God, shun all this; pursue righteousness, godliness, faith, love, endurance, gentleness. Fight the good fight of the faith; take hold of the eternal life, to which you were called" (1 Tim. 6:11-12). "Do your best to present yourself to God as one approved by him, a worker who has no need to be ashamed, rightly explaining the word of truth" (2 Tim. 2:15). Further examples abound, but these give the tenor of "Paul's" counsel to his young pastoral associates.

Sound Teaching

Timothy and Titus are especially encouraged to promote "sound doctrine" and to refute various teachers of false doctrine, some of whom "Paul" names, while others are categorized in the stock language used to describe opponents during this period. Timothy is "to instruct certain people not to teach any different doctrine and not to occupy themselves with myths and endless genealogies that promote speculations" (1 Tim. 1:3-4). A long list of vices (1 Tim. 1:9-11) concludes with "whatever else is contrary to the sound teaching that conforms to the glorious gospel," while opponents are defined as "whoever teaches otherwise and does not agree with the sound words of our Lord Jesus Christ" (1 Tim. 6:3). Timothy is urged: "Hold to the standard of sound teaching that you heard from me, . . . guard the good treasure entrusted to you" (2 Tim. 1:13-14), while Titus is charged: "But as for you, teach what is consistent with sound doctrine" (Titus 2:1).

Church Order

Sound doctrine will be promoted by sound organizational structures led by carefully approved people with appropriate virtues:

> Now a bishop/overseer must be above reproach, the husband of one wife [Gk; NRSV: "married only once"], temperate, sensible, respectable, hospitable, an apt teacher, not a drunkard, not violent but gentle, not quarrelsome, and not a lover of money. He must manage his household well, keeping his children submissive and respectful in every way—for if someone does not manage his own household, how can he take care of God's church? (1 Tim. 3:2-5)

Similar descriptions are given for other officeholders: deacons, elders, and "widows who are really widows" (as opposed to the widows who are causing trouble for the author). Women's leadership is almost completely excluded and is usually described as problematic for the community. The author's low opinion of women in general is no secret in these letters (1 Tim. 2:11-15; 5:11-15; 2 Tim. 3:6-7; Titus 2:3-5), although Timothy's mother and grandmother are singled out as exceptions to the rule (2 Tim. 1:5). The household code in Titus 2:3-10 urges the submissiveness of younger women and slaves in particular.

Good Works

The author has "Paul" write to Timothy "so that if I am delayed, you may know how to behave in the household of God" (1 Tim. 3:15). Women are to be dressed "with good works" (1 Tim. 2:10); for a "widow" to be enrolled, "she must be well attested for her good works, as one who has brought up children, shown hospitality, washed the saints' feet, helped the afflicted, and devoted herself to doing good in every way" (1 Tim. 5:10). The rich "are to do good, to be rich in good works, generous and ready to share" (1 Tim. 6:18). Everyone is "to live lives that are self-controlled, upright, and godly," since God needs "a people of his own who are zealous for good deeds" (Titus 2:12, 14). "Remind them to be subject to rulers and authorities, to be obedient, to be ready for every good work" (Titus 3:1). "Insist on these things, so that those who have come to believe in God may be careful to devote themselves to good works" (Titus 3:8).

SO NOW WHAT? RECOMMENDATIONS FOR INTERPRETING THE DEUTERO-PAULINE EPISTLES

We all read from a point of view: as a Paul scholar, church reformer, and evangelical feminist, I struggle with these texts written in Paul's name. As I suggested with respect to Isaiah of Jerusalem and Second Isaiah, even assuming the best intentions of the later writer to complement the thought of the earlier prophet does not excuse subsequent readers from the task of assessing how well the prophetic mantle (or in this case the apostolic mantle) is being worn. Regarding Paul and the Deutero-Paulines, the ideas of the historical apostle Paul have been taken in a markedly conservative direction that has been very costly to the subordinate members of the households they prescribe. Because of their canonical placement among the genuine letters of Paul, the convention of reading them as if they were Paul's letters has been so widely followed, and the line between Paul and "Paul" has become so blurred that even the genuine letters of Paul have not been available for church reform, because they are read through the conservatism of the Deutero-Paulines.

Colossians and Ephesians are both theologically sophisticated developments of Pauline theology toward an imperial cosmic Christology, a realized eschatology, a centralized and hierarchical church under the headship of Christ, and an ethics based on the household codes of the surrounding culture. Because of these tendencies, they lent themselves nicely to the political theology of Augustine, which supported the Constantinian arrangement with the empire that the church enjoyed from the fourth century onwards. The same tendencies often still promote an increasingly triumphalist understanding of the church, one which assumes that reform is unnecessary and disparages local churches in favor of the universal "mother church" coextensive with the empire and the cosmos. There is little incentive for self-critique and little support for the less powerful members of the institution from whom the gift of reforming anger might come.

It is more difficult to credit the author(s) of the Pastoral Epistles with theological sophistication: they consistently flatten Paul's most important theological concepts into simplistic and predictable moralism. One contemporary Pauline scholar quips that if Paul wrote the Pastorals he had a lobotomy first! They reflect a process of formalization of church structures and an overwhelming concern for the guarantee of stability. God's people *do* need structures and standards (forms of doctrine to defend against error, organizational structures to do the work of the church, ethical standards to guide Christian life). Nevertheless, the prophetic role of the church is almost eclipsed in these writings. The communities prescribed in these letters seem entirely safe from the wildfire of the Holy Spirit of God.

It helps me to remember that these same scriptures that are "difficult texts" for me (texts that challenge my ability to read them with generosity and patience) are sources of comfort and inspiration to my conservative brothers (especially) and sisters in Christ "for whom Christ died" (Rom. 14:15). This is true, for example, of many Christians in the United States, particularly in the South and the Midwest, and of many Christians in Great Britain and Europe, where the Bible (and particularly Paul) is read more traditionally. It is also true of the rapidly growing Pentecostal churches of Africa, where conservative church teachings mesh easily with local traditions that ascribe witchcraft to women, particularly to older women, who would otherwise be natural leaders. At the same time, a circle of African women theologians is calling not only African Christians but all of us to reread these texts in the light of their social and political consequences for women and for others who have been marginalized by their use. They are joined by women and men from every continent, who rightly challenge us to find ways of reading Colossians, Ephesians, and the Pastoral Epistles that do not continue to do harm.

In preserving both the letters of the historical Paul and the

Deutero-Pauline epistles, the church's tradition holds together strong disagreements that are still unresolved at present. I am called, as an interpreter of the New Testament *for the church*, to honor that tension and to stay in conversation with others, precious in the sight of God, with whom I disagree. I am also called to stay "in conversation" with these ancient writers, who either read the historical Paul very differently than I do, or, as I think, were so troubled by Paul that they found it necessary to correct his theology at several points (particularly his political theology) by writing other letters in his name. In light of the decisions they made then, it is an occasion for thanksgiving that many in the church today are *not* so frightened by Paul's liberating gospel and are eager to recover the voice of the apostle Paul, in addition to the voices of those who sought to "improve" his theology to conform to the surrounding culture. An interpreter's decision to read Paul and the Deutero-Paulines separately (and comparatively) allows the church to choose among canonical options for ordering its life together with greater clarity. It respects the tradition represented by the Deutero-Pauline letters by critiquing it from within that same tradition of interpreting Paul. This interpretive strategy is one way of "loving the neighbor" when that neighbor is a text that has brought about tremendous hardship, for great numbers of people, over a very long period of time.

RESOURCES FOR FURTHER STUDY

Barrett, C. K. "Pauline Controversies in the Post-Pauline Period," *NTS* 20 (1973-74): 229-45.

Bassler, Jouette M. "1 Timothy, 2 Timothy, Titus." In *HarperCollins Study Bible,* ed. Wayne A. Meeks. New York: HarperCollins, 1993.

Beker, J. Christiaan. *Heirs of Paul: Paul's Legacy in the New Testament and in the Church Today.* Minneapolis: Fortress, 1991.

Brown, Raymond E. *The Churches the Apostles Left Behind.* New York: Paulist, 1984.

———. *An Introduction to the New Testament.* New York: Doubleday, 1997.

Collins, Raymond F. *Letters That Paul Did Not Write.* Good News Studies. Wilmington, Del.: Michael Glazier, 1988.

Johnson, Luke T. *Letters to Paul's Delegates: 1 Timothy, 2 Timothy, Titus.* Valley Forge, Pa.: Trinity Press International, 1996.

———. *The Writings of the New Testament.* Philadelphia: Fortress, 1986.

Kittredge, Cynthia Briggs. *Community and Authority: The Rhetoric of Obedi-*

ence in the Pauline Tradition. Harrisburg, Pa.: Trinity Press International, 1998.

Lincoln, Andrew T. *Ephesians.* Word Biblical Commentary 42. Dallas: Word, 1990.

Lohse, Edward. *Colossians and Philemon.* Trans. W. R. Poehlmann and R. J. Karris. Hermeneia. Philadelphia: Fortress, 1971.

MacDonald, Dennis. R. *The Legend and the Apostle: The Battle for Paul in Story and Canon.* Philadelphia: Westminster, 1983.

Martin, Clarice J. "The Haustafeln (Household Codes) in African American Biblical Interpretation: 'Free Slaves' and 'Subordinate Women.'" In *Stony the Road We Trod: African American Biblical Interpretation,* ed. C. H. Felder, 203-31. Minneapolis: Fortress, 1991.

Meeks, Wayne A., ed. *HarperCollins Study Bible.* New York: HarperCollins, 1993.

Newsom, Carol A., and Sharon H. Ringe, eds. *The Women's Bible Commentary.* Louisville: Westminster/John Knox, 1998.

Redding, Ann Holmes. "Together, Not Equal: The Rhetoric of Hierarchy and Unity in Ephesians." Forthcoming, Union Theological Seminary.

Sampley, J. Paul. "Colossians, Ephesians." In *HarperCollins Study Bible,* ed. Wayne A. Meeks. New York: HarperCollins, 1993.

Schüssler Fiorenza, Elisabeth, ed. *Searching the Scriptures.* Volume 2, *A Feminist Commentary.* New York: Crossroad, 1994.

Stockhausen, Carol L., *Letters in the Pauline Tradition: Ephesians, Colossians, I Timothy, II Timothy and Titus.* Wilmington, Del.: Michael Glazier, 1989.

9

Catholic Epistles

Hebrews, James, 1 Peter, 2 Peter, Jude

A. Katherine Grieb

Introduction to the Writings as a Group

THE TERMS "GENERAL" and "Catholic Epistles" often used to describe the writings in this chapter (Hebrews, James, 1 and 2 Peter, Jude) are catchall categories that obscure the rich diversity of these texts. At first, this looks like the "everything else" section of the New Testament. A closer examination, however, reveals the strikingly distinctive features of these writings. Hebrews is a profound reflection on the pastoral implications of the humanity and divinity of Jesus Christ, comparable to Romans in its rhetorical and theological use of the scriptures. James makes one of the strongest statements anywhere in the Bible of the need to be single-minded with respect to the things of God and to pay attention to coherence between speech and action. First Peter addresses the complex situation of communities in Asia Minor weighing their Christian commitments with their desire to accommodate themselves to the culture around them. Jude and 2 Peter mount a strong defense of Christian identity and distinctiveness in the context of a permissive pagan society.

These writings resist efforts to group them in a single category, whether as to contents, authorship, or genre. Unlike the Deutero-Pauline letters, they do not share attribution to an apostolic author (since Hebrews, properly speaking is anonymous, not pseudonymous). And, while each of them has at least some epistolary features, neither

James nor Hebrews fits easily into the genre of letter. The writings are sometimes labeled "Catholic" because of their alleged connection to "early Catholicism" (a hypothetical construct that once seemed useful to Protestant scholars, but now is increasingly suspect) or because they are not attributed to Paul, who was assumed to be the quintessential Protestant (by the same scholars). They were called "general" or "catholic" (universal) by the Eastern Church because they seemed to address more than one community or even the church universal, but this is not obviously true for Hebrews, Jude, or 2 Peter, nor is it clear whether the "general" language at the beginning of James and 1 Peter describes the addressees or is being used metaphorically. So I place no interpretive weight on the category "catholic epistles" but discuss the texts individually, except for Jude and 2 Peter, since 2 Peter is dependent on Jude literarily. After reviewing matters of authorship, place, date, genre, and reception, since (unlike the Deutero-Paulines) each of these writings has had a checkered career in the life of the church, and briefly summarizing the argument or concerns of these authors, I will comment very briefly on what is at stake in interpreting them today.

The Letter to the Hebrews

Authorship and Reception

Like its own description of Melchizedek, Hebrews appears in the New Testament canon "without father or mother or genealogy" (Heb. 7:3), but with all the brilliance and sharpness of a finely cut diamond. Hebrews does not identify its author, and while it shares certain themes with Paul and was attributed to Paul in some early canonical lists, Tertullian and other ancients (especially those at Rome) knew it was not Pauline, as the present canonical order shows. This caused difficulties for its canonical acceptance, but Hebrews (especially 1:3) proved so valuable in the orthodox defense of Christ's full divinity against the Arians during the trinitarian controversies that Rome was finally persuaded about 400 to accept it as the fourteenth letter of the apostle. However, the issue of authorship remained far from settled. Tertullian thought Barnabas wrote it. Origen thought Luke might have translated it, but finally confessed that "only God knows" who wrote it. The Greek of Hebrews is highly sophisticated, with complex sentences composed of balanced, rhythmic cadences, and with rhetorical embellishments such as repetition and alliteration to delight the ear. Its style is clearly not Johannine, even if its magnificent beginning resembles John's Prologue. Luther (who rejected the book [German Bible, 1522]) proposed Apollos as its author, based on the description of him in Acts 18:24-28. More recently, Adolf von Harnack suggested Paul's co-worker Prisca (Priscilla in Acts). Whoever the author was, he or she was well trained in rhetoric, at home in the world of Plato and Greek philosophy, a gifted scholar of the Scriptures of Israel (like Philo of Alexandria) and familiar with a variety of interpretive strategies for crafting a powerful homiletical argument.

Addressees

The audience for Hebrews must have been educated Christians (Heb. 6:1-3) who knew their Scriptures well, or the complexity of the argument would have overwhelmed them. There are a few clues about their social situation: they have experienced some suffering or at least some of them had been imprisoned and had had their property confiscated (10:34), but they had not yet suffered to the point of death (12:4). The author worries that they are discouraged (hope and faith are major themes of Hebrews) and undergoing temptation (2:18) to renounce their Christian commitment (12:16-17). In the author's view, they do not appreciate the dangers of apostasy (denying the faith under pressure [6:4-6; 12:17]) but have become "sluggish and dull of hearing" (5:11) with "drooping hands and weak knees" (12:12). This does not suggest a context of present active persecution of Christians, but instead recalls past trials and appears to expect more.

Place and Date

The only geographical or chronological clues found in Hebrews itself are the closing greetings of "those from Italy" (13:24), which suggests Rome as the location of the addressees. External evidence supports Rome (1 Clement, written from Rome about 95 C.E., quotes Hebrews extensively). Any date between the death and resurrection of Jesus (about 30 C.E.) and 95 is theoretically possible. Scholars argue about whether to date Hebrews before or after the destruction of the temple at Jerusalem in 70 C.E. To some extent, this is a misplaced debate, since the author focuses not on the details of the temple but on those of Israel's tabernacle or tent in the wilderness. Nevertheless, Hebrews does describe sacrifices that are still going on daily (8:3; 9:7; 13:11), and, while that situation is not impossible after the destruction of the temple, a date after 70 is unlikely. Moreover, given the role of the sacrificial system in the author's argument, it is difficult to imagine that the destruction of the temple would not have been mentioned if it had been known.

Genre

Even the genre of Hebrews is widely debated. The canonical title "The Letter to the Hebrews" was almost certainly not original, but added later. Despite its early date (about 200 C.E.), it is a description based on the contents (the author's extensive use of Scripture and interest in Israel's sacrificial system) and the epistolary ending. Its compressed and highly alliterative prologue and the precision of its argument have led some to classify it as a treatise. Harold Attridge calls it an "epideictic oration, celebrating the significance of Christ." Hebrews calls itself a "word of exhortation" (13:22), or sermon (see Acts 13:15 for a synagogue sermon by Paul that is also called a "word of exhortation"). Today some distinguish between a homily (tied to the biblical text) and a sermon (more topical), but this distinction does not work for Hebrews, which both quotes extensively from biblical texts and has Jesus Christ as its primary subject.

The Argument of Hebrews

In the context of "the last days," Hebrews 1:1-3 asserts the superiority of Jesus Christ over all that has gone before in Israel by contrasting two divine revelations: one by the prophets and the other by a preexistent Son through whom God also created the world (reflecting Israel's wisdom tradition; see Wis. 7:25-27; Prov. 8:22-31). This "high" Christology is worked out in the first major section of the argument (1:4-4:13) by demonstrating the superiority of the Son over angels (1:4-2:18) and Moses (3:1-4:11), followed by a meditation on the power of God's word (4:12-13, another Wisdom motif; see Wis. 7:23; Isa. 55:10-11).

The superiority of the Son over angels is demonstrated in a chain of seven biblical quotations (1:5-14) matching the descriptions of the Son in the introduction (1:1-3). Within the argument, God speaks to the Son (in words never spoken to an angel) through Psalm 45:6-8 (Heb. 1:8-9), addressing him as God, one of the very few New Testament texts where Jesus is called God. Moral exhortation follows (2:1-4) in a warning to heed the great salvation declared by the Lord and "attested to us by those who heard him" (2:3), locating the author in the generation after the first disciples of Jesus. Then follows a description of Jesus as the representative human described in Psalm 8 (2:9), the pioneer of human salvation through his suffering (2:10), and one who had to become human in every respect "so that he might become a merciful and faithful high priest" (2:17) to atone for the sins of the people. Because he was tested by what he suffered, he is able to help those who are being tested now (2:18). The author carefully underlines the pastoral significance of the incarnation for the community.

The superiority of the Son over Moses (3:1-4:11) is demonstrated by contrasting Moses, who was faithful in God's house as a servant, with Jesus "the apostle and high priest of our confession" (3:1), who was faithful over God's house as a Son (3:1-6). Again, christological reflection leads to moral exhortation, as a homily based on Psalm 95 warns the community not to be disobedient like the generation who wandered in the wilderness and failed to enter God's rest (3:7-4:7). The author puns on the names Jesus and Joshua (identical in Greek) to argue that there still exists a Sabbath rest for the faithful people of God and urges the community to enter into that rest (4:8-11). There follows (4:12-14) the justly famous description of the word of God "as living and active, sharper than any two-edged sword," able to discern reflections and thoughts of the heart.

The next section of the argument shows the superiority of Jesus' priesthood over the levitical priesthood (4:14-7:28). Hebrews 4:14-16 restates the theme: we have a great high priest who has passed through the heavens to the presence of God, having become fully human and being tempted in every way as we are, yet without sin, so that in him we may approach the throne of God with boldness to seek mercy. Like the high priest of Israel, Jesus was chosen by God, as shown in the royal coronation psalms (5:1-6). In a bold move, the author redescribes Jesus' prayers to God and obedient suffering before his death as the process of his consecration "as a high priest after the order of Melchizedek" (Ps. 110:4; Heb. 5:7-10). Exhortation follows, warning about the dangers of apostasy and the impossibility of subsequent restoration to the community (5:11-6:8). The author then expresses confidence that they will persist in "hope" (following the example of Abraham, who patiently endured), a hope that enters the inner shrine behind the curtain where Jesus has gone on our behalf, "a high priest forever after the order of Melchizedek" (6:9-20).

After these several "teasers" about Melchizedek, the author devotes 7:1-28 to midrashic expansion on the story of Abraham's meeting with Melchizedek (Gen. 14:17-20), artfully playing with the meaning of his name and office to demonstrate that he is both "king of righteousness" and "king of peace," a worthy type of Christ. Since Abraham paid a tithe to Melchizedek (and, figuratively speaking, Levi of many generations later was already "in the loins of Abraham"), then in principle Levi also paid a tithe to Melchizedek, showing that the priesthood of Jesus (after the order of Melchizedek) is superior to the levitical priesthood. This superiority is reinforced by a Platonic argument about "the one and the many": many levitical priests making many sacrifices for sins do not compare with the one high priest chosen by God to make a sacrifice once for all in his death on the cross.

The superiority of Jesus' sacrifice in the heavenly tabernacle (the new covenant) over the sacrifices of the levitical priests in the earthly tabernacle (the old covenant) is the theme of the argument's next section (8:1-10:18). Meditation about Jesus as a high priest before God leads the author to reflect on the heavenly sanctuary. Exodus 25:9, 40; 26:30 tells how God showed Moses the heavenly model after which the earthly tabernacle was built (Heb. 8:2-7). The Platonic view of reality, in which the form (idea) of a thing is more real than the copy (instance) of it, reinforces Exodus 25-26. Since the levitical priests serve only the earthly shadow (copy) of the heavenly sanctuary, Jesus' heavenly ministry is superior to theirs, just as he mediates a new covenant (Jer. 31:31-34) superior to the covenant with Moses, which is now "old" and passing away (8:13). A detailed comparison of Jesus' death as an atoning sacrifice (9:5; see also Rom. 3:25) and the ritual for the Day of Atonement (Yom Kippur) carried out in Israel's tabernacle (Lev. 16) follows. Hebrews contrasts the high priests of Israel, who went into the Holy of Holies every year with the blood of bulls and goats, with Jesus, who went "once for all time" into the heavenly sanctuary with his own blood (9:11-12). Having offered himself once to bear the sins of many, he will appear a second time to save those eagerly waiting for him (9:28). Hebrews 10:1-18 underlines the point, stressing that God prefers a single act of obedience to multiple sacrifices. Psalm 40:7-8 describes the obedience of Jesus: "Behold, I have come to do your will," spoken by the Son to God (10:5-9). Since Jesus' one obedient sacrifice has permanently atoned for the sins of the sanctified, they no longer need to offer sacrifices for sin.

The argument's next section calls the community to faith and endurance by imitation of Jesus and participation in his priesthood (10:19-12:29). Through the way opened by Jesus' blood, the community should enter the sanctuary with faith, hope, and love, meeting together as they await the Day of the Lord (10:19-25). More exhortation warns them that to sin deliberately is to risk judgment: "It is a fearful thing to fall into the hands of the living God!" (10:26-31). This severe warning is balanced by the author's expressed confidence in them: they are not "those who shrink back" but God's righteous ones who live by faith (Hab. 2:4), as they proved by enduring a hard struggle with sufferings previously (10:32-39).

Since they still "need endurance" (10:36), Hebrews provides the famous definition of faith as "the assurance of things hoped for, the conviction of things not seen" (11:1), and retells the stories of faithful men and women of Israel's past who demonstrated faithfulness (11:2-40; see Sir. 44). After a powerful summary of the sufferings of Israel's martyrs, the author stresses that none of these faithful ancestors received what was promised, because God is bringing to perfection all of the past in the community's own time of the last days (1:1), after they themselves endure suffering (11:39-40). The climax of the series of exemplary faithful ancestors is, of course, Jesus. "Surrounded by so great a cloud of witnesses" the community is to keep their eyes on him, "who endured the cross, despising its shame" and is now at God's right hand (of power), lest they grow weary during persecution (12:1-3). The mystery of suffering is redescribed as divine discipline (12:4-13; see comments below). Exhortation to pursue peace, holiness, and God's grace follows. Esau, who sold his birthright for a meal and later had no chance to repent and inherit his blessing, is featured as a negative example (12:14-17). The wilderness generation (afraid to approach Mount Sinai to hear God's word to Moses) is contrasted to this generation, invited to Mount Zion, to hear the gracious word of Jesus (10:18-24). They dare not refuse, however, since no one escapes the One warning from heaven: "Our God is a consuming fire" (Deut. 4:24; Heb. 10:25-29).

The final exhortation (13:1-19) and conclusion (13:20-25) provide a rhetorically satisfying end to the argument. Here moral exhortation includes specific recommendations for hospitality, solidarity with the persecuted, sexual holiness, economic contentment, support of and obedience to leaders, sound doctrine, regular worship, sharing of possessions, and prayer that the author too will act honorably in all things (13:1-19). Once again, as throughout Hebrews, the exhortation's center is christological reflection. "Jesus Christ is the same yesterday, today, and forever" (13:8) warrants remembering those who spoke the word of God to the community and imitating their faithfulness. Jesus' suffering "outside the city gate" mandates going outside the community and being willing to bear the abuse he endured (13:12-13). "For here we have no lasting city, but we are looking for the city that is to come" (13:14) recalls the contrast between the heavenly tabernacle and its earthly shadow, and between the temporary (including suffering) and the eternal (God's reality). The exhortation closes with a prayer that "the God of peace who brought again from the dead our Lord Jesus" will perfect the community in holiness. The author shares news of Timothy, sends greetings to their leaders and to the community from those in Italy, and prays for God's grace upon them all (13:20-25).

Interpreting Hebrews Today

Hebrews is widely neglected by today's church, less familiar with the Old Testament, especially the specific elements on which Hebrews' argument depends: Melchizedek, the levitical priesthood and sacrifices, the wilderness tabernacle, and the Day of Atonement. Hebrews' Platonic worldview is equally foreign. Rejecting Greek philosophy, modernity identifies reality with materiality or physicality. With respect to Hebrews' challenge to endure suffering, the persecuted church in Sudan has an interpretive advantage over the academy, which tends to focus more on aspects of Hebrews that have been abused. There are some: Hebrews 12 has been misread to glorify suffering, warrant child abuse, and perpetuate the patriarchal idea of an illegitimate child. These misreadings often mistake its description for prescription. Hebrews neither endorses suffering nor recommends it, but redescribes experienced persecution and feared suffering in theological terms, using the familiar analogy of parental discipline of children to suggest a way of trusting God in the midst of otherwise meaningless pain. Israel's prophets had already wrestled with the problem of God's justice in the midst of personal suffering (Jer. 15:15-18; 20:7-18) and Job (6:4) complains that God is using him for target practice! In our own century, Dietrich Bonhoeffer wrote, from a concentration camp, of learning how to take the bitter cup of suffering from God's good hand.

Hebrews is often called anti-Jewish because of its new covenant language and its use of negative examples from Israel's past. But Hebrews uses many positive historical examples (see chap. 11): the new covenant comes directly from Jeremiah, and privileging one's own way of being Jewish over everyone else's was common among Second Temple Judaisms, as the Dead Sea Scrolls attest. Was the Qumran community anti-Jewish? The horrors of the Tremendum (Holocaust) rightly cause Christians to reflect deeply about both our Bible and our biblical interpretation. We still have much work to do, both confessing past sins and reforming present practices. Any part of the church that (unlike Hebrews) no longer understands itself as part of Israel will have difficulty with the argument of Hebrews. But if (with Hebrews) we understand ourselves as the part of Israel that believes Jesus is the Messiah (Christ), then we will continue to talk (and sometimes to argue) with Jews about theological truth claims and the interpretation of Scripture. We do that best by confessing our past sins and repentance of them, then by stating the differences between us honestly, while we work for agreement wherever possible. Most of us would not do that exactly as Hebrews did, but Hebrews is not anti-Jewish for that reason. In short, Hebrews is too valuable to be dismissed. These are some of the most powerful words ever written about Jesus Christ: they were meant to be preached.

The Letter of James

Authorship, Date, Place, Genre

Traditionally the "James" of 1:1 has been identified with "James, the Lord's brother" (Gal. 1:19), head of the Jerusalem church (Acts 15:13; 21:18), who was martyred shortly before the Jewish War of 66-70 C.E. (Josephus, *Antiquities* 20.9.1). Features of James suggesting but not requiring an early date and Palestinian location include Jewish symbols (twelve tribes, 1:1; firstfruits, 1:18; synagogue, 2:2; *Shema* 2:19); the patriarchs as moral examples; esteem for the law (1:25; 2:8-12; 4:11-12); and interest in Jesus' teachings. James (Greek for Jacob) was a common name (in the New Testament alone several other people are named James). Moreover, James the Lord's brother was so respected that others wrote in his name to honor him and to claim his authority (*Protoevangelium of James, Apocryphon of James* and two apocalypses). It is not necessary to decide for a date after the circulation of Paul's letters, and, therefore, for pseudonymity. We may never know, since the author describes himself only as "a servant (slave) of God and of the Lord Jesus Christ" (1:1). The epistolary aspect of James consists of its greeting "to the twelve tribes of the Diaspora" (1:1), which probably refers to the readers' self-identification with Israel, not their ethnic background. Not a treatise or sermon (like Hebrews), James is well described as Christian wisdom literature. Its pattern of short sayings and commands mixed with longer exhortations resembles the discourse form of Jesus' Sermon on the Mount and the teaching aphorisms of Proverbs, Sirach, and Wisdom.

Reception by the Church

James was accepted relatively late by the church because of early doubts about its apostolic origins, although its powerful moral exhortation was greatly valued. During the Protestant Reformation Luther rejected it as "a right strawy epistle," compared to the "chief proper books" (German Bible, 1522). Luther disliked James because he thought it conflicted with Paul's teaching on faith righteousness (in 2:14-26) and because of its "low" Christology (doctrine of Christ). Since then, James has been studied largely as a foil to Paul, a tradition already begun by the *Pseudo-Clementines* (fourth century, from sources dating to 150-220?). This interpretive strategy usually reduces its significance to a few often misunderstood verses. More recently, partly because of William Stringfellow, Elsa Tamez, and Pedrito Maynard-Reid, James has come into its own as one of the most socially conscious books of the Bible.

The Wisdom of James

James is not a sustained argument but a discourse on topics of moral exhortation that concern him and his community: trials and temptations, not showing partiality to the rich, matching words with deeds, wealth and poverty, keeping the whole law, faith leading to works, the powerful tongue, the Wisdom from above versus human wisdom, desire as a cause of war, judging one another, patience in suffering, faithful prayer until the coming of the Lord. James warns consistently against double-mindedness (4:8), which includes praying while doubting God's word and power (1:6-8), saying one thing and doing another (2:1; hypocrisy in 3:17), expressing concern but not following through with action (2:14-17; 4:17), and blessing and cursing with the same mouth (3:9-12). James describes a rigorous and demanding ethic. He wants doers of the word, not just hearers (1:22-25) or judges (4:11-12); the whole law is to be kept, not just some of it (2:8-12); teachers will be judged with greater strictness (3:1); friendship with the world is adultery and enmity with God (4:4); there should be no swearing (5:12). The author does not suffer fools gladly (4:13-16) or put up with spiritual nonsense (1:13-16). On the other hand, James provides real help in times of trial (1:2-4), in temptation (1:12, 4:7-8), in suffering and sickness (5:13-15), in conviction of sin (5:15-20), and in prayer (5:7-11).

James is written to and for the poor (2:1-7) with words the rich should also overhear (1:9-11; 4:1-10; 5:1-6). John Elliott suggests that the reference to the Disapora in 1:1 suggests "transience" and the situation of "refugees" living somewhere only temporarily. This would explain James's particular concern for the marginalized and most vulnerable members of society: day laborers and migrant workers (5:1-12), orphans and widows (1:27), those without food and shelter (2:15). The examples James chooses as models of faith are interesting in this regard: Abraham (2:21) was called to leave home and go somewhere God would show him; Rahab (2:25) was a Canaanite who identified with Israel; Job (5:11) was marginalized by his suffering and afflicted by his friends; Elijah (5:17) was alone in the wilderness and pursued by Ahab and Jezebel; the prophets (5:10) experienced trials, persecution, and martyrdom; "the righteous one" (5:6) may refer to Jesus (cf. Acts 3:14; 7:52) or to the righteous suffering ones of the Psalms (e.g., Ps. 140:12-13; Wis. 2:12-20). All of them were vulnerable and in need of both God's integrity, which James assumes (1:5, 17-18; 2:19; 4:8), and the church's support, which he commands.

Interpreting James Today

Unlike Hebrews, most of what James says is clear even at first reading, and it is brief, which makes it invaluable for Bible study in most contemporary churches. James sounds a powerful call to make Christian faith consistent with the practice of justice. His sensitivity to the economically marginalized and the vulnerable, his insistence that words of love issue in works of mercy, his analysis of the relationship between greed and military action, will all be challenging to wealthy Christians (most of us: as I write this, the per capita income in Haiti or in Ethiopia is one dollar a day), who may be tempted to follow Luther. James also has wisdom for anyone tempted to reduce Christianity to progressive social and political reforms and therefore to dismiss conservative Christianity. His loyalty to the teachings of Jesus and love for the law, his warnings about judging others, blessing God and cursing God's children with the same tongue, his stress on long-suffering patience and faithful prayer, and his concern for the whole community call us to reconsider our own commitment to Christ (2:1). James is a demanding spiritual director, and there are few Christians who would not benefit from some honest introspective hours spent with him.

THE FIRST LETTER OF PETER

Authorship, Date, Place, Genre, Reception

This writing sounds as much like Paul as it does like James, yet it claims to come from Peter (1:1). It was probably written by a disciple of Peter, from Rome, sometime after his martyrdom there under Nero about 64/65 C.E. Because 1 Peter is cited by or known to several early-second-century witnesses (2 Pet. 3:1, Polycarp, Papias) a date before 100 C.E. is likely. Other internal evidence suggesting Rome as its origin is the mention of "Babylon" in 5:12-14 (see Rev. 17:1, 5), a name used for Rome after the Roman destruction of the temple in Jerusalem in 70 C.E. Since there is no hint of the official persecution of Christians in Asia Minor which occurred in the 90s, a date between 70 and 90 is reasonable. First Peter's addressees are the elect "exiles of the Diaspora" in named districts (Pontus, Galatia, Cappadocia, Asia, Bithynia) of northern Asia Minor (1:1-2). It was probably an actual letter (it has standard epistolary features), meant to circulate, not universally but to more than one community. The odd sequence (geographically speaking) may represent the delivery route (as in Rev. 2-3). Its place in the canon owes much to its attribution to Peter, which was not challenged in the first centuries. But, since other writings also attributed to Peter (the *Gospel of Peter, Apocalypse of Peter*) remain extracanonical, the quality of 1 Peter itself seems also to have been appreciated by the early church.

The Argument of First Peter

First Peter is written in excellent Greek, using a rich vocabulary and quotations from Scripture to support its carefully crafted argument. After the initial greeting, the author uses a blessing (1:3-12) instead of the more familiar thanksgiving paragraph. A baptismal homily based on Psalm 34 probably forms the basis of the argument in 1:3-4:11, followed by a conclusion (4:12-5:14) restating the homily's major themes. Baptismal language appears in 3:18-22. Alternatively, Raymond Brown suggests that between the initial greeting (1:1-2) and the closing (5:12-14) are three sections dealing with Christian identity and dignity (1:3-2:10), Christian conduct among pagans (2:11-3:12), and Christian conduct in the face of harassment (3:13-5:11). Other structural divisions are also possible: one of the characteristics of 1 Peter's style is the skillful use of connectives blending separate sections of the argument into a seamless whole.

The argument is powerful: after reminding the addressees of their participation in Israel's story and blessings, using imagery from the exodus from Egypt, the first Passover, the Sinai covenant, and the wilderness wanderings, 1 Peter calls on the community to manifest their distinctiveness from the dominant pagan culture of the Roman empire. Using a combination of biblical texts with the common theme "stone," 1 Peter describes Jesus Christ as the stone rejected by the builders (Ps. 118:22) over which others stumble (Isa. 8:14) but which Christians trust as the precious cornerstone (Isa. 28:16). They are to come to that "living stone" and, like living stones themselves, be built into a spiritual house (2:4-8). As God's chosen people (1:2; 2:9-10) called out of darkness into God's marvelous light (2:9), they are to be holy as God is holy (1:13-16), renouncing their former religious beliefs and immoral behavior (1:18; 4:3-4). But the envisioned social distinctiveness of living as God's elect among pagans would also be costly to them. The extent to which 1 Peter urges it is seriously called into question by the author's use of the household code (2:13-3:7) to describe the behaviors which constitute that holiness appropriate to Christians.

Roman society was thoroughly patriarchal. Its primary social structure, the hierarchical household, expressed core social and philosophical values (Aristotle, *Politics* 1.2.1-2), which included the subordination of wives, slaves, and children to their husbands, masters, and fathers. (Versions of the household code appear also in Colossians, Ephesians, and the Pastorals; see the chapter on Deutero-Pauline letters). Suspicions about "foreign religions" included fears that they would overturn traditional hierarchical patterns and cause women to rebel (Cicero, *Laws* 2.14-15). Since Romans expected foreign religions to cause sexual immorality, disobedience within households, and sedition against government, 1 Peter stresses sexual modesty and holiness for women (3:2-4), obedience of wives to husbands (3:1-6), subjection of slaves even to unjust masters who abuse them (2:18-25; see 1:14 for a word on obedient children) and subjection of the whole community to governing institutions (2:13-17).

Unlike Colossians and Ephesians, where the household code functions as the rhetorical climax of each letter, and where the realized eschatology of the texts requires subordination as the very structure of new life in Christ (Eph. 5:22-24), in 1 Peter household subordination is not an end in itself but a means to the greater end of living in peace with pagan neighbors, as the code's introduction shows (2:11-12). By contrast, the rhetorical climax of 1 Peter features tribulations of the coming end-time and the need for the community, including its leaders, to behave appropriately during the expected ordeal. The style of the arguments is also different. Unlike the powerful christological warrant of Ephesians, the argument here rests on the example of Sarah's obedience to Abraham. Missing are the appeals to pathos, (the apostle Paul in chains [Col. 4:18; Eph. 6:20]) and the rhetorical cunning that introduces the household code while the community has its eyes closed in prayer (Col. 3:16ff.; Eph. 5:18ff.). By contrast, 1 Peter's straightforward and pragmatic argument follows logically from the combination of the community's role as a chosen people and their situation of suspicious pagan neighbors.

A major theme of 1 Peter is the nonretaliation of the community, in imitation of Christ, to acts of aggression inflicted on them by pagan outsiders. Its opening verses describe obedience to Jesus Christ as being sprinkled with his blood and link new birth with his resurrection (1:1-3). His community, which suffers trials (1:6), loves him without seeing him (1:8), knowing that his sufferings were predestined (1:11) and that they have been ransomed with his blood (1:19). Therefore the author exhorts them (2:11) "for the Lord's sake" (2:13) to be subject to human institutions. Slaves (the community members most likely to suffer physical abuse) are urged to endure unjust suffering because Christ suffered for them. His refusal to return abuse when he was abused is recommended as a model of trusting God's justice in the midst of absurd pain (2:20-25). The entire community (3:9) is urged not to repay evil for evil or abuse for abuse. They are not to be afraid, but to be ready to explain their faith with gentleness and to endure suffering if it should be God's will, "because Christ also suffered" and was raised from the dead (3:14-18). Therefore (4:1) they should also trust God, knowing that their persecutors will have to answer to God, who judges the living and the dead (4:5). Those reviled for the name of Christ, who suffer "in a Christian way" are blessed (4:14-19). The author has "Peter" assure

them that he witnessed the sufferings of Christ (5:1) and reminds them
that Christians everywhere are undergoing similar sufferings, which are
temporary and which God will end soon (5:10).

Interpreting 1 Peter Today

First Peter does not share James's view (4:4) that friendship with the
world is enmity with God and results in an adulterated or double-
minded faith. This letter tries to balance Christian morality with strategies for assimilating to the dominant pagan society, including adopting
its household code wholesale and stressing nonretaliation for slander
and physical abuse. The author describes an ethic "shared" by Greco-
Roman pagans and Christians, hoping that Gentile neighbors will glorify God because of the Christians' honorable deeds (2:12). Yet this
extremely optimistic view is tempered by realism that persecution from
these same pagan neighbors cannot be entirely avoided.

If the logic of Ephesians raises the question of what price should be
paid for church unity, that of 1 Peter raises the question of what price
should be paid for peace with pagan cultures, especially if it is unlikely
that the cost will achieve peace. Israel's prophets warned that peace
depends on justice (Isa. 32:17) and truth (Zech. 8:16) and warned
about false prophets who say "peace" when there is no peace (Jer. 6:14;
8:11; Ezek. 13:10, 16). In the shared tradition of Matthew and Luke,
Jesus denied coming to bring peace exactly at the point of the household (Matt. 10:34; Luke 12:51) and instructed disciples to pronounce
peace only upon households worthy of peace (Matt. 10:13; Luke 10:5-
6), while the Johannine Jesus promises peace not as the world gives
(14:27). Christians are clearly called to peaceful nonretaliation in imitation of Christ. Are they also called to withhold peace from structures
of injustice, even at the risk of incurring suffering? Christians in the
United States civil rights and South African anti-apartheid movements,
and the Confessing Church in Germany thought so. Some of them paid
with their lives for a truthful peace based on justice.

THE SECOND LETTER OF PETER AND THE LETTER OF JUDE

Authorship, Date, Place, Genre, Reception

The letter attributed to Jude, a brother of Jesus (Mark 6:3) is difficult to date. A few scholars assign it to Jude himself, locating it in the
50s from Palestine, in which case it is one of the earliest Christian writ-

ings. Many others think it is pseudonymous (written in Jude's name) and date it around 90-100, possibly from Alexandria. It takes the form of a polemical letter. Already by the early second century it was copied by 2 Peter. By about 200, it was acknowledged as Scripture in both the West (Muratorian Fragment, Tertullian) and the East (Clement of Alexandria). Origen himself liked it but noted that others rejected it, probably because of its use of apocryphal texts (*1 Enoch, Testament of Moses*) and other nonbiblical traditions. Finally, by 400, it was accepted into the canons of the West and the Greek-speaking East. Syriac-speaking churches accepted it in the sixth century. At the Protestant Reformation, Luther rejected it (German Bible, 1522) along with James, Hebrews, and Revelation. There has been no continued debate about Jude, which has been considered theologically unimportant and has had minimal impact on the church.

Second Peter presents itself as Peter's "last will and testament" (1:12-15), a summary of his teaching as he wanted it remembered after his death (about 64/65), but most scholars believe its origin from Rome (about 90-110) explains its attribution to the apostle associated with Rome. Almost everyone thinks the author of 2 Peter used Jude's Letter, adapting its material for his own purposes. It is probably the latest writing in the Christian canon. Of the twenty-seven canonical books, 2 Peter had the least support in antiquity. Unknown or ignored in the West until about 350 (Jerome rejected it because of stylistic differences from 1 Peter), in the East Origen noted disputes about it and Eusebius did not accept it as canonical. Nevertheless, by the early sixth century, it was accepted by the Latin, Greek, and Syriac churches. Unlike Jude, 2 Peter survived Luther's scrutiny, but as recently as the twentieth century the Lutheran scholar Ernst Käsemann attacked it as his parade example of intolerant, repressive "early Catholicism," leading some to press for its excision from the canon. Käsemann's argument has been criticized on two grounds: first, whether his assessment of 2 Peter as a product of "early Catholicism" is sound; second, whether any interpreter(s) may delete from the Bible books that oppose their own theological positions. This argument has led to more interest in 2 Peter than might be expected and to considerable debate about the history, role, and function of the canon among Orthodox, Protestant, Roman Catholic, and other theologians.

The Argument of Second Peter and Jude

The reference to Balaam (Num. 25:1-4; 31:16), the false prophet who led Israel astray by giving bad advice (Jude 11; 2 Pet. 2:15-16) provides an important contextual clue to the logic of these letters. The authors assume that since idolatry always leads to sexual immorality (see also Wis. 12-13), those who are urging Christians to act like their pagan neighbors in sexual affairs must be false prophets like Balaam. Jude "finds it necessary to write" (3) to warn the church about church leaders who claim that their visionary revelations release them and their followers (and all truly spiritual people) from external moral authority (8) and who demonstrate their Christian freedom in sexual immorality (7). Jude describes them as intruders who have stolen in among them and who are to be condemned as ungodly, since they pervert God's grace into licentiousness (4). He is eloquent in his anger, describing the opponents as "reefs" (12) upon which the church's ship will break apart, waterless clouds, wild waves of the sea, wandering stars (12-13), comparing them to the fallen angels, whom God chained in deepest darkness (6), and to the cities of Sodom and Gomorrah, which God destroyed with eternal fire (7). "They are grumblers and malcontents; they indulge their own lusts, they are bombastic in speech, flattering people to their own advantage" (16). "It is these wordly people, devoid of the Spirit, who are causing divisions" (19).

Over against their dangerous message, Jude insists that Christian faith is inseparable from moral obedience to Christ. His purpose is to urge his readers "to contend for the faith" (3) by living out the gospel in faith, hope, and love (20-21). They are to have mercy on those who are wavering "by snatching them out of the fire" and to have mercy on the others "by hating even the tunic defiled by their bodies" (23). Presumably this language refers to refusing to get anywhere near the opponents and their followers.

The author of 2 Peter builds his argument on the logic of Jude's letter. It seems probable that his first readers knew that Peter was dead, and that the literary convention of writing in the name of a famous apostle was the author's way of expressing the normative value of apostolic teaching after the death of the apostolic generation. The pastoral situation described in 2 Peter is apparently the opposite of that described in 1 Peter, where pagans were fearful that Christian immorality would destroy their culture. Here it is the higher ethical standards of Christianity that are a problem for the church, distancing it from the more permissive pagan society and calling attention to its distinctiveness. In 2 Peter, as in Jude, the opponents are portrayed as arguing that Christians are free from moral constraints. In addition, 2 Peter applies the language about "scoffers" from Jude 18 directly to the problem of the delayed *parousia* (the second coming of Jesus Christ) and to "scoffers" who say, "Where is the promise of his coming?" (3:3-4). The author has some answers for them: they laughed at Noah, too, when he warned about the flood (3:5-7); God operates with a different timetable (3:8); and postponement of judgment is God's act of mercy to allow repentance (3:9). "But the day of the Lord will come," when the earth and all of its contents will be destroyed by fire (3:10).

Interpreting 2 Peter and Jude Today

The delay of the *parousia* still worries many Christians: almost two thousand years have passed since the early church expected the immediate return of Jesus. There are also still "scoffers" who use this apparent contradiction to disqualify the entire Christian gospel. The arguments of 2 Peter are actually quite sophisticated when considered carefully. They point, in three different ways, to the great abyss (the infinitely qualitative difference) that separates God's ways from our ways: God's actions are unpredictable from human experience and knowledge; God cannot be limited by human concepts of time and space; and God's mysterious mercy is incredible to humanity, which consistently tries to shape God in its own unmerciful image. We learn much from 2 Peter's reflections on the relationship between eschatology (the doctrine of last things) and ethics.

Jude's use of extracanonical literature has posed an unnecessary theological problem for Christians with a wooden theory of inspiration, who assume that the author of an "inspired" writing was supposed to know which other writings were also inspired. (Or the reverse: since the text of Jude quoted nonbiblical texts and traditions and Jude was inspired, these other writings must also be inspired.) Either way, the logic is dubious. A better position recognizes the work of the Spirit in the writers and in their readers, both ancient, as in the process of canonization, and contemporary ("Fresh light shall yet break forth from God's Word," as John Robinson wrote in his hymn) rather than locating "inspiration" in the text as if it were some property of the text, like being blue or glowing in the dark.

Origen found Jude "packed with sound words of heavenly grace," and Richard Bauckham argues that Jude's advice about his opponents "combines a realistic sense of the danger they pose to his readers with a pastoral concern for their salvation." But the highly polemical language used by the author to describe his enemies challenges many of us today, who find Jude and 2 Peter at best negative, at worst reactionary.

How do we deal with biblical texts we don't like? Or, since the authors of these texts were Christians (like most of the readers of this book), how do we relate to other Christians we don't like? These early writers chose one strategy. Perhaps we can learn from the history of the reception of Jude and 2 Peter that polemical words do not serve the church over the long run as well as constructive criticism and positive exhortation of the kind that James gives. However, I would deny that there is never a time to condemn the idolatrous lies of the contemporary culture. Could we imitate the passion of these writers, if not their polemics, to combat the materialism, consumerism, and militarism around us and within us? Because of the difficulty of understanding their allusions and their tone, they are rarely studied, but they do show us how some church authorities responded to apparent dangers as Christians began to divide from within. If we reject their polemics, they also challenge us to do better in our own day.

RESOURCES FOR FURTHER STUDY

Attridge, Harold W. *The Epistle to the Hebrews.* Hermeneia. Philadelphia: Fortress, 1989.

———. "Hebrews." In *HarperCollins Study Bible,* ed. Wayne A. Meeks. New York: HarperCollins, 1993.

Balch, David L. *Let Wives Be Submissive: The Domestic Code in First Peter.* SBL Monograph Series 26. Chico, Calif.: Scholars Press, 1981.

———. "1 Peter." In *HarperCollins Study Bible,* ed. Wayne A. Meeks. New York: HarperCollins, 1993.

Bauckham, Richard J. *Jude, 2 Peter.* Word Biblical Commentary 50. Waco: Word, 1983.

———. "2 Peter, Jude." In *HarperCollins Study Bible,* ed. Wayne A. Meeks. New York: HarperCollins, 1993.

Brown, Raymond E. *An Introduction to the New Testament.* Anchor Bible. New York: Doubleday, 1997.

Elliott, J. H. *A Home for the Homeless: A Social Scientific Criticism of 1 Peter, Its Situation and Strategy.* Minneapolis: Fortress, 1990.

Meeks, Wayne A., ed. *HarperCollins Study Bible* New York: HarperCollins, 1993.

Johnson, Luke T. *James.* Anchor Bible. New York: Doubleday, 1995.

———. *The Writings of the New Testament.* Philadelphia: Fortress, 1986.

Lane, William L. *Hebrews.* 2 volumes. Word Biblical Commentary 47. Dallas: Word, 1991.

Laws, Sophie. *A Commentary on the Epistle of James.* Harper's New Testament Commentaries. San Francisco: Harper & Row, 1980.

————. "James." In *HarperCollins Study Bible,* ed. Wayne A. Meeks. New York: HarperCollins, 1993.

Maynard-Reid, Pedrito U. *Poverty and Wealth in James.* Maryknoll, N.Y.: Orbis, 1987.

Newsom, Carol A., and Sharon H. Ringe, eds. *The Women's Bible Commentary.* Louisville: Westminster/John Knox, 1998.

Schüssler Fiorenza, Elisabeth, ed. *Searching the Scriptures.* Volume 2, *A Feminist Commentary.* New York: Crossroad, 1994.

Stringfellow, William. *Count It All Joy.* Grand Rapids: Eerdmans, 1967.

Tamez, Elsa. *The Scandalous Message of James: Faith without Works Is Dead.* Trans. J. Eagleson. New York: Crossroad, 1990.

10

Revelation

Claiming the Victory Jesus Won over Empire

WES HOWARD-BROOK

BLUEPRINT FOR THE END?

"MY NEIGHBOR TELLS ME that the book of Revelation says that before Jesus returns, believers will be raptured but everyone else will suffer under a one world government run by the Antichrist? What do you think?"

In teaching adult Bible study classes in Catholic and mainline Protestant congregations, I have often received questions like this. Ever since the incredibly popular book by Hal Lindsey in the 1970s, *The Late, Great Planet Earth,* many Americans and others have "discovered" the branch of Christianity known formally as "premillennialism" (meaning that the "Rapture"—the literal "lifting up" of believers from the earth—would take place *before* the thousand-year reign of Christ) but sometimes referred to by its practitioners as "prophecy studies." One of the results of this phenomenon has been to polarize people's reactions to Revelation more than to any other biblical text. Response has been divided into several camps. The most vocal are those who occupy themselves with various end-of-the-world scenarios developed by taking biblical verses out of their contexts and trying to "apply" them to current world events. At the other end are those who see such efforts as silly at best and dangerous at worst, and throw out the baby with the bathwater by seeing Revelation itself as the problem. Another response is taken by mainstream academic biblical scholars, who tend to study Revelation in its original context but without taking seriously its claims to visionary experience or ongoing prophetic power.

Yet the questions that drive people to "biblical prophecy" remain, and Revelation continues to be a source of potential answers to basic aspects of the human struggle. The basis for its answers, however, is not the provision of a "blueprint" for the imminent end of the world but an "apocalyptic" perspective on the always-ongoing *now* of human existence. Revelation was not meant to be a "code" requiring deciphering, but a powerful, poetic expression of a visionary perspective on God's battle against what it calls "the great city," and which we might call "empire" (Rev. 11:8; 16:19; 17:18; etc.). If its imagery seems confusing or overwhelming to us, it is likely because of two factors. First, most people these days are unfamiliar with the historical tradition of visionary literature—both in and out of the Bible—of which Revelation is but one example. Second, Revelation's message is nothing less than the bringing forward of *all* of biblical tradition, expressed through the complex mosaic of scriptural allusions which comprise both its plot and its imagery. The more one becomes familiar with the rest of the Bible, the more transparent Revelation's own story becomes. As one's familiarity with these traditions grows, Revelation's goal becomes ever clearer: to call followers of Jesus who have become comfortable with the privileges and products of empire to "come out" and to live instead in the Holy City, New Jerusalem, where the church is to have its home.

What Is "Apocalyptic" Literature?

The word "apocalyptic" is used today by secular media to refer to wars, earthquakes, and other kinds of powerful, violent events. But at its root, it has nothing to do with violence at all. The word comes from the Greek *apokalyptō*, meaning "to lift the veil." Apocalyptic literature, then, purports to lift the veil that blinds us to the truth of our social and religious situation.

There are two aspects of apocalyptic, the *mystical* and the *political*. The mystical aspect starts from the recognition that for all of the powers God has given humanity, our ability to perceive reality remains finite. In other words, there is more to life than meets the eye—or the ear. No matter how smart or astute we may be, we cannot on our own look at the world with God's perspective. But from time to time, certain people have been given the gift of such a perspective. Such an experience is not given, however, simply for the personal joy of the mystic, but on behalf of the struggling community of faith of which the mystic is a part. The apocalyptic seer's historical mission was, like the prophets, to speak a word of divine truth amidst competing human claims to authority.

The second aspect was the political task of stripping away illusions generated by empire which seduced and threatened God's people into submission. In our world, we are confronted by such seductions daily by advertising and global corporate-owned media reports of "the news." Such experiences are not unique to our time and place. God's people have constantly been harassed by empire's assaults throughout biblical memory. The apocalyptic visionary used his or her experience to "unveil" empire's lies and to remind people what living according to God's own ways was like.

Some scholars have suggested that apocalyptic is a "last resort" for those who have "given up" on politics. If by "politics," one means putting one's trust in the power of human empire, this is certainly true. But in the wider sense, there were no writers in the ancient world more vitally concerned with social relationships than the apocalypticists. Because they had experienced God's perspective on reality, they were able more clearly to see the demonic nature of much of what claimed to have divine legitimacy. Rather than being a "last resort," apocalyptic literature provided the most powerful means available to convince people that God was vitally concerned with the daily lives of those oppressed by empire.

The struggle between God's ways and those of empire is expressed throughout the Bible, from the building of the first city by Cain in Genesis 4, through the exodus from Egypt and Israel's own monarchical empire, and out the other end into Babylonian exile. But the roots of apocalyptic were planted during the time after exile.

The Bible reports the wrenching pain of Judah's elite as their world was destroyed by Babylon, and they were forcibly marched from their homeland into exile. But we must remember that this experience affected only a small percentage of people calling themselves "Israelites." The large majority of people were peasant farmers who had been forced by debt into becoming day laborers and slaves to the elite. *Their* experience of the Babylonian invasion was not exile but its opposite: *jubilee!* For with the destruction of the Jerusalem temple, the debt records were also destroyed, enabling the people to return to their ancestral land. For over fifty years (from 587 to 532 B.C.E.), these peasants lived in peace. But with the toppling of Babylon's empire by Persia, the former Jerusalem elite were allowed to return, not as free people but as colonial subjects of the new empire. The claims of the returnees to restored power were met with bitter resentment by the peasants, whose land and children were again threatened by the arrogance of the world's powerful. The elite's version of events was reported in the books of Ezra and Nehemiah, as supported by the "prophet" Haggai. The key to their program is expressed in the Persian king's decree: "All who will not obey *the law of your God and the law of the king*, let judgment be strictly executed on them, whether for death or for banishment or for confiscation of their goods or for imprisonment" (Ezra 7:26, emphasis added).

But this program of dual allegiance to God and empire was not accepted by all. A voice on behalf of the oppressed poor rose up in opposition, whose words are recorded in Isaiah 56-66. In traditional prophetic style, he blasts those who would treat the poor among God's people as fodder for the imperial project of rebuilding Jerusalem and its strategically important temple. In place of this sellout, "Third Isaiah," as he is known to scholars, promises that God is again proclaiming jubilee, a time in which even strangers and foreigners who love God's ways will be welcomed into the land (Isa. 61). As a matter of worldly politics, Isaiah was a "failure." The colonial deal held. But Isaiah did not respond with despair. Instead, his prophetic vision foresaw a time when God would "create new heavens and a new earth; the former things shall not be remembered or come to mind. But be glad and rejoice forever in what I am creating; for I am about to create Jerusalem as a joy, and its people as a delight" (Isa. 65:17-18). This vision was not quite "apocalyptic." That is, it envisioned a *future* time in which God would wipe the slate free from empire's authority and restore God's exclusive reign. Its rhetoric is similar to Martin Luther King's vision in our own time of a day in which people would be judged by the content of their character rather than the color of their skin. It expressed hope and trust, but still saw God's reign as future-oriented.

But the seeds planted in this struggle began to bear fruit as God's people experienced further waves of imperial authority. Persia gave way to the Greek empire of Alexander the Great in 332 B.C.E., which in turn split into the northern Seleucid empire (centered in Syria) and the southern Ptolemaic empire (centered in Egypt). The Bible contains an amazing record of competing perspectives within Israel toward this Hellenistic rule. On the one hand were those who accepted Greek cultural values and sought to convince their fellow Israelites that there was no need to remain stubbornly isolated. On the other hand were those who saw such an accommodation as a sellout of the covenant that called God's people to a different way of life. We see this battle in the first book of Maccabees, which begins with the question of voluntary participation in the Seleucid-controlled culture. But as the book continues, the Seleucid king, Antiochus IV Epiphanes, has mandated that all peoples within his control abandon their ancestral ways to become "one people." The stakes are raised until circumcision or possession of a Torah scroll leads to the death penalty. Some resist and are brutally killed. Others despair over the possibility of resistance and give in to the "inevitable." But out of this incredibly difficult situation, a hero arises: Mattathias. When the imperial representative offers him honor and wealth if he will set an example for the people by offering sacrifice on the imperial altar, he loudly refuses on behalf of himself and his family. One Jew, however, goes up to the altar to sacrifice. Mattathias becomes incensed: he springs forward to kill the apostate, and while he's at it, the king's messenger too. A guerrilla war ensues, which is as much a civil war as an international one. When the dust and blood settle, Mattathias's children, the Maccabees, have won the war. But it is a bitter victory, which leads not to freedom and justice but to the corrupt and short-lived reign of the Hasmoneans, who are in turn defeated a hundred years later by the invading army of Rome.

Meanwhile, another voice expressed a perspective on this struggle, the prophet Daniel. Through a series of dream-visions, Daniel 7-12 offers a look "behind the veil" cast by the Seleucid reign. From this perspective, Daniel saw the current empire as simply one in a series of "beasts." These rapacious creatures will be succeeded by "one like a human being" (7:13). What Christians assume to refer to Jesus, the "son of man," Daniel meant to refer to "Michael, the great prince and protector of your people" (12:1). What appears "from the ground" to be an armed conflict between the Maccabees and the Seleucid army and its supporters is given a "heavenly" perspective as a cosmic battle between beasts and "the human one." Listeners are called to trust that this cosmic battle is sure to be won by God's representative. Thus, rather than take up arms against the oppressor, Daniel's narrative calls God's people to practice *hypomonē*, the apocalyptic virtue par excellence. Usually translated "patience" or "endurance," the word means "faithful resistance," a stubborn trust in God's exclusive power that will not bend to the demands of empire. To support those who are bold enough to maintain such trust in the face of suffering and death, Daniel's vision reveals something new: "Many of those who sleep in the dust of the earth shall awake, some to everlasting life, and some to shame and everlasting contempt. Those who are wise shall shine like the brightness of the sky, and those who lead many to righteousness, like the stars forever and ever" (12:2-3). It is the promise of resurrection—not as a separation of "soul" from body at death, but as restoration of the flesh/spirit unity at "the end times"—that is offered as sustenance for the faithful. With Daniel's vision, apocalyptic became a full part of the biblical arsenal of nonviolent weapons in resistance to empire.

"JOHN TO THE SEVEN *EKKLĒSIAI* THAT ARE IN ASIA . . ."

By the time of Jesus and his followers, apocalyptic had become the most popular genre of anti-imperial literature. A huge number of both Jewish and Christian apocalyptic texts have survived from the roughly two-hundred-year period framing Jesus' ministry, including portions of the canonical Gospels, such as Mark 13. Some noncanonical texts, such as 4 Ezra (also known as 2 Esdras), are quoted by New Testament writers. They form a common treasury of imagery and ideas to encourage God's people to remain faithful in hard times. By the time John had his vision in the late first century of the common era, apocalyptic had been established for generations as a powerful vehicle for expressing the call to remain loyal to God alone.

Revelation, unlike Daniel and many other noncanonical apocalyptic texts, is addressed to a very specific audience, which enables us to explore in more detail the situation into which its message was proclaimed. Its visionary author, known only as John, found himself on the island of Patmos, "because of the word of God and the testimony of Jesus" (1:9). Many have assumed that this phrase refers to a state of exile, because Patmos was well known for its penal colony. If so, it means that John was a member of the privileged elite who turned his back on his privilege, because only the elite experienced the "luxury" of exile. Lower-ranking people (like Jesus) were dispatched through crucifixion or beheading. But it may simply be that John's presence on Patmos was part of a missionary or pastoral journey similar to Paul's, as suggested by the relationship he has with seven Christian communities in the Roman province of Asia (part of modern Turkey) on the mainland near Patmos. In either case, John claims no official authority as apostle, elder, or presbyter. Rather, he describes himself as "your brother who shares with you in Jesus the struggle (*thlipsis*) and the kingdom (*basileia*) and the faithful resistance (*hypomonē*)" (1:9, author's translation). John is simply a believer with a vision, called to proclaim the vision to those with whom he shares the way of discipleship.

A key question that we must address about this relationship has divided scholars for decades: Was John writing to support Christians suffering under Roman persecution? The first of the three attributes by which John describes himself (*thlipsis*) has suggested this to some. However, the word does not necessarily imply literal persecution, but the difficult day-to-day struggle with which God's people have perennially been faced: to live God's ways surrounded by neighbors who live the ways of other gods. In fact, there is almost no evidence that Christians in Asia experienced systematic persecution under the emperor Domitian, whose reign extended through the late first century and into the beginning of the second. Recent studies have shown that the Roman empire had little concern with Christians for the simple reason that they were not numerous enough to draw much attention from official circles. To understand why John feels that fidelity to Jesus requires such a struggle, we must pause to look at life in the cities of Asia.

While the Gospels speak of a land-based society focused on long-term, village and small town relationships, Revelation addresses an *urban* audience. Unlike our modern cities, which tend to sprawl into all available space, ancient cities were strictly demarcated by the walls built to protect inhabitants from invading enemies. Thus, these cities were crowded almost beyond our imagining. Narrow streets filled with animals and their wastes and lack of human sanitation made them not only unpleasant but also disease-ridden. The overwhelming majority of people were desperately poor, many spending their days seeking sustenance through day labor or begging. Those who practiced some sort of trade might manage to make ends meet, but could rarely achieve any measure of financial or social security, especially given the dangerous conditions engendered by poor construction, hordes of desperate people, and lack of public security services. The few on top lived in abundant luxury, enjoying the spoils of the imperial economy and its treasures gathered from throughout the Mediterranean.

The glue holding this together was a combination of local and imperial cult practice, serving as "religion" in the literal sense of *re-ligio*, a binding together again of separated pieces. Religion was not an option exercised in response to existential questioning, as it is for many today. Rather, it was the essential means of avoiding dangerous isolation, which could leave one helpless in the face of crime, disease, or ill health. Asian cities contained worship of a wide variety of divinities, brought in by the diverse inhabitants who comprised the population. Unlike our cities, where population control is of great concern, high infant and child mortality and the consequences of war and urban violence led most cities to experience steady decline in numbers unless population was

increased by factors from outside the city itself. Despite the crowding
and danger, it was in the interest of the Roman economy to maintain a
stable population base in important cities such as Ephesus (one of the
seven to which John wrote) to assure a steady flow of trade and commerce. For this reason, the empire placed surviving soldiers or freed
slaves in cities, who brought their indigenous religious traditions with
them. In addition, the cities contained a huge number of persons forced
off their land by the growth of the Roman *latifundia*, enormous agricultural estates that swallowed up farmland in the name both of imperial
trade and poetic ideals of the "good life." Good, that is, for the owners;
not so good for those forced off their land into urban day labor or debt
slavery. These people too brought their religions to the cities of Asia.

As a binding force, these local religious practices linked urban people from various lands into a practical unity that served as both
protection and a means for developing business and other social relationships. But those seeking more than simply day-to-day needs set
their sights higher. Within the patronage system that organized the
imperial society, greater goals were attainable only by an exchange of
wealth for honor. We see remnants of this kind of network in our day
when we look to "patrons" of arts or building campaigns, whose
money is given in exchange for the donor's name inscribed in marble,
steel, or stone. So, if the elite of a city such as Ephesus sought to show
its rivals in Pergamum how important they were, they might work to
"buy" financing for a temple building (used primarily for commercial
affairs) for the price of giving honor to the emperor whose "benefi-
cence" enabled the building project to proceed. This process eventually
developed, beginning with the cities of Asia, into the set of practices
known as the "imperial cult," through which the emperor Domitian
himself was worshiped as divine.

Thus, both local and imperial cult practices of religion had their primary effects at the level of person-to-person and city-to-city relations,
rather than being mandated from Rome. For people who claimed to be
followers of Jesus, this meant that their own religious practice could be
found threatening, not by elite Roman officials but by neighbors, fellow
tradespeople, or potential customers. John's apocalyptic narrative is
addressed, then, not to people needing comfort in times of persecution
but largely to persons all too comfortable "passing" within the local
imperial environment.

We can see this situation reflected in Revelation 2-3, the messages to
the *ekklēsiai*. I chose to use the original Greek term, which is usually
translated as "churches," for several reasons. First, two millennia of

Christianity have burdened the word "church" with many associations that would not have been made by Revelation's original audience, including the reference to a building or religious institution. John, like Paul and Luke (in Acts), described the gathered discipleship community with a term that has its origins in Greek democracy. An *ekklēsia* is an assembly of the "called out," that is, the representative body of the larger community that comes together to make decisions on issues of communal concern. In other words, it is essentially a *political* rather than a theological term. It was used by the translators of the Hebrew Scriptures who produced the Septuagint to convey the Hebrew *qāhāl*, the assembly in Israel designated in the Torah (e.g., Deut. 9:10). Another reason for using this term here is the special role of the image of being "called out," which, as we shall see, is central to Revelation's challenge to discipleship (e.g., 18:4). John writes to the "angels" of these *ekklēsiai* in Asia to express the risen Jesus' judgment and encouragement for each community's degree of fidelity to the gospel way. Across the seven *ekklēsiai* we find a range from those which are successful in the world's eyes but are condemned by Jesus (Ephesus, Laodicea) to those most commended for their willingness to be ostracized as the price for faithfulness (Smyrna, Philadelphia). In between are the *ekklēsiai* of Pergamum, Thyatira, and Sardis, whose message mixes criticism and encouragement. Note that the word given to each angel (i.e., the community's collective spirit) is heard by all seven. Discipleship is not simply a matter of "personal salvation," but depends on the perseverance of the entire network of local communities. Just as Paul in Acts urges far-flung *ekklēsiai* to show their concrete concern for the sisters and brothers in the *ekklēsia* in Jerusalem through the taking up of the famine relief collection, so John tries to show each community how it is interdependent with its sister *ekklēsiai* in Asia. The book thus opens and will close with a message of concrete, pastoral concern to real communities of discipleship, not abstractions or prophetic predictions awaiting a future fulfillment.

SCROLLS, SEALS, TRUMPETS, AND BOWLS: REVELATION'S "PLOT"

Once John has conveyed the set of messages to the *ekklēsiai,* he begins the description of his vision. While the imagery he uses may seem confusing, bizarre, or even outrageous to us, it would have been clear enough to those familiar with both the apocalyptic tradition and

Hebrew Scripture. Although Revelation never quotes Scripture, hardly a verse goes by that does not contain one or more intertextual references to biblical texts. Still, John wrote not systematic theology but apocalyptic poetry. Therefore, one can hardly claim—especially in the face of the widely divergent interpretative roads taken within the history of interpretation—that the reading offered here is "correct." But when one reads the text in light of both the traditions through which John expressed his visions and the world of his original audience, many aspects of the "mystery" of Revelation become clear.

A preliminary question one must ask is about the relationship between the series of sevens found in Revelation 5-16: seals, trumpets, thunders, and bowls. Many scholars have argued that the narrated sevens (excluding the thunders, which John is told not to write down [10:3-4]) are a series of variations on a single theme of judgment. That is, the seals, trumpets, and bowls are each saying the same thing but with slightly different imagery. However, the sevens are not three series loosely connected like beads on a necklace. Rather, they are interwoven within the story of the two scrolls: the first sealed with seven seals and held in the right hand of the One on the heavenly throne, which only the Lamb can read (5:1-7), and the "little" scroll, which is held open in the hand of an angel and offered to John to eat (10:1-10). While poetry cannot be said to have a "plot" in the same way as can prose narrative, one can find within John's imagery a story, indeed, *the* story of God's relationship with humanity from the beginning through the time of Jesus and beyond. Let us see briefly how these septets reveal this story to us.

John's vision takes him to the other side of "the veil," where he sees the heavenly court engaged in loud and joyous worship of the One on the throne. The content of the worship reverberates with politically charged rhetoric: overt challenges to the imperial cult's proclamation of the emperor as divine. For example, "You are worthy, our Lord and God, to receive glory and honor and power, for you created all things, and by your will they existed and were created" (4:11). It is God alone who is "worthy" to receive laud because God is not simply the holder of temporal power garnered through military might, but is the creator of all things. This theme will echo through each of the seven scenes of "heavenly liturgy" placed throughout Revelation at key points.

After this initial celebration, John sees the sealed scroll, but is immediately driven to bitter tears because "no one in heaven or on earth or under the earth was able to open the scroll or to look into it" (5:3). But his weeping is interrupted by one of the twenty-four elders who comprise the heavenly court (along with angels and cherubim), who tells him that "the Lion of the tribe of Judah, the Root of David, has conquered, so that he can open the scroll and its seven seals" (5:5). John thus hears the word "lion," but when he looks he sees instead "a Lamb standing as if slaughtered" (5:6). A common feature of Revelation is how what John *hears* is reshaped in terms of what he *sees*. "Lion" suggests power and might; the "Lion of the tribe of Judah" suggests in particular the political Messiah stemming from David who would rid Israel of the Romans by force of arms. However, John sees not this powerful figure but its apparent opposite: a Lamb, and one seemingly dead at that! For those who abhor what they perceive to be Revelation's embrace of violent vengeance, it is essential to recognize at the outset that Revelation's proclamation is of the *conquering power of a slaughtered lamb*. The Jesus John follows defeated empire not with empire's own sword but with the sword of his mouth, that is, with his divinely inspired word and witness (1:16; 2:12, 16; 19:15, 21).

It is this conquering Lamb who is the only one in all of creation "worthy" to break the seals and open the scroll. As he begins this process, we see released a series of four horses and riders, each with authority to wreak havoc of one kind or another. We might immediately wonder about the apparent contradiction between the nonviolent power of the Lamb and the terrible onslaught that the horses and riders cast onto the earth. The key is to remember that the *seals are not the scroll*. Jesus the Lamb is not "causing" the violence described by the seals but rather is *unveiling* it. The seals are precisely the powers of empire to keep the scroll—the word of God—sealed up and hidden from view. Only the conquering Lamb, by his triumphant trust that God's life-giving power is greater than empire's death-dealing violence, has understood this relationship between empire and God's word so as to break empire's stranglehold on God's people.

Now we can see that the first four seals express both the primary means by which empire gains its power and how each of those powers is constantly at risk of crumbling. The white horse with the bow and crown (signaling to the original audience the Parthians, who remained a constant threat to stability of the empire's eastern boundary) represents international war, which both brings about empire and threatens its longevity. The second, red horse is war of a different kind: civil strife that renders empire fragile from within. The third, black horse with the scales and the proclamation of massive economic inflation signifies the imperial economy, which thrives on exploitation but risks both famine to the poor masses ("a quart of wheat for a day's pay") and infighting among the elite clambering over each other for competitive advantage ("don't harm the olive oil and the wine"). Finally, the fourth, pale horse expresses the power of death through the common prophetic image of "sword, famine, plague, and beast" (e.g., Jer. 15:2-3; 34:17).

With this final horse we get a hint of the broader structure upon which John's vision is based. For the sequence of sufferings that Jeremiah announced as the price to be paid by those who refuse to abide by God's covenant was already traditional in his time. Its root is in the series of "covenant curses" in Leviticus 26.[1] These curses follow from the blessings that accrue to those who practice the divine mandates of keeping the sabbatical and jubilee years, as described in Leviticus 25. These mandates call for both economic and environmental justice: the sabbatical is first for the *earth itself* and then for humanity. If God's people live in harmony and *shalom* with one another and the earth, then all will be well. But if they "continue hostile" to God and God's ways, they should not be surprised to experience the opposite of *shalom*. Leviticus 26 presents four sets of "sevenfold" punishments in terms echoed in Revelation's fourth seal. These punishments are not to be seen as arbitrary judgments, like a parent taking away a child's allowance for doing something dangerous. Rather, they are what parenting manuals might call "natural consequences," the bad things that flow predictably from bad behavior. In other words, if, despite being warned, you put your hand in the fire, don't complain to Mommy when you get burned!

We can begin to see how Revelation's imagery combines a prophetic critique of empire and its followers with the concomitant power of God's judgment. It is part of Revelation's apocalyptic insight that from God's perspective, judgment is not something held for the future ("wait until your father gets home!") but is *simultaneous with sin*. In the same way, though, God's mercy is also simultaneous, as we hear in the fifth seal in response to the insistent cry of "How long?" by those "under the altar" who "had been slaughtered for the word of God and for the testimony they had given" (6:9). They rightfully demand that there be some evidence that their witness-unto-death will bear fruit. God's response is that they receive a "white robe" and "rest a little longer."

---

[1] Some scholars note that the final version of Leviticus may have been compiled during the exile, that is, around the same time or even after that of Jeremiah. We cannot argue this question here, but simply recognize it while keeping the focus on how the imagery was used across many different biblical contexts, regardless of when those texts were finally written in their current form.

In other words, empire and its practitioners are both judged/punished and given mercy *at the same time*. From our side of the veil, this is a paradox. *We* can offer either mercy or judgment/justice, but not both at once. But *God*, whose ways are not our ways, is not bound by this limitation. John's vision opens him and therefore his audience to perceive the world as God does, where mercy and justice can and do happen together.

The penultimate sixth seal follows, in which all—starting from the "kings of the earth and the magnates and the generals and the rich and the powerful" and ending with "everyone, slave or free"—hide themselves from "the wrath of the Lamb" in fear. Again we are faced with the apparent God of vengefulness and violence. This scene is immediately followed by the sealing of God's faithful ones ("heard" to be twelve thousand from each of Israel's tribes but "seen" to be a "great multitude that no one could count, from every nation, from all tribes and peoples and languages" [7:9]) and a joyous liturgy. Is this a cruel celebration of the suffering of sinners? To grasp John's message, we must pause to see how he uses the contrasting pair "earth" and "heaven." Those who cower in fear in their perception of God's and the Lamb's impending wrath are "inhabitants of the earth." This phrase is used repeatedly in Revelation to refer not to all humans on the planet but to those whose loyalty lies on "this side" of the veil. That is, those whose identity is with human-made systems of domination (empire) anticipate the experience of divine presence as threatening and frightening. Those whose identity is "in heaven," however, anticipate this identical experience as cause for raucous celebration. While the term "heaven" (*ouranos*) refers literally to the sky, John uses it consistently to refer more broadly to *wherever and whenever God's life and reign are at the center of community*. Thus, heaven is neither spatially in the sky nor temporally after death but expresses the apocalyptic awareness of the *bifurcation* of reality. On the streets of Ephesus or Pergamum (or Paris or Seattle) are both "inhabitants of the earth" and those who "dwell in heaven." The God who is perceived by followers of the Lamb as loving and just is perceived by the followers of empire as wrathful and violent.

We see this choice of perspective in the series of seven trumpets, which makes up the "content" of the first scroll. The open scroll reveals a "litany of thirds" which threaten (but do not totally destroy) the earth's sources of bounty, an attempt to remind "earth dwellers" of the provisional nature of all earth-bound systems (8:7-12). They end, though, with an apparent "failure." Those who remain alive "did not repent of the works of their hands or give up worshiping demons and idols of gold and silver and bronze and stone and wood, which cannot see or hear or walk. And they did not repent of their murders or their sorceries or their fornication or their thefts" (9:20-21). The external acts of idolatry (in Revelation's original context, the practice of the local and imperial cults) both cover and attempt to legitimize the behaviors that follow, the four "cardinal sins of empire," to which we will return when we look at Babylon. From this hindsight, we can see what the seven trumpets are naming and why they "fail" to generate repentance. A key to unraveling John's imagery comes in the description of the demonic cavalry associated with the sixth trumpet (9:13-19). John says that the power of these fire-, smoke-, and sulfur-breathing beasts "is in their mouths and in their tails; their tails are like serpents, having heads; and with them they inflict harm (*adikousin*, "do injustice")." A look at an Isaiah text sheds light on this image:

The people did not turn to him who struck them, or seek the LORD of hosts. So the LORD cut off from Israel head and tail, palm branch and reed in one day—*elders and dignitaries are the head, and prophets who teach lies are the tail;* for those who led this people led them astray, and those who were led by them were left in confusion. (Isa. 9:13-16, emphasis added)

In other words, John's vision shows him how it is the "elders and dignitaries" of the people whose lies and deceptions—their justification of empire and its practice by God's people—are the "head" while the false prophets (like "Jezebel" [Rev. 2:20; also, 16:13; 19:20; 20:10]) are the "tail." God will "cut them off," but meanwhile, those who are confused and led astray by their smoke(and fire and sulfur)-screen refuse to repent. That is, they continue to believe that they can walk empire's ways and God's ways at the same time. But the truth is, they cannot. And the consequence of trying to do both is the experience of God's threats of judgment as expressed through the trumpet images and their numerous echoes of the plagues against Egypt, which also failed to bring about repentance.

The failure leads immediately to the revealing of the second scroll, the "small" and open one given to John to eat. It leads to a different response through a different means from the first scroll. What then is this first scroll which contains this "failed" message? It is the story of God's relationship with humanity up to the time of Jesus. It expresses the historical failure of threats of divine judgment to lead to repentance, a circumstance repeatedly decried by Israel's prophets. Only the Lamb understood this history and revealed God's "new way," first revealed to Daniel but not understood by him (Dan. 12:8-9). Jesus' resurrection revealed that the "end-times" predicted to Daniel had begun with the first Easter. In place of threats of judgment, therefore, Jesus showed trust in a God who called for the practice of nonviolent witness and the apocalyptic virtue of *hypomonē* which are to be rewarded with resurrection.

This is what we see in the second scroll's story of the two witnesses slaughtered by the inhabitants of "the great city" (11:7-8). The death of the two prophetic pests is celebrated by "inhabitants of the earth" by an exchange of presents, but the celebration is cut short when "the spirit of life from God entered" the dead witnesses and they stood up (11:11). The experience of resurrection terrifies those who side with empire in the battle for hearts and minds, because it shakes the frail reed upon which imperial authority always rests. Yet the experience leads some to "give glory to the God of heaven," an expression extolled later by an angel bearing "an eternal gospel" (14:6-7). The two witnesses, described as "two olive trees and the two lampstands" (11:4), are not to be identified with specific historical persons nor with two generic individuals but are, according to the symbolic logic of the story, two *ekklēsiai* (1:20). Revelation calls not for heroic individualism but for faithful witness by the discipleship community as a whole. This is what Jesus' ministry, death, and resurrection revealed and therefore what is the mission of the communities that claim his name.

What, then, of the seven bowls in Revelation 15-16, which appear simply to offer more violence? We see at the end of this series the consistent refusal of repentance by people who know who God is but choose empire's ways anyway (16:8-11). Their suffering represents the "justice" side of the justice/mercy paradox (16:5-7). Their punishment is the consequence of their refusal to repent. As harsh as it may seem to people raised in a "liberal" environment (which is itself frequently a veil over systemic imperial sinfulness), God's gift of freedom implies the possibility of suffering for sin, which possibility God does not take away. Repentance and healing are always available, but unless they are freely chosen, people may experience the painful consequences of walking the way of death rather than the way of life. In this sense, "hell," like "heaven," is not an afterlife place but a condition of life experienced by people who have *chosen* to turn from God's ways. John's vision does not revel in this prospect, but unveils it as a truth-telling warning to those who believe that their relationship with empire has no consequences.

WHERE DO YOU LIVE?
BABYLON OR NEW JERUSALEM?

Revelation's "plot" ends with this stark and horrifying image of hell-on-earth. What remains is the portrait of the two apocalyptic cities, Babylon and New Jerusalem. Again, John's vision of the cities is not about the future but about the bifurcation of reality which presents the choice of "citizenship" each moment of our lives.

The core of the Babylon vision is Revelation 18. One challenge for many readers in our time is John's use of female imagery (whore and bride) to "embody" the cities. There is no denying that such language can be and has been abused to denigrate women and even to justify violence against women. Feminist scholar Barbara Rossing has emphasized that John's attention is directed not to real-life women but to *cities* conventionally referred to in female imagery. There is absolutely no basis for applying Revelation 18-21's metaphors to human beings. In John's time, "whore" signified both "illicit intercourse" and wealth gained and used illicitly. Similarly, "bride" was a symbol for purity and relational loyalty. Perhaps the best we can do is to acknowledge the harm that this language has caused and to try to focus on John's real message: the call to live in the realm of God's sovereignty.

The description of the already-fallen "great city" matches the imperial sins of which "inhabitants of earth" refused to repent at the end of the first scroll (9:20-21):

Murder: "In you was found the blood of prophets and of saints, and of all who have been slaughtered on earth" (18:24).

Sorcery: "Your merchants were the magnates of the earth, and all nations were deceived by your sorcery" (18:23).

Fornication: "Kings of the earth have committed fornication with her" (18:3).

Theft: The cargo list of imperial imports gained through exploitation and slavery (18:12-13).

Throughout the portrait of "the great city," we see how the sinfulness refers not to private vice (literal "fornication" or "theft") but to the structural injustice of empire. While the immediate context for John's vision was the Roman empire of his day, it is clear that Babylon is not merely a symbol or code for Rome, but rather, that Rome was the then-current manifestation of the eternal enemy of God's reign, "the great city." The term has its roots in Genesis 10, where Nimrod, the first "mighty warrior" on earth, is described as the builder of cities, including "the great city," Nineveh (Gen. 10:8-12). In Revelation, John shows how the term applies to all human empires when he refers to "the great city that is called in the spirit Sodom and Egypt, where also their Lord was crucified" (11:8). Throughout the Bible, "city" represents the place of human arrogance, violence, and opposition to God, beginning with the first city, Enoch, built by the first murderer, Cain (Gen. 4:17). The exodus call out of Egypt became the paradigm for the life of God's people. They would best know their God and themselves when they were away from the influence and temptation of empire (cf. Gen. 12). Thus, Revelation's call is to "Come out of her, my people, so that you do not take part in her sins!" (18:4). As befits the use of "fornication" as an expression of illicit intercourse (socioeconomic, not sexual), the call to "come out" commands God's people to stop engaging in such intercourse with the great city. There is irony here as well: it is not a warning not to "go in," but a command to "come out." God's people are found in the midst of Babylon!

For the *ekklēsiai* in Asia, the challenge was not to leave the urban setting, the option chosen by the Jewish covenanters who left Jerusalem to live at Qumran by the Dead Sea. Rather, it was to live God's ways outside the influence and control of empire while remaining physically in its midst. The call parallels that of John's Gospel to be "in the world" but not "of the world." So where and how are God's people to live?

Anthony Gwyther (co-author of *Unveiling Empire*) has noted that one reason that many Christians today find the call to "come out" of Babylon difficult is that they perceive the alternative to be "perpetual Lent." Does God want God's people to be denied the pleasures of life? Is discipleship but a dour asceticism? Not according to Revelation's description of the "holy city" in Revelation 21-22. New Jerusalem is described with the most lavish array of jewels, gold, and flowing water. It is not a matter of rejecting "wealth" or pleasure, but of distinguishing between "the best that money can buy" and what God gives as a free gift (21:6; 22:17). Babylon/empire is seductive indeed. "She" is not a streetcorner hooker with smeared lipstick looking for her next drug fix, but a luxurious, four-star hotel call girl, dressed in the finest attire. What Revelation tries to get its audience to recognize is that "her" glory is *illusion*. A good prostitute (whether offering sex or other "sold" services) convinces her/his customers that what they offer is given freely for "love." But this is a lie. It is simply a commercial transaction which profits from attempting to satisfy the desires of the heart with commodities (cf. Rev. 18:14).

In contrast, what God offers in the New Jerusalem is *truly* a gift of love. There is no entrance fee, no password, no class privilege required to enter its open gates and drink from its ever-flowing water of life. God is not a distant potentate in a grand temple accessible only to the few, but a "camper" in the midst of the people (*skēnē,* "tent," 21:3). Outside the holy city are only those who choose not to enter, those who continue to practice empire (21:8; 22:15).

What did this mean to John's original audience? What does it say to us today? Simply that the *ekklēsiai* are to be where New Jerusalem is found. Rather than being a "Sunday morning thing," the life of discipleship is both a liturgical celebration of joy which proclaims God's exclusive reign *and* a life lived day to day in that recognition. The only way that disciples can experience New Jerusalem is when the *ekklēsiai* engage in the concrete practice of covenant-based economic and social relationships. For instance, consider two attitudes toward economic exchange. In a market economy, most buyers see their goal as getting the product or service for as low a price as possible. There is no concern over the time, energy, or expense required by the seller. All is self-interest. But in the covenant economy that John's vision restores to its central place in the biblical story, one sees the "other" not as "seller" but as "sister" or "brother." When one is in relationship with a farmer or craftsperson, one knows their need and does not try to take advantage of it. At the same time, producers do not attempt to extract the highest possible price, but recognize the need of the purchaser to eat, be housed in dignity, and so forth. The church, John proclaims, is meant to be the community in which such relational economics are practiced. And as we noted at the outset in looking at the messages to the seven *ekklēsiai,* each community is to struggle not in isolation but in relationship to all others. Those of the First World blessed by abundance (and privileged by empire) are to share freely, out of love rather than obligation or altruism, with those in the Two-thirds World, who have been systematically victimized by centuries of imperial oppression and exploitation. It is worth remembering this, as many U.S. congregations engage in expensive building campaigns while Latin American *ekklēsiai* struggle simply to eat and avoid slaughter by death squads.

As one living amidst the privilege of empire, I do not find Revelation's message easy or comforting. But I do hear the truth of God proclaimed in its powerful imagery. How much I yearn to live in the illusion! But in the end, the life of discipleship is a call to walk in the truth. Unless I believe that New Jerusalem is a more joyous and satisfying experience than that of the false pleasures of Babylon, my faith itself is a sham. This means engaging in the constant and sometimes exhausting process of staying awake, alert to the daily seductions by which I am lured into compliance with empire's ways. Without a small faith community in which to attempt experiments in alternative economics, I would feel lost. But when we do manage to participate in honest expressions of song and story, the "great city" seems miles away indeed.

RESOURCES FOR FURTHER STUDY

Barr, David. *Tales of the End: A Narrative Commentary on the Book of Revelation*. Sonoma, Calif.: Polebridge Press, 1998.

Boyer, Paul. *When Time Shall Be No More: Prophecy Belief in Modern American Culture*. Cambridge, Mass.: Belknap Press, 1992.

González, Justo L. *For the Healing of the Nations: The Book of Revelation in an Age of Cultural Conflict*. Maryknoll, N.Y.: Orbis, 1999.

Howard-Brook, Wes, and Anthony Gwyther. *Unveiling Empire: Reading Revelation Then and Now*. Maryknoll, N.Y.: Orbis, 1999.

Krodel, Gerhard A. *Revelation*. Minneapolis: Augsburg, 1990.

Manley, Roger. *The End is Near! Visions of Apocalypse, Millennium and Utopia*. New York: Dilettante Press, 1998.

Richard, Pablo. *Apocalypse: A People's Commentary on the Book of Revelation*. Maryknoll, N.Y.: Orbis, 1995.

Rossing, Barbara R. *The Choice Between the Two Cities: Whore, Bride and Empire in the Apocalypse*. Harrisburg, Pa.: Trinity Press International, 1999.

Schüssler Fiorenza, Elisabeth. *Revelation: Vision of a Just World*. Minneapolis: Fortress, 1991.

Strozier, Charles B. *Apocalypse: On the Psychology of Fundamentalism in America*. Boston: Beacon Press, 1994.

Thompson, Keith. *Angels and Aliens*. New York: Fawcett Columbine, 1991.

Thompson, Leonard L. *The Book of Revelation: Apocalypse and Empire*. New York: Oxford University Press, 1990.

About the Contributors

MICHAEL H. CROSBY lives with other Capuchin Franciscans in a ministry to poor and marginalized folk in Milwaukee. He advises groups in the Midwest on socially responsible investing. He has lectured and given retreats around the world and has written over a dozen books on spirituality in contemporary society, including *House of Disciples: Church, Economics and Justice in Matthew* (Orbis, 1988).

NEIL ELLIOTT is the author of *Liberating Paul: The Justice of God and the Politics of the Apostle* (Orbis, 1994) and has published articles on the apostle Paul in the context of Roman imperialism; he teaches New Testament studies in the Twin Cities.

JUSTO L. GONZÁLEZ is a United Methodist minister who was born in Cuba; he is engaged in writing and promoting the theological education of Latinas and Latinos. He has published over seventy books, as well as hundreds of articles, at both the academic and the popular level, most recently, *Acts: The Gospel of the Spirit* (Orbis, 2001).

A. KATHERINE GRIEB teaches New Testament theology at the Virginia Theological Seminary in Alexandria, Virginia, and at the Servant Leadership School of the Church of the Savior in Washington, D.C., where she is part of the Friends of Jesus Church. She also serves as part of a clergy team for St. Stephen & the Incarnation, an inner-city Episcopal parish. Her book *The Story of Romans* will be published by Westminster John Knox in 2002.

RICHARD A. HORSLEY is chair of the Study of Religion Program, University of Massachusetts, Boston. He is the author of numerous books on the social and economic context of first-century Palestine, including *Bandits, Prophets and Messiahs: Popular Movements in the Time of Jesus* (Trinity Press International, 1999).

WES HOWARD-BROOK teaches and writes from his home at Patmos in the Woods Retreat House outside of Issaquah, Washington. He is the author of several books, including *Becoming Children of God: John's Gospel and Radical Discipleship* (Orbis, 1994) and co-author of *Unveiling Empire: Reading Revelation Then and Now* (Orbis, 1999).

CHED MYERS holds a degree in New Testament from the Graduate Theological Union. He is author of several books on Mark, including *Binding the Strong Man: A Political Reading of Mark's Story of Jesus* (Orbis, 1988). He works as a theological animator and popular educator with Bartimaeus Cooperative Ministries in Los Angeles, California.

SHARON H. RINGE is Professor of New Testament at Wesley Theological Seminary and a member of the adjunct faculty of the Universidad Bíblica Latinoamericana. She is an ordained minister in the United Church of Christ and the author of several books on the Gospels and on biblical interpretation, including *Luke* (Westminster Bible Companion) (Westminster John Knox, 1995).

Index

Acts of the Apostles, 103-21; apostles in, 104; authorship of, 103-4; history and, 104-5; humor in, 108-9; idealizing Paul the missionary, 151; justice in, 114-15; Lukan agenda in, 104-7; the margins in, 115-16; message for the people in, 112-13; outpouring of Spirit in, 111; and Roman government, 119-20; as second Lukan volume, 64, 67, 103-4; sharing in, 112; subversion in, 107-9, 112, 116-19; "we passages" in, 103-4; "Western" text of, 107-8; women and, 66

Acts of the Holy Spirit. *See* Acts of the Apostles

agapē (love): in John, 92, 95, 96, 99, 102

angels: superiority of Son over, in Hebrews, 171-72

Antichrist: in 1 John, 100, 101; in Revelation, 188

anti-Judaism: in Hebrews, 175-76; in Roman writers, 124

Antioch: and Jesus movements, 9; and term *Christianoi,* 9

Antipas: as ruler of Galilee and Perea, 4

Apocalypse of John, 127; *see also* Revelation

apocalyptic: as Jewish resistance literature, 43-44; meaning of word, 189; mystical, 189-90; and Paul, 127; political, 189-90; in sermon in Mark, 43; writings, 127, 189-93

apocalyptic moments: in Gospel of Mark, 51, 53, 54-55; *see also* Transfiguration

apostle: in John, 98; meaning of, 98; Paul as, 123

assemblies (*ekklēsiai*), 19; as base communities, 130; political connotations of, 125; *see also* ekklēsia

Attridge, Harold: on genre of Hebrews, 171

authority (*exousia*), 23, 34

banditry, 4, 7

baptism: in Colossians 152-53; into death of Christ, 153-54; of John, 22-23, 24-25; Pauline idea of, 140

Barrett, C. K.: on post-Pauline literature, 151

Bauckham, Richard: on Jude, 185

Beloved Disciple: in John, 94; as witness to resurrection, 98, 99

Bible: as story of God's ways and empire, 190-93

birth: as master metaphor of Gospel of John, 83, 89, 91, 97

birth narratives: in Luke, 68-70

blindness: in John, 88-89

Blount, Brian: and African American reading of Mark, 42

boundaries: of Israel in Matthew, 26-28; Jesus' breaking of, 34; of the temple, 28-30

Brown, Raymond E.: on Deutero-Pauline letters, 149; on 1 Peter, 180

campaigns of challenge, 48-49, 53

Catholic Epistles, 168-87; Hebrews, 169-76; James, 176-79; 1 Peter, 179-82; 2 Peter and Jude, 182-86

chiastic structure: in Johannine passion narrative, 96-97; in John, 82, 86-87, 96-97; in Matthew, 20

Christianoi, 9, 14

Christology: in Colossians, 152-53; of Hebrews, 171-75; of James, 177; and John, 82, 89

church order: in Pastoral Epistles, 163

circumcision: baptism as, 153; as capital offense, 192; Gentiles and, 138-40

The New Testament—
Introducing the Way of Discipleship